LIBRARY OF DAVIDSON COLLEGE

Books on regular loan may be checked out for two weeks. Books must be presented at the Circulation Desk in order to be renewed.

A fine of five cents a day is charged after date due.

Special books are subject to special regulations at the discretion of library staff.

OCT 12 1974
OCT 14 1976
NOV 29 1983
NOV -4 1992

Library of
Davidson College

7.75
Met

GREEK PHYSICAL EDUCATION
CLARENCE A. FORBES

AMS PRESS
NEW YORK

The Century Education Series

GREEK PHYSICAL EDUCATION

BY

CLARENCE A. FORBES

ASSISTANT PROFESSOR OF CLASSICS
UNIVERSITY OF NEBRASKA

THE CENTURY CO.
NEW YORK AND LONDON

Reprinted from the edition of 1929, New York
First AMS edition published 1971
Manufactured in the United States of America

International Standard Book Number: 0-404-02449-1
Library of Congress Number: 78-136383

AMS PRESS INC.
NEW YORK, N.Y. 10003

PREFACE

This history of the theory and practice of physical education among the ancient Greeks was undertaken at the suggestion of Professor W. A. Oldfather, of the University of Illinois. To him all thanks are due for encouragement, advice, and help freely given at every turn.

Though concerned with a specialized topic of Greek antiquities, the book is also a chapter in the history of education. Hence in its composition the purpose was steadily kept in view of making it as usable and comprehensible for those interested in education, as for those interested in the classics. Those unacquainted with Greek will find that the Greek alphabet is for the most part confined to the footnotes, and that the few words or phrases which form exceptions to this rule are translated or explained. The lack of adequate English equivalents necessitated the repeated use, in a transliterated form, of certain Greek words, e. g., *paidotribes*, *eiren*, and *kosmetes*. Such of these words as are reasonably well domesticated in the English language, and are to be found in standard and reliable dictionaries, were left with little or no explanation. Others are defined where they first occur in the text, and again, for purposes of reference, in the glossary.

References in the footnotes were made as succinct as possible. Books and articles are referred to simply by the author's name, with volume and page, the date being given only where necessary to distinguish between two or more works of the same author. Thus "Poland 90" refers to page ninety in the book of F. Poland, *Geschichte des griechischen Vereinswesens*, Leipzig, 1909. All works thus briefly referred to in the text or footnotes will be found listed with full data in the bibliography, which is arranged alphabetically by authors. Abbreviations such as *IG*, *RE*, and *BCH* indicate collections of inscriptions or papyri, encyclopedias, and periodicals. All these abbreviations are explained in a list which just precedes the index; many of them are in everyday use among classical scholars, and others are those adopted by the compilers of the new (9th) edition of Liddell and Scott's *Greek Lexicon*.

Considerable pains have been taken with the bibliography, in the endeavor to make it full and accurate. It is the most complete bibliography of the subject that has ever been published, and the author hopes that it may be of real service to those desirous of becoming acquainted with the kindred literature.

Finally, warm thanks are extended to Dr. Rachel Sargent, of Naperville College, Illinois, for reading the larger part of the book in manuscript and for assistance in many matters; and to the author's wife, for active aid and sympathy at every stage of the book's progress.

C. A. F.

Lincoln, Nebraska.

CONTENTS

CHAPTER		PAGE
I	Introduction: The Beginnings	3
II	The Spartan Agoge	12
III	Physical Education in Crete	44
IV	Athens before 335 B.C.	54
V	Theories of the Philosophers	93
VI	The Athenian Ephebia	109
VII	The Remainder of Greece and the Greek World	179
VIII	Conclusion	258
	Appendix	263
	Glossary	265
	Bibliography	271
	Abbreviations Employed for Periodicals and Collected Works	289
	Index	295

GREEK PHYSICAL EDUCATION

διαφέρει δὲ πάμπολυ μαθὼν μὴ μαθόντος καὶ
ὁ γυμνασάμενος τοῦ μὴ γεγυμνασμένου.

PLATO.

GREEK PHYSICAL EDUCATION

CHAPTER I

INTRODUCTION: THE BEGINNINGS

Physical education played a larger part in Greek life than it has in the life of any nation before or since. The Oriental civilizations of earlier centuries paid scant attention, if any, to gymnastic exercises and to physical development. Modern nations lead a life so busy and complicated, so distracted with business affairs, and with the pleasures of the cinema, automobile, radio, and books, that little time or thought is left for the promotion of the body's welfare. It is difficult for one who lives in the rush and confusion of the twentieth century to imagine the simplicity of life in ancient Greece. With far fewer external sources on which to draw for recreation, the Greek naturally turned to gymnastic sports; instead of being diverted by radio programs or some elaborate form of amusement, he literally diverted himself by a natural use of the resources which nature had given him. Instead of being swept from day to day in a mad whirl of activities, he had, if he belonged to the middle or upper classes, leisure enough so that he might spend hours daily conversing in the market-place or exercising in the gymnasium.[1] He was so constituted and so trained that he could make a worthy use of his leisure (and this is a true test of a man); he did not squander his free time in frippery and nonsensicalities, but devoted it to his physical and mental betterment. His word for leisure (σχολή) became our word for "school." There was no such thing as home life in ancient Greece, and when the men were thrown together, they took a real pleasure in stripping, rubbing themselves with oil, and giving their bodies free play in vigorous, blood-quickening sports. Their habitual existence in the open air and the light, loose character of their clothing were standing invitations to gymnastic activities.[2]

The Greeks stood alone among the nations of their day in their passion for physical exercises. Foreigners or "barbarians," as the Greeks called them, were amazed to see the Greeks wrestling, boxing, running, and jumping; why men should raise such an ado about nothing was beyond their comprehension. Anacharsis of Scythia, on seeing for the first time the activities of a Greek gymnasium, is represented by Lucian[3] as convinced that the Greeks were insane. Plato[4] recognized the love of gymnastics (φιλογυμναστία) as peculiarly Greek, and the thought is

[1] Aristotle felt (*Pol.* ii. 6. 2 [p. 1269a 34ff.]) that in a well-ordered state the citizens simply must have leisure. Cf. *ibid.* vii. 13. 16ff. (p. 1334a 11ff.).

[2] G. Glotz *La civilisation égéenne* 10.

[3] In the lively sketch called the *Anacharsis*.

[4] *Symp.* 182B.

echoed by a modern writer on Greek gymnastics, Julius Jüthner:[1] "Among no people of antiquity or of the present day have gymnastics attained such a significance and experienced such a magnificent development as among the Greeks, and as a fully developed art of physical culture they are surely a native product of the Greek national character." *Gymnasiis indulgent Græculi*, says a voice from Roman times,[2] and the citations could easily be multiplied to prove how enthusiastic the Greeks were over physical education.[3] No self-respecting city was without a gymnasium, and Pausanias[4] expresses doubt whether it was proper to call a place a city at all if it lacked one.[5] Large cities had as many as four or five, and Athens had seven.[6]

Now in seeking to understand the nature and history of Greek physical education, it is necessary to define what is meant by the term. Physical education must be sharply distinguished from athletics. These are akin, in that both have the exercises of the body as a groundwork, but they employ the exercises in wholly different ways, and for different purposes. The athletes who took part in the games at Olympia and elsewhere did not acquire their pro-

[1] *RE* VII. 2035.

[2] Trajan in Plin. *Ep.* x. 40.

[3] See Oehler *RE* VII. 2005.

[4] x. 4. 1.

[5] Oehler (*l. c.* 2005-8) lists 128 places where we know that gymnasia were located; that we have knowledge now of every one that existed is, of course, not to be expected.

[6] Oehler (*l. c.*) listed nine, but see my discussion below (page 222, n. 4).

ficiency at school, nor were paid teachers essential to their training; they had nothing to do with any school system, and their activities were distinct from those of organized physical education. When group instruction is given by recognized teachers, who receive remuneration for their efforts, and whose duty it is, not to train athletes, but to develop strong, sound, supple bodies, prepared to face the manifold needs of daily life—this we may call "physical education." In this field, as in many others, the Greeks were supreme; they aimed straight at the goal, and attained it nobly.

In the earliest Greek times physical education as a system was unknown. Even then, however, men had the instinct to exercise and test their prowess in rivalry with their fellows.[1] In the pages of Homer we read of the heroes holding funeral games in honor of Patroclus, and we discover that men even so early had skill in boxing, wrestling, running, chariot-racing, the javelin and discus throw, and other sports. The epics naturally represent only the heroes and aristocrats as engaged in the games, but probably the common people too had their sports;[2] the bards did not mention them because they were not interested in the affairs of the common people. They did not train themselves for the contests, as athletes did later on, nor was there any conscious purpose of promot-

[1] Philost. *Gym.* xvi.
[2] Here the writer agrees with Bondurant (4), as against Gröschl (3), Jüthner (*RE* VII. 2038), and I. Müller (136).

INTRODUCTION: THE BEGINNINGS

ing their physical development by so exercising. The skill which they displayed and the familiarity with these exercises would suffice to prove that gymnastics had already reached a high stage of development, but we have this directly attested by archæology besides.[1] So far back did athletic sports go that the Greeks attributed their beginnings to the gods. Hermes Enagonios (ἐναγώνιος) was said to be the inventor,[2] and he was represented as the father or the lover of the maiden Palæstra[3] (a personification of the school of wrestling and other exercises). This tradition was not uniform, and sometimes Theseus was named as the inventor of gymnastics.[4] Hercules and Apollo were two other deities closely connected with the palæstra.

Scant traditions of instruction in physical exercises extend back to Homeric times. The older and more experienced frequently coached the young in hunting and gymnastic sports, as well as in the military arts. Nestor gives sage advice to his son Antilochus on how to win in the impending chariot race.[5] This is not, of course, organized and systematic physical education. About the education of Heracles there were many

---

[1] Boxing was well known in Crete in Minoan and Mycenæan times. See Jüthner *RE* VII. 2035; Hyde 1ff.

[2] Hor. *C.* i. 10. 3f. See the discussion of Jüthner *l. c.* 2071f. and Preller-Robert *Gr. Mythol.* I. 415ff.

[3] Philost. *Imag.* ii. 32. Serv. on *Æn.* viii. 138.

[4] Paus. i. 39. 3. Schol. Lucian *Iup. trag.* xxi. (ed. Rabe p. 65). For varying reports see Schol. Pind. *Nem.* v. 89 (ed. Abel p. 169).

[5] *Il.* xxiii. 306ff.

traditions,[1] the commonest being that Chiron gave him private lessons.[2] Chiron was famous as a gymnastic teacher, and we owe to Maximus of Tyre (28.1c) a description of his simple, Spartan methods: "He brought about the pink of condition in those who came to him, employing for this end the chase, mountain-climbing, and running. He made his pupils sleep on rushes, eat the spoils of the hunt, and drink spring-water."

With more zeal and regularity gymnastics were carried on by the Dorians, whose penchant was for such of the exercises as were warlike. The many city-states of Hellas were chronically at war with their neighbors or with one another,[3] and from this circumstance arose the necessity of making preparation for war one of the absolutely essential parts of education.[4] Nilsson (340) carries the beginnings of the Spartan educational system very far back in primitive days.[5] The ancients ascribed its foundation to Lycurgus, but the mythical character of Lycurgus is now generally recognized. Nilsson believes, however, that to some one man, or group of men working harmoniously, we must assign the remote beginnings of the Spartan organization of

[1] Many of them are given by Theoc. xxiv. 104ff.
[2] Philost. *Her.* ix. pp. 707–8.
[3] See, Æschylus' epitaph and the remarks of Zimmern (70) on the Greek attitude that war was the normal thing. A study of Plato's *Republic* leads to the same conclusion, and further evidence is given by Seitz (18).
[4] Barth (1920) 106.
[5] "*Vielleicht . . . vor der Eroberung Lakoniens.*"

education. The system seems such an integral part of the Spartan constitution that we can hardly imagine the one existing without the other. The best we can say, then, is that the primitive features of Spartan education, discussed in Nilsson's article, make us certain that it was started in the earliest times of the state's existence.

Similarly for Crete we must allow great antiquity to the educational system. It resembles in many essential aspects that of Sparta, and betrays the same traces of primitive origins.[1] In the period of the Minoan civilization, the Cretans allowed the women to participate in gymnastic games and even to engage in bull-fights.[2] Such freedom for women was a rarity in Greek history, but Sparta granted similar privileges to her women in the historical age. It was a persistent tradition of antiquity that Sparta's constitution was modelled on that of Crete; Lycurgus, it was said, when he was ready to frame laws for his country, first visited Crete and studied the arrangements there.[3] The tradition can not be credited, for the Dorians certainly settled the Peloponnesus before they spread to Crete, but its growth is due to the previous existence of the Minoan civilization on the island. As a matter of fact, neither the Cretans nor

---

[1] Nilsson 314.
[2] Bruno Schröder 10–11.
[3] Plut. *Lyc.* iv. Aristot. *Pol.* ii. 7. 1 (p. 1271b 22ff.). Cf. Strab. x. 4. 9 (477 Cas.), who gives Plato and Ephorus as authority; cf. also Cic. *Tusc.* ii. 14. 34.

the Spartans were affected by the Minoan culture and practices, but later generations knew vaguely of this old civilization in Crete, and carelessly made it the source of many later institutions. The new settlers in Crete and Laconia simply retained and developed their own common institutions, without borrowing from their neighbors or predecessors. The origins of physical education in Crete were, then, we must believe, slightly posterior to the Spartan beginnings.

In Athens gymnastics for educational purposes neither began so early in history nor were they prosecuted with such one-sidedness as among the Dorians. The Athenian scheme of physical culture, unlike the two we have just mentioned, betrayed no marks of primitive ideas and practices. The earliest educational laws of Attica were promulgated, or rather codified, by Solon; they were not the laws of a creator, like the so-called Lycurgean laws, but simply provided regulation for a system already in full operation.[1] We are unable to lay our finger on any moment in Athenian history and say: "Here began physical education." It would be surprising if we could. Let us be satisfied with an approximation of the century and say the seventh. From Pisistratus onwards, at any rate, gymnastic education had a considerable place at Athens, and it already had a firm foothold before that time.

[1] Girard (1891) 185.

INTRODUCTION: THE BEGINNINGS

The three localities, Sparta, Crete, and Athens, to which we have now called attention, are the ones which will concern us most in the following pages. We know very little about physical training among the Dorians save in Sparta and Crete, and where we can gather hints about it, the model of Sparta seems to have been imitated.[1] The non-Dorian part of the Greek world fell into step with Athens in this respect as in many others. We shall now set forth the history, the rise and bloom, the decay and fall of physical education in the three Greek countries where we know it best, then follow it in its subsequent spread through all the lands which Greek ideas and practices penetrated. We shall find that its development runs parallel to the general course of Greek history.

[1] See below, pp. 242–243.

CHAPTER II

THE SPARTAN *AGOGE*

The earliest Greek civilization from which we have a fair body of well-grounded knowledge is that of Sparta. The educational system there was termed the *agoge*.[1] Since its creation was ascribed to Lycurgus,[2] it was sometimes called the Lycurgean *agoge* (Λυκούργειος ἀγωγή). As to-day in the United States, education was made compulsory for every son of a citizen.[3] Besides being compulsory, the régime under which the Spartan boys lived was very severe. No other part of the Greek world, in fact, had a system so rigid, methodical, and exacting. Its desirable features commended themselves to Plato,[4] to Xenophon (who based thereon his sketch of education in the *Cyropædia*), and to Plutarch, while its bad features elicited unequivocal condemnation from Aristotle (see below, page 14).

The purpose of physical education at Sparta was governed by the peculiarities of the state. The only genuine Spartans (*Spartiates*) were a mere handful,

---

[1] ἀγωγή: Plut. *Ages.* i.; Polyb. i. 32. 1.
[2] Plut. *Lyc.* xiv ff.
[3] Plut. *Ages.* i.
[4] Cf. the many imitations in the *Laws*. Dantu (19) sees in the *Timæus* (87D), where the need of maintaining an equilibrium between body and soul is emphasized, a plain criticism of Spartan educational methods. This is possible, but unproven. In general, Plato highly favored the Spartan ἀγωγή.

THE SPARTAN *AGOGE*

who declined to enlarge their numbers to any appreciable extent by assimilating foreigners or by any other method. On the other hand, frequent wars with their neighbors kept depleting their ranks. They lived in the midst of overwhelming hosts of oppressed serfs, the helots, who were always ready to rebel. If, then, they thought, they must ever be fighting with their neighbors, and at the same time striving to hold the helots in subordination, it was necessary that every Spartan citizen be an able-bodied fighting-man. In order to attain this object, the state assumed complete control of the fortunes of all its citizens, from birth to the grave.

Individuals did not matter; only the State mattered, and no sacrifice was too great to make in its interest. If a weakling babe was born, a council of elders ordered it ruthlessly exposed on Mt. Taygetus to die. Those who were permitted to live, lived not for themselves, but for Sparta, and under a system of education reared up by the state. Aristotle with his communistic ideals admired this public education: "One might well praise the Spartans for their display, as a body politic, of very great zeal in regard to their children." [1] To insure that each one should be strong, hardy, brave, obedient—this was the goal of the training to which they were subjected from early years.[2] Music, art,

---

[1] Aristot. *Pol.* viii. 1. 3 (p. 1337a 31–2).

[2] *Ibid.* vii. 2. 5 (p. 1324b 8–9) ἐν Λακεδαίμονι καὶ Κρήτῃ πρὸς τοὺς πολέμους συντέτακται σχεδὸν ἥ τε παιδεία. See Krause (1851) 119 and 121; Fr. Cramer I. 304; Mahaffy 77. Philost. *Gym.* xix and Quint. i. 11. 18 point out that even dancing at Sparta was directed to this serious purpose.

and literature counted for nothing in this narrow-minded policy, save as in some trifling way they could subserve this end. In the highest degree Spartan education was utilitarian, and a "liberal education" was undesired and, indeed, incomprehensible. The resemblance to Crete in this respect will appear later; how unlike the situation at Athens this was I need hardly suggest. Aristotle gives a severe but justified criticism:[1] "The Lacedæmonians brutalize their children by laborious exercises which they think will make them courageous." Haase (373) grants that this reproach was partly merited in Aristotle's time, and fully merited in the following age, but considers it invalid for the earlier time. It really appears that Sparta had some artistic culture, for example in painting and ceramics, in the seventh century; but this was overthrown in the wide and sweeping changes made in the Spartan constitution and ways of daily life in the sixth century. Haase has in fact been justified by the results of archæology and later research.[2]

This leads us to say that the Spartan *agoge* undoubtedly passed through some changes from time to time, as must have been the case in the shake-up of the sixth century, to which we have just referred. Of these changes we can perceive at best only the vague effect, and we know none of the details. The *agoge* became

---

[1] *Pol.* viii. 3. 3 (p. 1338b 11ff.) tr. Jowett.
[2] See Wilcken *Gr. Geschichte* (1924) 189–90.

more severe and stringent with the exodus of culture, and a few centuries later we find it in decay. Beyond general indications of this sort we can not go. In the following description of the *agoge* evidence derived from all periods is employed, and the pieces fitted together into a harmonious whole. Lack of chronological data forces us to assume that what was true in one period was equally true before and after that, unless we have some special reason, in rare cases, to believe the contrary. So intense was the Spartan conservatism that few changes can have been made, even in the course of centuries. Freeman (12) aptly illustrates this conservatism by the fact that the Spartan officials caused to be scourged any one who tried to change the rules of the ball game.

Now we will consider more in detail who must and who might be enrolled in the "Laconic *agoge*."[1] As I have indicated, all the sons of citizens [2] were under obligation to submit; exception was made to this rule only in the case of an heir presumptive to the throne.[3] If the heir apparent did not care to be exempted, there was nothing to prevent his taking part in the *agoge;* and it is likely that Cleomenes III was one who did not avail himself of his privilege of exemption.[4] The younger sons of the kings never shared

[1] Λακωνικὴ ἀγωγή, Xen. *Lac.* ii. 14.

[2] οἱ πολιτικοὶ παῖδες, as they were termed by Phylarchus ap. Ath. vi. 102 = *FGrHist.* lxxxi. F43.

[3] Plut. *Ages.* i.

[4] Plut. *Agis et Cleom.* xxix. 1 tells us that he had σύντροφοι (=μόθακες) and this implies his submission to the ἀγωγή; yet he had a non-Spartan,

in this special privilege, and we know that two of the greatest among them, Leonidas and Agesilaus, passed through the system.[1]

Two other groups in addition to the citizens' sons were allowed in the *agoge*. The latter were permitted to choose among the illegitimate children of *Spartiates* by helot women, one or more (the number being determined by the ability of the father to support them) to be their companions and foster-brothers, and to go through the *agoge* with them.[2] As their fellow-pupils, they were useful in many respects. Ælian (*V. H.* xii. 43) states that they served as antagonists of their comrade-masters in the daily exercises. If they persisted through the *agoge*, their reward at the end was freedom.[3] Ælian also gives us the names of three of these *mothakes* who reached the heights of fame: Callicratidas, Lysander, and Gylippus.[4]

philosophical training (*Ibid.* xxiii. 2). Kahrstedt (127) thinks it hardly possible that limits of time would have permitted him to undergo the ἀγωγή also, unless in a modified form, but Kahrstedt fails to observe that the ἀγωγή was modified, and had become comparatively insignificant in the days of Cleomenes. See below, page 32.

[1] K. O. Müller II. 295–6.

[2] These were called μόθακες (Æl. *V. H.* xii. 43; Phylarch. *l. c.*) or μόθωνες (Harpocr. *s. v.*). They were not numerous (Kahrstedt 53). That they were bastard children of *Spartiates* appears from Xen. *Hell.* v. 3. 9; see Nilsson 329.

[3] Æl. *l. c.* Freeman 17 says this was probably true in late times, but thinks Plutarch (the writer can not find this in Plutarch; the reference should be to Ælian) wrong in dating the custom as early as Lycurgus. The opposite view, to which the writer adheres, is expressed by Nilsson 329.

[4] Niese in *RE* VII. 1967 doubts the truth of this statement for Gylippus.

The second class allowed to share in the *agoge* was composed of foreigners who came to Sparta when children, or were born in Sparta to foreign parents. They might be the sons of guest-friends of powerful Spartans, or of men who were eating the bread of exile in Laconia (Freeman 15). Like the *mothakes*, they must have been few in number.[1] They were called "foster-sons of Sparta" (τρόφιμοι), and corresponded partly to the metics in other Greek states.[2] Phocion caused his son to go to Sparta and become one of the *trophimoi*, in order to have the training of the *agoge*,[3] and Xenophon, admirer of things Spartan, sent his sons to Sparta for the same purpose.[4]

Freeman (16) observes that Sparta was thus a predecessor of Athens as an educational center. While this can not be gainsaid, yet it is doubtful if the number of foreigners who went to Sparta for their education was at all large. The Spartan system was too narrow-minded, while the Athenian education was so rounded and complete that it made an international appeal, and drew students from everywhere. We can trace this, as a matter of fact, from the fifth century on to the latest times. Pericles declared that Athens was the school of Greece; in the fourth century Isocrates[5] speaks of people flocking from Sicily, Pontus, and other places, to be educated in Athens, and a letter attributed to Æschines (xii. 13) declares that the par-

[1] See next paragraph.
[2] Kahrstedt 53.
[3] Plut. *Phoc.* xx.
[4] Diog. Laert. ii. 54.
[5] *de Perm.* 224.

ents of Bœotia and Ætolia send their children to Athens to share in the education there. In the second century and thereafter, the ephebia, and still later its successor, the University of Athens, brought countless students together from all over the Greek and Roman world. Sparta must have made a contemptible showing as an educational center, when compared with Athens.

K. O. Müller (II. 295) has pointed out that there were inferior types of *agoge* intended to give some sort of training to the other inhabitants of the Spartan domain who were excluded from the real *agoge*. A passage in Athenæus (xv. 15) contrasts the *periœci* with "the boys of the *agoge*," assuring us that the education of the former was wholly different from that of the latter. The "demotic *agoge*" (δημοτικὴ ἀγωγή), of which we hear in Polybius (xxiv. 7. 1), was an inferior sort of *agoge* for some of the lower classes, and it is not impossible that there were several degrees.

Left at home under the care of his parents in his earliest years, the son of a Spartan citizen was drafted by the state as soon as he reached his seventh birthday.[1] For the process of making strong, hardy, obedient fighting-men to defend the state, Sparta felt that she could not begin too early. It was no boyish, carefree, happy life that awaited the lads whose destiny it was to pass through the *agoge*. They were immediately grouped into "herds" (βοῦαι). The

[1] Plut. *Lyc*. xvi. 7 and Busolt-Swoboda II. 694. Kahrstedt (45 n. 3) observes that no birth register was followed, with the result that occasional inaccuracies of a year or two arose.

name *herds* was perhaps used advisedly, for in very truth the existence which the boys now led had something in common with that of cattle. Each herd ate together, partaking of food that was anything but attractive and far from abundant. If too well fed, the Spartans philosophized, the boys will lack ambition and get fat and lazy. Certainly the elders were zealous and spared no pains to avoid such a contingency.[1] The state regulated the food and probably did the purchasing, but the expense had to be borne by the individual parents. This must have worked a hardship in poor families, and poor boys, who were perhaps not given by their parents even the small amount required by the state, must have been frequently reduced to stealing and foraging in order to allay their pangs of hunger.[2] The boys also slept together in true barracks fashion, but the state was unkind in the matter of beds. None of any sort were furnished, and the boys were forced to go down to the banks of the Eurotas and gather rushes to serve as their couch. How soft and comfortable such pallets were may be imagined, but this was a characteristic feature of the *agoge*.

[1] See below, page 33.

[2] Freeman (15) and Drever (13) wrongly think the sons of poor citizens were automatically excluded from the ἀγωγή by the expense. The penalty for not submitting to it was loss of citizenship (Plut. *Ages.* i.; cf. K. O. Müller II. 295; Kahrstedt 127). Aristotle says (*Pol.* iv. 7. 5 [p. 1294b 22–4]): "For the sons of the poor are brought up with the sons of the rich, who are educated in such a manner as to make it possible for the sons of the poor to be educated like them." The expense for such food as the Spartans ate must have been slight, and besides they could have recourse to theft, as the author has said above, to eke out their scanty supplies.

Nothing luxurious, or even comfortable, was allowed for an instant; Spartan boys must be hard and tough in body and spirit. A test of their courage and their power of resistance was the flogging (διαμαστίγωσις) at the altar of Artemis Orthia—a brutal rite under the name of religion—of which more later.

The size of the herds we do not know. Boys of different ages were not mixed together in a herd, and even the herd leader (βουαγός) was of the same age.[1] No doubt the herd leader was chosen for his ability and for his Spartan qualities of obedience and endurance (Freeman 18). Special names were given to the boys who were all of the same age, and so performed their gymnastics together in the herds; for the boys of each year from the time they entered until they reached their fourteenth year, there were designations comparable to our high-school and college terms: *freshman, sophomore, junior, senior*,[2] although the six grades cor-

---

[1] Hesych. s. v. βουαγόρ; Nilsson 313. The βουαγός retained his title throughout life as an honorary appellation. This circumstance has led some (e. g., Szanto *RE* III. 572) to believe that the βουαγός was an *eiren* (see below).

[2] Hdt. gloss (Stein's ed. maior of Hdt., Vol. 2, p. 465): 8 ῥωβίδες (Baunack *Philol.* LXX. [1911] 367 would emend to βωβίδες and connect the word with βοῦα and the Cretan-Laconian ox-god; hence we might translate it as "herd-children;" Bechtel, however, *Gr. Dialekte* [1923] II. 377, simply says the word is "unerklärt"), 9 προμικιζόμενοι "preparatory youngsters," 10 μικιζόμενοι "youngsters," 11 πρόπαιδες "preparatory boys," 12 παῖδες "boys," 13 μελλείρηνες "preparatory ephebi." The source of this valuable gloss is Aristophanes of Byzantium ὀνομασίαι ἡλικιῶν (Preger *AM* XXII. [1897] 338). Only the last four of these age classes are attested by the inscriptions of the imperial epoch (Kahrstedt 342); the reason is, as Nilsson has shown, that these are records of παιδικοὶ ἀγῶνες, and to these the two youngest groups were not admitted, as being too weak and unskilled.

respond more nearly to our eight elementary school grades, which we number but do not name. From the thirteenth to the fourteenth year the boys were called *melleirens*, "preparatory ephebi," and from the fourteenth to the twentieth they were *eirens*, "ephebi."[1] On attaining the twelfth birthday and becoming technically "boys," they were subjected to more stringent discipline. The exercises generally were graduated to suit the different ages (Plut. *Lyc.* xvi). Nilsson (311) points out that the division of boys into age classes by single years ceased when they reached physical puberty at fourteen, and remarks that the term *sideunai* referred loosely to the younger *eirens* aged fifteen or sixteen,[2] while the older ones on the threshold of manhood were called "ball-players."[3] The latter term, now substantially attested by many inscriptions,[4] is plainly indicative of the exercise which was a prime favorite among them at this age.[5]

[1] Busolt-Swoboda II. 696. As Nilsson (310) remarks, these statements on the age classification at Sparta clash sharply with the old theory that *melleirens* were 18–20, *eirens* 20–30 (Fournier 13; Grasberger III. 58–9; Gilbert I. 70 [E. T. p. 63]), but he shows that the Herodotus gloss is not inconsistent with Plut. *Lyc.* xvii. Busolt-Swoboda (*l. c.*) have shown a slight error of Nilsson's in assuming a gap from 14 to 15, when boys had ceased to be *melleirens* and had not yet become *eirens*. Nilsson was following Plut. (*l. c.*) εἴρενας δὲ καλοῦσι τοὺς ἔτος ἤδη δεύτερον ἐκ παίδων γεγονότας, but failed to observe that Plutarch meant παῖδες in the technical sense (boys of 12). Busolt-Swoboda (II. 697) also show that Hdt. ix. 85 can not be adduced, as it is by Kahrstedt, to refute the belief that *eirens* were 14–20.

[2] Phot. *Lex. s. v.* συνέφηβος.   [3] σφαιρεῖς, Paus. iii. 14. 6.

[4] *IG* v. 1. 674–87, with the discussion prefaced to this group by Kolbe, p. 144.

[5] K. O. Müller (II. 296) remarks that Spartan boys were fond of ball at all ages, and had games between organized teams. Kahrstedt (343)

The herds were subdivisions made for convenience in arranging gymnastic classes. For more general purposes, the boys were divided into troops or *agelai* (ἷλαι or ἀγέλαι),[1] each composed of four herds (Kahrstedt 344). The leadership of these troops or companies was entrusted to *eirens;* in all probability only one *eiren* was assigned to each troop (Xen. *Lac.* ii. 11), and, if it could be arranged, each *eiren* headed a troop of which he himself was an alumnus.[2] He chose the herd leaders and directed the exercises. Indeed each troop formed a community by itself; in their exercises, games, meals, sleep, and all phases of their daily life, the individuals of a troop were almost never alone, almost never without an *eiren*, a herd leader, or an older citizen to curb them (Xen. *Lac.* ii. 10f.).

Even when encamped away from home in time of

holds that the σφαιρεῖς were not an age division, but a sporting club of youths already graduated from the *agoge*.

[1] The two terms were probably used synonymously at Sparta: Busolt-Swoboda (II. 695), comparing Xen. *Lac.* (ii. 11) with Plut. *Lyc.* (xvii. 2). Hesychius *s. v.* βουαγόρ contradicts this, making ἀγέλα = βοῦα.

[2] Kahrstedt 343. The members of an ἴλη were of different ages, unlike the members of a βοῦα. Very likely only the older *eirens*, sometimes called πρωτείραι (Hesych. *s. v.* κατὰ πρωτείρας; Phot. *Lex.* (cxl. 21) κατὰ πρωτείρας: πρωτείραι οἱ περὶ εἴκοσιν ἔτη παρὰ Λάκωσιν), were eligible to these positions of command (Nilsson 312). Naturally we shall discard the theory of Kahrstedt (343 n. 4) that πρωτείραι were first-year *eirens;* the passage in Photius compared with our revised notions of the age of *eirens* demonstrates that they were the oldest, not the youngest. Neither is his suggestion that the remaining *eirens* were employed in the secret service (κρυπτεία, cf. Plut. *Lyc.* xxviii. 3ff.) tenable; if the *eirens* were as young as we now believe, surely they were not ripe for such bold and desperate work as was required in the secret service. Plutarch does not say that *eirens* did the work of the secret service, but says it was done by the young men (νέοι), a term which ordinarily meant those in their twenties rather than in their teens.

war, the Spartans were not released from all their program of daily physical exercises. Only mild exercises were required of them under these circumstances, however, so that Plutarch suggestively remarks (*Lyc.* xxii) that the Spartans alone among men enjoyed war as a rest and recreation from the training for war. Twice a day, before breakfast and again before the evening meal,[1] they marched and drilled, and sometimes threw the javelin and discus.[2] They exercised in divisions, one after another, as the Persian scout observed at Thermopylæ (Hdt. vii. 208). Agesilaus not only demanded this exercising in his army,[3] but even prevailed on Sparta's allies to emulate their comrades in arms, with the best of results on their physique (Xen. *Hell.* v. 3. 17).

One of the phases of the Spartan training to physical and mental endurance was the cruel flogging, called *diamastigosis* (διαμαστίγωσις), at the altar of Artemis Orthia. The religious origins and significance of this rite I leave to the students of religion, but its usefulness in teaching the lads to bear pain and suffering concerns us in our history of physical education. Every year [4] some of the noble and highly-esteemed [5] lads [6]

---

[1] Xen. *Lac.* xii. 5–6.
[2] *Ibid. Hell.* iii. 4. 16.
[3] *Ibid.* and 18; *Ages.* i. 25 and 27.
[4] Plut. *Inst. Lac.* xl. (239 C–D).
[5] Philost. *Vit. Apoll.* vi. 20; Tert. *ad Mart.* iv.
[6] Cic. *Tusc.* ii. 14. 34 says *pueri*, but Plut. *Arist.* xvii. 10 refers to their age more exactly by calling them ephebi. Probably they were *eirens*. The scholiast on Hom. *Od.* iv. 245 referred to them as νέοι, "young men."

entered a contest, the object being to see which one could endure longest the severe lashing.[1] The winner was given the title of "altar-conqueror" (βωμονίκης), and was allowed to keep the title throughout life.[2] His victory was no easy one, for his blood flowed freely under the stinging lash,[3] and he was bound to refrain from whimpering and pretend to a Stoic cheerfulness.[4] His parents were there watching him and encouraging him to endure,[5] and the priestess who stood by made the scourgers ply the lash hard, by pretending that she could no longer bear the weight of the wooden image of Artemis which she held veiled in her hands, whenever they showed signs of remitting their blows (Paus. iii. 16. 10–11). The most horrible aspect of this custom was that the lads not infrequently died under the scourge rather than utter a cry.[6] Perhaps the rite, at least in the form familiar to us, was of comparatively late origin; it is not mentioned by any author earlier than Xenophon, and Xenophon's allusion (*Lac.* ii. 9) is far from clear. Of course its establishment was attributed to Lycurgus, but that means nothing. Dio Chrysostom (lxxv. 3 Budé) speaks of it as a practice still existing in the first century of the Christian era.

---

[1] Hyg. *Fab.* 261; Plut. *Inst. Lac. l. c.*

[2] *IG* v. 1. 652, 653, 653b, 654, and see Szanto *RE* V. 325. Statues were set up in their honor: Lucian *Anach.* xxxviii.

[3] Greg. Nazianz. *Or.* iv. p. 109. Sext. Emp. *Pyrrh. Hypot.* iii. 208. Lucian and Philost. *l. c.*

[4] Cic. *Tusc.* ii. 14. 34 and v. 27. 77. Plut. *Inst. Lac. l. c.* ἱλαροὶ καὶ γαῦροι.

[5] Lucian and Tert. *l. c.*

[6] Lucian and Plut. *Inst. Lac. l. c.* Cic. *Tusc.* ii. 14. 34.

The regular exercises of the Spartans included, besides the game of ball already mentioned, (1) running, an ancient and natural form of exercise, (2) wrestling, (3) archery, (4) throwing stones and javelins, (5) boxing, (6) the pancratium,[1] (7) hunting, and (8) bareback riding.[2] Their training was almost wholly physical, and little or no attention was paid to the instruction of the intellect (Plut. *Lyc.* xvi. 10). The stress laid on gymnastics[3] bore fruit in the Greek games as well as in war. The oldest games at which athletic contests were regularly held, the Olympic, were established in the Peloponnese, although not on Laconian or Argive soil. To Heracles, national hero of the Dorians, was ascribed the first renewal of the Olympic games; and Aristotle said (Plut. *Lyc.* i) that Iphitus, king of Elis, was helped in making laws for the games by Lycurgus. The circumstance that nothing more than an olive crown was the award of

[1] The common belief that boxing and the pancratium were forbidden at Sparta is exploded by Jüthner (*RE* VII. 2041), who points out that Spartans were merely prohibited from entering these contests in the national games, because defeat, except in the case of a disabling injury, was determined by one of the contestants giving up, a thing that no Spartan should ever form the habit of doing. To the Spartan Pollux was attributed the discovery of the technique of boxing; Philost. *Gym.* (ix.) calls boxing a Spartan invention; Cic. *Tusc.* (v. 27. 77) gives a description of the pancratium as Cicero had personally seen it at Sparta; no warlike people would overlook such useful preparatory exercises as boxing and the pancratium. See further Xen. *Lac.* iv. 6; Philost. *Gym.* lviii, *Imag.* ii. 6; Plat. *Protag.* 342 B–C.

[2] Hesych. *s. v.* ἵππαρχος and ἡνιοχαράτης. Krause (1841) II. 672; K. O. Müller II. 297. Riding was not a favored sport, nor one in which the Spartans became adept.

[3] See, for example, Dio Chr. xxxvii. 26 Budé παρὰ Λακεδαιμονίοις δέ, ὅτι φιλογυμναστεῖ.

Olympic victory was a manifestation of Doric simplicity. Before the twentieth Olympiad, the victor lists of Olympia prove that all the victors, if not all the contestants, were Peloponnesians—good evidence of the marked development of gymnastics in that section of the Greek world. Until the late sixth century before Christ, Sparta led the world in the field of gymnastics.[1]

In this state system of physical education, there were fewer functionaries than one might expect. The Athenian *sophronistes*, *paidotribes*, and *gymnastes* were never introduced into Sparta, and the *hoplomachos* was a late importation.[2] It has been seen that the older and more capable boys gave instruction to those who were younger or had had less initiative.[3] In addition to this, every citizen at Sparta considered himself personally charged with the instruction and especially with the discipline of the youth of the state who were enrolled in the *agoge*.[4] It was, however, impossible that this carefully organized educational

[1] For the substance of the above paragraph the writer is indebted to Jüthner (*RE* VII. 2040).

[2] Mentioned in one inscription (*IG* v. 1. 542) of the late second or early third century of the Christian era, one of the last inscriptions referring to physical education at Sparta; and referred to by Vegetius *de Re Milit.* prol. bk. 3 (a work of the fifth century).

[3] Van der Bach (38) remarks that before the exercises of the gymnasium and palæstra became recognized disciplines, each person had to teach himself, or get help and advice from his fellows; to some extent this always held true at Sparta.

[4] Plut. *Lyc.* xvii. 1 καὶ προσεῖχον οἱ πρεσβύτεροι καὶ μᾶλλον, ἐπιφοιτῶντες εἰς τὰ γυμνάσια, καὶ μαχομένοις καὶ σκώπτουσιν ἀλλήλους παρατυγχάνοντες, οὐ παρέργως, ἀλλὰ τρόπον τινὰ πάντες οἰόμενοι πάντων καὶ πατέρες εἶναι καὶ παιδαγωγοὶ καὶ ἄρχοντες. Cf. *ibid.* xvi. 5 and *Agis et Cleom.* xxxiii. 3 τὰ μὲν πολλὰ μελετώντων τῶν νέων καὶ τῶν πρεσβυτέρων διδασκόντων.

system should function without some supervision on the part of a corps of regular officials. The citizens, therefore, chose a school superintendent, the *paidonomos*. According to Plutarch (*Lyc.* xvii. 2), the *paidonomos* was selected from among the best and most worthy inhabitants of Sparta.[1] The people realized that, constituted as their state was, the conduct of the *agoge* was of the utmost importance, and should be in capable hands. Xenophon (*Lac.* ii. 2) tells us some of the duties and privileges of the *paidonomos:* he could summon the boys to a school assembly on occasion; he had general supervision of the school system; and he had disciplinary powers in case any of the lads should display laziness. Generally speaking, his authority was absolute, and he was responsible to no one. In the case of *eirens*, he still had control, but cognizance was taken of the greater maturity of the *eirens*, and he was forbidden to punish them for any serious misdemeanor without first consulting the ephors.[2] K. O. Müller (II. 297) observes that our concept of the importance of the *paidonomos* is increased by finding that even the chosen band of knights [3] was under his authority. As disciplinary

---

[1] παιδονόμος ἐκ τῶν καλῶν καὶ ἀγαθῶν ἀνδρῶν ἐτάττετο—very wise and proper policy.

[2] Xen. *Lac.* iv. 6; Kahrstedt 219 and 251. Kahrstedt still held the old belief that an *eiren* was at least twenty years old (see his statement to this effect p. 243); apparently he did not know Nilsson's article), hence says the *paidonomos* could not punish the *eirens* for the reason that they were liable to military service.

[3] ἱππεῖς: Xen. *Lac.* iv. 6.

assistants, the superintendent had an unknown number of *mastigophoroi*. Their name, "whip-bearers," has an unpleasant ring; it is eloquent of the methods employed in Spartan education. Xenophon (*Lac.* ii. 2) tells us that the *mastigophoroi* were young men; their duty was to punish the boys "so as to effect in them genuine good-behavior and real obedience."

A rare and noteworthy feature of Spartan education was the admission of girls. The purpose here again was utilitarian: girls had to grow up sturdy and hard if they were to be the mothers of Spartans.[1] That the girls were proud to be disciplined in physical education for this end is plain from the charming anecdote in Plutarch's life of Lycurgus (xiv. 8). Gorgo, the wife of Leonidas, heard the comment of some woman from abroad: "You Spartan women are the only ones who rule over your men." "Ah, yes," replied Gorgo, "that is because we alone among women give birth to *men*" (μόναι γὰρ τίκτομεν ἄνδρας). Little is known of how the girls were trained, and it is impossible to believe that they were submitted to a close-knit organization comparable to that of the boys. Still they were arranged in bands or herds, just as the boys were. The word ἴλη (troop, company) is applied to

[1] Xen. *Lac.* i. 4. Plut. *Lyc.* xiv. Cic. *Tusc.* ii. 15. 36. Critias *FHG* II. 68. Philost. *Gym.* xxvii. Another reason is given by Barth (1920) 107: "*In Sparta allein nahmen die Mädchen an Übungen teil, weil sie nach den dortigen Gesetzen zur Verteidigung der Stadt in Notfalle die Waffen zu ergreifen hatten.*" This is a rather too strong re-statement of Plut. *Apophth. Lac., Lyc.* 12.

THE SPARTAN *AGOGE*

them in Callimachus:[1] "Come forth, Athena! A company pleasing to thy heart awaits thee, the maiden daughters of Acestor's mighty sons;" and the word ἀγέλα (band) is connected with them in Pindar.[2] It may be that there were sixty allotted to a band: compare the attractive scene drawn for us by Theocritus.[3] "For lo, we maidens are all of like age with her, and one course we were wont to run, anointed in manly fashion, by the baths of Eurotas. Four times sixty girls were we, the maiden flower of the land."

Even in Sparta, however, the girls did not frequent the same gymnasia as the young men did, and the state provided separate exercise places for their use.[4] When speaking of gymnasia in the primitive time, one should not think of buildings, for Sparta, like Crete, had only δρόμοι, plain athletic fields with no buildings. Under a roof was no place for a Spartan to exercise; he was expected to spend his life *sub divo et trepidis in rebus*. According to Livy (xxxiv. 27), one of the δρόμοι, apparently the principal one, was not in the city, but out in the fields. It is easy to con-

---
[1] *Hymn* v. (*Bath of Pallas*) 33f. tr. A. W. Mair.
[2] *Fr.* 112 Bergk⁴ Λάκαινα μὲν παρθένων ἀγέλα.
[3] 18. 22ff. Wilamowitz

ἄμμες δ' αἱ πᾶσαι συνομάλικες, αἷς δρόμος ωὑτός
χρισαμέναις ἀνδριστὶ παρ Εὐρώταο λοετροῖς
τετράκις ἑξήκοντα κόραι, θῆλυς νεολαία.

The writer quotes Lang's translation.
[4] Nicol. Damasc. *Eth.* 35 (*HGM* I. 150) γυμνάσια δ' ὥσπερ ἀνδρῶν ἐστιν, οὕτω καὶ τῶν παρθένων. Contrast the custom at Ceos and seemingly at Locri (see page 242 below).

jecture that it was on the banks of the Eurotas.[1] In later days there were gymnasia erected on the athletic field.[2]

Modern girls, the author is told, rarely wrestle, but the Spartan girls did regularly.[3] Neither do girls nowadays customarily engage in the "weight events," but at Sparta the vigorous maidens hurled both javelin and discus.[4] Indeed, the only exercise practiced by Spartan girls that is still engaged in by girls of the twentieth century is running.[5] Like the young men, they had contests to test their strength and skill in rivalry, and sometimes went on expeditions to Mt. Taygetus, where they clambered over rough country, up and down the mountain ridges.[6] They dressed sensibly for their exercising, feeling no Victorian scruples, and realizing that athletic bodies like theirs were deserving of pride,

---

[1] Cf. Theoc. *l. c.* The ancients generally, before the invention of the complex bathing establishments, liked to have a river for bathing purposes near the exercise grounds.

[2] Paus. iii. 14. 6. Krause (1841) II. 666.

[3] That they wrestled nude with the young men as described by Eur. *Androm.* 597ff. (a passage falsely interpreted by Nicol. *Prog.* [Walz *Rhet. Gr.* I. 276]), *credat Iudæus Apella*. The exaggeration is due to Euripides' hostility toward Sparta (Haase 373). The scholiast on Juvenal iv. 53 shows that they did sometimes wrestle with men.

[4] The shot-put and hammer-throw were unknown to ancient Greece.

[5] On the running of the Spartan girls see Philost. *Gym.* xxvii. For an exaggerated and poetically colored description of their exercises, see Propert. iii. 14. 1ff. One should add to the exercises named above jumping, dancing, and ball playing. (Grasberger III. 503). The leg exercise described in Ar. *Lysist.* 82 was apparently a favorite; Pollux iv. 102 says that one Spartan woman jumped and kicked her buttocks with her heels one thousand times in succession, a feat which was recorded on her tombstone.

[6] Sen. *Med.* 77ff.

not shame.[1] K. O. Müller gives the lie to the tradition that they were watched when they were at their exercise either by the younger or the older men; idle spectators loafing around were not allowed in Spartan gymnasia.

The question naturally arises, for how many years were the Spartan girls subjected to physical education under state supervision? Our only hint in answer to this question is contained in Plato's *Laws* (viii. 833C–D). Girls, the philosopher says, should exercise from the age of thirteen until they reach eighteen, unless they marry first. They may, if they wish, continue their training until the age of twenty, but under no circumstances longer than that, and never after they become brides. How closely modelled after actual conditions in Sparta these recommendations were can not be discovered. Certainly the women gave up exercises in public when they married, but often they continued them in private. The married Lampito in Aristophanes (*Lysist.* 82) attributes her buxom beauty and vigor to exercises of a gymnastic character.[2] Some think it more probable that

---

[1] "*Nackt oder leicht bekleidet*," K. O. Müller. II. 308; cf. Ov. *Her.* xvi. 149f.; Propert. iii. 14. 4; Eur. *Andromˌ* 595ff.; and Plato's ideal, *Resp.* v. 452A. The passage on physical education of women in the *Laws* (viii. 833C–D) was composed with the Spartan system in mind. On account of the short woolen garment, slit up the sides, which the girls wore when exercising (if they wore anything), they were often called φαινομηρίδες, "thigh-showers;" see Ibycus *Fr.* 61 (Bergk[4] III. 252); Pollux ii. 187 and vii. 55. Possibly they sometimes used a cincture as their garb for sport; cf. the bronze of a Dorian girl in Bruno Schröder, Tafel 110a.

[2] Bussemaker and Fougères in Dar.–Sagl. II. 1703.

the girls, like the boys, began their training at seven, rather than at thirteen.[1] Like the boys, too, they must have been in the charge of the *paidonomos* and the other educational officials until they were married.

Such was the organization of physical education in Sparta's prime. With the fall of Spartan power at the battle of Leuctra, in 371, the old system of education fell into neglect and decay. We know that this decay was posterior to the time of Socrates, for in one of the conversations recorded in the *Memorabilia* (iii. 5. 15) Socrates commends the Spartans for their diligence in gymnastics, and contrasts with them the Athenians. In the time of Aristotle, however, the Spartans were no longer such perfect physical specimens as they had been in the earlier days, and their morale had declined together with their bodies. In fact, Sparta had lost nearly all her former virtues, and was on the wane.[2] In the latter half of the third century before Christ, there were two Spartans who wished to resuscitate the Lycurgean *agoge* in its pristine vigor. These men were the kings Agis IV and Cleomenes III. Fortunately, we have their biographies, written by Plutarch, and are able to glean hints of their activity in educational reform. Of Agis Plutarch says:[3] "He set his face against pleasures. He put

[1] Exarchopulos 145.

[2] Plut. *Agis et Cleom.* iii. 1 τῶν πλείστων ἐξέπεσεν ἡ Σπάρτη καλῶν, καὶ ταπεινὰ πράττουσα παρ' ἀξίαν διετέλει μέχρι τῶν χρόνων ἐκείνων, ἐν οἷς Ἆγις καὶ Κλεομένης ἐβασίλευον. See Busolt I. 494.

[3] *Agis et Cleom.* iv. 2 tr. Perrin (whose translation is used also in the following extracts).

away from his person the adornments which were thought to befit the grace of his figure, laid aside and avoided every extravagance, prided himself on his short Spartan cloak, observed sedulously the Spartan customs in his meals and baths and general ways of living, and declared that he did not want the royal power at all unless by means of it he could restore the ancient laws and discipline (τὴν πάτριον ἀγωγήν)." Since Spartan life was built on the *agoge* as a necessary foundation, Agis deemed it fitting that even the highest elected officials of Sparta, the ephors, should be concerned with the operation of the educational system. To the lot of the ephors he assigned the duty of reviewing the youth periodically. Let Ælian (xiv. 7) tell the details:[1] "And besides, it was written in the law that every ten days the youth stripped naked should pass in public review before the ephors. Now if they were solid and vigorous, resembling the works of the sculptor and the engraver, as a result of the gymnastic exercises, praise was accorded them; but if their physique displayed any flabbiness or flaccidity, with fat beginning to appear in rolls because of laziness, then were they beaten and punished. The ephors were concerned also to inspect their equipment in detail, lest any part of it fall short of the proper orderliness." Such were the pains lavished by the

[1] Ælian's statements are from Agatharcides, who gives almost the same details in Ath. xii. 74 = *FGrHist*. lxxxvi. F10. For the attribution of the ephors' concern in education to the time of Agis, see the commentary of Jacoby on Agatharcides *l. c.*

ephors. The *paidonomos* and his helpers must have striven with diligence to keep the boys in perfect trim for these frequent reviews. The boys themselves doubtless took pride in a clean-cut appearance. Unhappily, this rejuvenation of the *agoge* did not meet with favor in all quarters; Agis' career was cut short when he was put to death by the ephors; and we can hardly think that his attempt at restoring the "ancestral *agoge*" was deeply or enduringly effective.

Indeed, in the biography of Cleomenes, who partook of the spirit of Agis, we are told as much.[1] "Of course, then, the condition of the city was not pleasing to him. The citizens had been lulled to sleep by idleness and pleasure; the king was willing to let all public business go, provided that no one thwarted his desire for luxurious living in the midst of his wealth; the public interests were neglected, while every man was eagerly intent upon his own private gain; and as for practice in arms, self-restraint in the young, hardiness, and equality, it was even dangerous to speak of these now that Agis was dead and gone." So had the mighty Sparta fallen! And what interests us most, they "had lost all ambition to maintain the ancient Spartan discipline (τὴν ἀγωγήν)."[2] This deplorable state of affairs Cleomenes was eager to change. After biding his time until he had acquired sufficient power to eject the ephors and his other leading opponents, he started in to reform the state according to his matured

[1] Plut. *op. cit.* xxiii. 1.   [2] *Ibid.* xxiv. 1.

convictions. Partly because he used the "big stick" methods so well adapted to the Spartans, partly because he was capably advised by his philosopher friend and instructor, Sphærus, his attempt succeeded better than that of Agis. But let Plutarch once more tell the story:[1] "Next he devoted himself to the training of the young men and to the 'agoge' or ancient discipline, most of the details of which Sphærus, who was then in Sparta, helped him in arranging. And quickly was the proper system of bodily training and public messes resumed, a few out of necessity, but most with a willing spirit, subjecting themselves to the old Spartan régime with all its simplicity." The result of this renaissance of the old Lycurgean educational system was immediately visible. None were more surprised than the Spartans to find that within a short time the youth of their power was renewed like the eagle's, and once more they domineered over the Peloponnese and were recognized as the supreme power in Hellas.[2] Cleomenes' subsequent downfall and Sparta's submission can not be attributed in any way to the renewed *agoge*, but rather to a combination of circumstances—chiefly treachery, as Plutarch reports.[3] Antigonus on seizing Sparta did away with all of Cleomenes' reforms, and the

---

[1] *Op. cit.* xxxii. 3f.

[2] Plutarch (*Ibid.* xxxix. 4) tells us expressly that this came about because they resumed their ancestral customs and returned εἰς ἴχνος ἐκείνης τῆς ἀγωγῆς.

[3] *Ibid.* xlix. 2, on the authority of Phylarchus *FGrHist.* lxxxi. F59.

Lycurgean *agoge* sank back into a slough of despond about 220 B.C.

In the year 188 [1] came temporary disaster. Though the *agoge* had fallen very low in internal decay, still Philopœmen, the head of the Achæan alliance which overthrew Sparta, thought it best to raze this ancient system along with Sparta's walls. Accordingly, the children and youths of ephebic age were all forced to abandon their accustomed methods of training and change to the utilitarian education of Achæa.[2] Grasberger (III. 580) points out what a humiliating blow this must have been. Even if the *agoge* was no longer what it had been in Sparta's great days, nevertheless its antiquity made it sacred to the conservative Spartans, and they surely bowed their heads in grief at the loss of this proud tradition of their forefathers, far more than at the destruction of their newly erected walls. Happily, they did not have to submit to the abominated Achæan education for long. Four years later, when the Roman power was gaining ground in the Peloponnese, the Spartans petitioned to the lords of the Mediterranean to be rid of the Achæan educational system,[3] and their request was granted. "Having obtained permission from the Romans," says Plutarch,[4] "they abandoned the Achæan polity, and resumed and re-established that which had come

---

[1] Niese *Geschichte der gr. u. makedon. Staaten* III. 44.
[2] Plut. *Philop.* 16. Paus. vii. 8. 5, viii. 51. 3. Cf. K. O. Müller II. 295.
[3] Liv. xxxix. 33, cf. xxxix. 36–7.
[4] *L. c.* tr. Perrin.

down from their fathers, so far as was possible after their many misfortunes and great degeneration." So once more there was a renewal of the "Lycurgean *agoge*, which was famed throughout the world" (Liv. xxxix. 36).

Our next knowledge of the history of the *agoge* is from the inscriptions of the period of Roman domination. The taste for archaizing was now abroad, and everywhere in the literature of the period we can discern a renewed interest in the ancient Spartan customs.[1] We even hear of Professors of Lycurgean Customs.[2] The upper age classes with which we were formerly familiar reappear in the inscriptions, the names for ten, eleven, or twelve-year-olds in different forms or with the spelling altered.[3] The *melleirens* and *eirens* reappear unchanged, while the two youngest classes (ῥωβίδες and προμικιζόμενοι) are not mentioned.[4]

By this time the ephebic system had taken its rise in Athens and spread to other parts of Greece, as we shall see later. Realizing the similarity of the *agoge* to the ephebia (both were for military ends), and no longer animated by the old-time jealousy, the Spartan lads began to call themselves *synephebi*,

[1] Jüthner *RE* VII. 2070.

[2] *IG* v. 1. 500 Οἱ διδάσκαλοι ἀμφὶ τὰ Λυκούργεια ἔθη.

[3] The word μικιζόμενοι is variously written μικιχιζόμενοι (*IG* v. 1. 276, 296, etc.), μικιχιδδόμενοι (*IG* v. 1. 288, 305, 323) and in other forms. The πρόπαις appears as πρατοπάμπαις (*IG* v. 1. 256, 270, 273, 279, 298, 340, 341), and the παῖς as ἀτροπάμπαις (*IG* v. 1. 278, 279).

[4] The reason for this is given above, page 20, n. 2.

"fellow-ephebi."[1] Another new term, indicative of brotherhood and fellowship, was one applied to the members of the same band (ἀγέλα): κάσεις, "brothers."[2] Hesychius gives us the further information that the term was employed also for the girls; this evidence is of importance for two reasons. First, it gives added weight to our belief that the girls as well as the boys were grouped in companies, and, second, it is the best evidence the writer knows of that girls were included in this revival of the old education. Further proof that Spartan girls still engaged in gymnastics in this epoch is the testimony of a scholiast[3] that "Palfurius Sura, the son of a man of consular rank, during the reign of Nero once wrestled with a Lacedæmonian maiden in a contest."

As for the places of exercise, probably no great changes were made. It is a fact now accepted that there were only gymnasia, no palæstræ, at Sparta. Yet in an inscription which belongs approximately to the age of Hadrian (*IG* v. 1. 493), we have an allusion to palæstræ at Sparta, used as exercise places for boys. Very likely the palæstra was introduced into Sparta at this late period, along with other things originating in Athens, such as the term *synephebi*, and the gymna-

[1] *IG* v. 1. 493 and many other inscriptions. Never, the writer thinks, was the term *ephebi* officially employed at Sparta: *IG* v. 1. 1583 is listed among *falsa et suspecta;* the frequent use of the word by Pausanias and Plutarch in referring to Sparta is inexact, or else is in the loose, non-technical sense of "young men."

[2] κάσιοι Hesychius. The modified nominative singular form, κάσεν, is the only form found in the inscriptions, where it recurs about forty times.

[3] Schol. Iuv. iv. 53.

siarchy (see next page). Since, however, this allusion is isolated and in a poem, the word may here be used loosely, as often happened, for gymnasium.

Two new groups of educational officials were added to or substituted for the ones formerly known. These were the "annual officers" (διαβέτεις) and the "overseers" (βίδεοι, βίδυοι, βιδιαῖοι). The former were seemingly lower in the *cursus honorum* than the latter,[1] but we have no accurate criteria to aid us in distinguishing their functions.[2] Kolbe conjectures[3] that the annual officers were six in number, because it seems that each one had charge of the youth of a tribe, and in the imperial period there were six tribes. The overseers were certainly six in number, as the inscriptional catalogs show us;[4] their chairman was called the "elder," and it was because of reckoning him out that Pausanias (iii. 11. 2) gave the number of the overseers as five.[5] An inscription recently found[6] proves that one could be an overseer more than once, but how long a single term of office was we do not know. The overseers supplanted the *ampaides* (ἄμπαιδες), of whom we no longer hear in this period.[7] Among their duties was arranging the contests at the Platanistas and other contests, according to Pausanias (*l. c.*), and they had offices in the agora.

Another innovation was the liturgical gymnasiarch,

[1] *IG* v. 1. 65.
[2] Zebelev.
[3] See his remarks in *IG* v. 1. p. 14.
[4] See indices to *IG* v. 1.
[5] Zebelev.
[6] *BSA* XXVI. 166, B8, l. 5 βίδεος δίς.
[7] Exarchopulos 67.

well-known in other states. We find him (*IG* v. 1. 20) furnishing oil for purposes of anointing, "according to the law," to men, youths, and boys. One Sextus Pompeius Theoxenus,[1] we learn, was a gymnasiarch "of high repute, a loyal subject and a patriot, good and just;" the city honored him for his munificence to the government. Some years later, the title "perpetual gymnasiarch" was given as a life-long designation of honor to those who acquitted themselves with distinction in their gymnasiarchal duties.[2] An inscription of the time of Marcus Aurelius or Commodus[3] cites Lysippus, son of Demænetus, for "surpassing the men of his time in the ambitious way in which he conducted the gymnasiarchy." As we shall see later was often the case at Athens and elsewhere, the gymnasiarchy at Sparta was often a personal expense as well as a charge. A certain Sextus Pompeius Spatalus was gymnasiarch twice, the second time at his own expense (i. e., he purchased the oil from his personal funds).[4]

The last traces we now have of this revival of physical education in Sparta fall in the early part of the third century of the Christian era.[5] Well may we feel surprise at the vitality that enabled it to endure so long. An *aleiptes* as teacher of athletes is mentioned in *IG* v. 1. 491, and another *ibid.* 569;[6] the

---

[1] *IG* v. 1. 464.   [2] *Ibid.* 468, 528, 529, 535, 549, 552.
[3] *Ibid.* 531.   [4] *Ibid.* 535.   [5] *Ibid.* 551, 601, 683.
[6] Also 542 and 543 (both of the late second or early third century after Christ), and 666.

THE SPARTAN *AGOGE*

monster athleticism swiftly crushed the life out of the ancient system. Neglect and sloth were the influences that were ruining Spartan education before Cleomenes, but in at the death came professionalism, finally spreading even to Sparta, which resisted it longer than any other country. The downfall of physical education was complete. By this time, interest in the care and development of the body was dying or dead all through the Greek world.

The results of the Spartan *agoge* were what a little reflection might lead one to expect. The system was devoid of symmetry and balance, in direct contradiction to the rule to which the remainder of Greece clung: "Moderation in all things." To be sure, what its founders aimed at, they did secure. Every Spartan possessed a splendid physique, and health unequalled in any other community of Greece; he could endure the stress of long marches and of battle without flagging; his courage and obedience were exemplary. The girls were fortunate above those of other states in being given an opportunity for outdoor life, and they developed their bodies to an excellent condition of health, beauty, and strength.[1] Yet, how much does

---

[1] Ar. *Lysist.* 78ff. As Lampito, the Spartan, enters, Lysistrata addresses her (tr. Rogers):

    O welcome, welcome, Lampito, my love.
    O the sweet girl! how hale and bright she looks!
    Here's nerve! here's muscle! here's an arm could fairly
    Throttle a bull!
Lampito: Weel, by the Twa, I think sae.
    An' I can loup an' fling an' kick my hurdies.

Sparta mean to civilization and how much does her contemporary Athens, with a different educational system, mean? The Spartans were not trained in such a way as to stimulate their intellect and stir their imagination. They were simply shaped into units in a mechanical fighting machine. "Parents who devote their children to gymnastics while they neglect their necessary education," said Aristotle,[1] "in reality vulgarize them; for they make them useful to the state in one quality only, and even in this the argument proves them to be inferior to others." Philosophers and poets did not spring from Sparta. The excessive amount of time devoted to gymnastics there, as later in Bœotia, kept the people from intellectual pursuits, and the results were saddening. Zimmern (185) speaks of "slow Spartan wits," and again he says: "Spartan minds, as Alcibiades knew, moved very slowly. One had to make their flesh creep before they would take in a new idea." In days of degeneracy, furthermore, immorality was occasioned by the *agoge*. The partial or complete nudity of youths and maidens at their exercises proved demoralizing, and led to unchastity between the sexes.[2]

Although we must grant, therefore, that the Lycurgean *agoge* achieved some fine results, and has much

[1] *Pol.* viii. 3. 4 (p. 1338b 32–6) tr. Jowett.
[2] Euripides (*Androm.* 595ff.) and Aristotle (*Pol.* ii. 6. 5 [p. 1269b 19–23]) complained of the lack of chastity of Spartan girls and thought it a result of the educational practices. Plato too observed the depravity of Spartan women, and for a time much later cf. Mart. iv. **55**. 6–7 *libidinosae Ledæas Lacedæmonos palæstras.*

to be said in its favor, yet we must also recognize that it did not make for a rounded existence, nor did it immediately or remotely contribute much to the sum of human happiness. It is to Athens that we must turn to find the ideal we are seeking. The occasion for Sparta's decline is well put by Aristotle:[1] "Most of these military states are safe only when they are at war, but fall when they have acquired their empire; like unused iron they lose their edge in time of peace. And for this the legislator is to blame, because he never taught them how to lead the life of peace."

[1] *Pol.* vii. 13. 15 (p. 1334a 6–10) tr. Jowett.

CHAPTER III

PHYSICAL EDUCATION IN CRETE

Our evidence on Cretan education is both incomplete and scattered. The chief source is Ephorus, whose work on the subject we know only through Strabo (x. 4. 16ff.), and next to him Aristotle, excerpts of whose work on the constitution of Crete, made by Heraclides Lembos,[1] we still have preserved. From several other authors, such as Plato and Hesychius, we can glean a little. The inscriptions have added to our store of knowledge the ephebic oaths, and have set us right on the age-terminology. Kahrstedt (352–3) has discussed the ages and some civic aspects of the education, while the most modern and correct treatment, albeit in a compact and encyclopedic form, is given by Busolt-Swoboda (II. 752ff.). In this discussion an attempt has been made to include all the pertinent information given us by the too-meager sources.

The resemblance of Cretan to Spartan education has been mentioned more than once already.[2] We feel ourselves on familiar ground when we find that the troops or bands (ἀγέλαι, *agelai*) were the basis of grouping in Crete, as in her Doric fellow-country of the Peloponnese. Here, too, we find the military aim

---
[1] These excerpts have usually been ascribed to Heraclides Ponticus.
[2] *Supra*, pages 9, 14, 29.

uppermost in the educational system; the emphasis on physical development is motivated by the desire to insure that the young men of Crete will display endurance and bravery when the test of war comes.[1] Since the goal to be reached was identical in the two countries, the exercises employed were partly identical. As at Sparta, education was completely under state control, and the state lent no encouragement to a literary, or, as the Greeks called it, "musical" education.[2]

From the famous inscription called the Law of Gortyn, found mostly in 1884, we learn something of the Cretan age-terminology. The word *anoros* (ἄνωρος,[3] "unripe") was applied to one who was sexually immature and had not yet reached his legal majority. When he became mature and was recognized in the eyes of the law as being of age, he was designated as *apodromos* (ἀπόδρομος or ἀπόδρομος ἠβίων), the word indicating that he was still excluded from the *dromos* or gymnasium. After some years he was received into fuller rights of manhood and entitled *dromeus* (δρομεύς). The identity of the stem in *apodromos* and *dromeus* is self-evident, and the reference is patently to the *dromos*.[4]

---

[1] Aristot. *Pol.* vii. 2. 5 (p. 1324b 8f.) ἐν Λακεδαίμονι καὶ Κρήτῃ πρὸς τοὺς πολέμους συντέτακται σχεδὸν ἥ τε παιδεία καὶ τὸ τῶν νόμων πλῆθος. Cf. Krause (1841) II. 692; Haase 374.

[2] Aristot. *Fr.* 611. 15 Rose γράμματα δὲ μόνον παιδεύονται, καὶ ταῦτα μετρίως. "Die geistige Bildung trat zurück hinter der einseitigen, übertriebenen Pflege der körperlichen Gymnastik."—Busolt-Swoboda II. 756.

[3] Col. xi. 19 has ἄνηβος.

[4] Wachsmuth 201. Still another Cretan term that had reference to the *dromos* was δεκάδρομοι, which Hesychius *s. v.* explains as οἱ δέκα ἐν τοῖς ἀνδράσι ἐσχηκότες, i. e., those who had been *dromeis* for ten years.

Another resemblance between Crete and Sparta crops up here, in that the exercise grounds of both countries were called *dromoi*. Not one of the Cretan gymnasia or *dromoi* has been found by archæologists or located approximately by epigraphical testimony. We only know that the inhabitants of Itanus, honoring Ptolemy Euergetes about 246 B.C., promised among other things to build a gymnasium to commemorate him;[1] no doubt their purpose was to name the structure the Ptolemæum. Whether or no they carried into effect their promise is uncertain.

Those belonging to the youngest of the three groups just named were also called, in popular, if not in legal diction, *skotioi*,[2] from the word *skotos* meaning "darkness." This term indicated that they remained in the figurative darkness of private life all through childhood, and were not brought under state control until they entered the next age group. Still a third term applicable within exactly the same age limits was *apageloi*,[3] indicating that the boys were not yet eligible to enter the troops or *agelai*. Now with the help of Hesychius we are able to determine the age at which boys ceased to be *anoroi*, *skotioi*, or *apageloi*, and entered the second age class. The turning point was the seventeenth birthday.[4] Less easy is it to determine

---

[1] *SIG*³ 463.

[2] Schol. Eur. *Alc.* 989 Κρῆτες δὲ τοὺς ἀνήβους σκοτίους λέγουσιν.

[3] ἀπάγελοι. See Caillemer in Dar.-Sagl. I. 131.

[4] Hesych. s. v. ἀπάγελος: ὁ μηδέπω συναγελαζόμενος παῖς, ὁ μέχρι ἐτῶν ἑπτακαίδεκα. See Caillemer *l. c.*; Szanto *RE* I. 769; Busolt-Swoboda II. 752.

the boundary line between the *apodromoi* and the *dromeis*. The parallels of Athens and Sparta are the only help we can get, and, as Kahrstedt (353) says, it is more reasonable to adduce the parallel of Sparta; we should therefore surmise that one became a *dromeus* at the age of twenty.[1]

To our surprise it appears that, according to the derivation of *apodromos*, Cretan lads were not allowed admission to the state *dromoi* until they were twenty or thereabouts.[2] This is directly at variance with the usage of Sparta and other countries. Again we see a variance with Spartan practice in the short duration of the training in the *agelai*, a circumstance which can be proved by the following argument. As we read in Hesychius, the boys could not join the bands until they reached their seventeenth year. The members of the bands were called *agelaoi*,[3] the Cretan equivalent for the word ephebi generally employed in Greece. Now a comparison of the passages quoted below in the notes, from Eustathius and Hesychius, shows that the terms *agelaoi* and *apodromoi* are synonymous, and can be used interchangeably in referring to the intermediate age class. This being so, the bands or *agelai* broke up when their members reached twenty, or whatever exact age it was when one became a *dromeus*,

[1] So also Busolt-Swoboda *l. c.*

[2] This is the plain statement of Eustathius 727. 22f. δηλαδὴ ἀπόδρομοι ἐν Κρήτῃ, οἱ μηδέπω τῶν κοινῶν δρόμων μετέχοντες ἔφηβοι. Doubtless they had exercise grounds of some sort (Nilsson 314, n. 4).

[3] Hesych. *s. v.* ἀγελάστους (which should be emended to ἀγελάους or ἀγελάτας): τοὺς ἐφήβους. Κρῆτες.

and thus a Cretan belonged to an *agela* only three years or a little more. As soon as he became a *dromeus* and stepped out of the *agela*, however, he was admitted to a *hetairia* ("band of comrades"); indeed, the *agelai* did not, strictly speaking, dissolve, but simply changed their name to *hetairiai*.

With these points cleared up, we may see the very considerable difference between the Cretan and the Spartan bands or *agelai*. We saw that in Sparta the members of a herd or *boua* were all of the same age, whereas in the *agela* the different ages were commingled. In Crete, on the other hand, the members of an *agela* were all of an age; it is, therefore, to the Spartan *boua* rather than *agela* that the Cretan *agela* is equivalent.[1] Neither were the members of an *agela* boys, as at Sparta, but they were of an age corresponding to that of the "ball players" (σφαιρεῖς), the older *eirens*. Two other points of difference already mentioned are the shorter duration of training in the *agela*, and the exclusion of the *agelaoi* from the *dromoi* in Crete. The leadership of the Cretan *agela* was entrusted to an official known as an *archos* (ἀρχός; the word means simply "leader").[2]

Now let us trace the course of the education, as best we may, from boyhood. In the first place, it is to be

[1] This is shown in detail by Kahrstedt (353).
[2] This is a case of epigraphical versus literary testimony. Aristotle *Fr.* 611. 15 Rose asserted that ἀγελάτης was the name for the leader of the ἀγέλα, but this is controverted by the inscription published in *AJ Arch.* XI. (1896) 587, which says τὰνς τιμὰνς ἐδούμεθα ἀγελάται, δούμην ἀρχῶι. An ἀγελάτης was, then, a member, instead of a leader of an ἀγέλα.

PHYSICAL EDUCATION IN CRETE

taken for granted that education was compulsory for all, as at Sparta. We do not hear of inferior types of education for the non-citizens, and Aristotle says [1] that the slaves, although allowed many privileges, were forbidden to practice gymnastics or to possess arms. The sons of citizens were left by the state under their parents' care very much longer than was the case in Sparta. Their fathers were accustomed, however, to take them to the *syssitia*, or common meals, of the men, and let them serve a sort of apprenticeship to the discipline they were later to face. The boys were made to sit on the ground, clad in poor, coarse cloaks, in which they shivered in winter. All the time listening to the conversation of the men, they served themselves with small portions and waited table for their elders.[2] With the triple purpose of developing them physically, preparing them for war, and providing amusement at the *syssitia*, the men set them on to childish fights with one another. Often the boys who visited one *syssition* were matched against those of another. To direct these "battles," which we can imagine consisted of fisticuffs and wrestling, there was one *paidonomos* set over the group of each table.[3]

[1] *Pol.* ii. 2. 12 (p. 1264a 21f.).

[2] Besides the account of Ephorus, additional testimony on this point is given by Dosiadas *FHG* IV. 399, and Pyrgion *FHG* IV. 486 οἱ νεώτατοι ἐφεστᾶσι διακονοῦντες.

[3] The above paragraph is based on Ephorus, as reported by Strabo x. 4. 20 (483 Cas.). The wide difference between the *paidonomoi* of Crete and Sparta should be observed. In the latter state, it will be recalled, there was but one *paidonomos*, who superintended the entire *agoge*.

On becoming *agelaoi* at the age of seventeen, the boys were taken from home by the state for life in the barracks. They now ate and slept together,[1] as at Sparta, but here the state furnished their food and supplied their other needs. The sons of the aristocrats were given the task of assembling the *agelaoi*. They plunged into this undertaking with competitive ardor, each one trying to get as large a number as possible in his band. It was like getting "pledges" for a college fraternity. Perhaps custom fixed some upper limit for the size of a band, lest some smart youth should gather an utterly disproportionate horde. Once all the pledges were made, the young assembler proudly handed them over to the *archos*, who was normally his father.[2] The *archos* directed their gymnastic exercises,[3] presided over their war-like games and contests, and took them out on hunting expeditions.[4] His authority was great enough to enable him to punish any case of rebellion or disobedience.

Mimic battles between the *agelai* were ordained for

---

[1] Strab. *l. c.* τρέφονται δὲ δημοσίᾳ. Aristot. *Fr. l. c.* τὰ πολλὰ κοιμῶνται μετ' ἀλλήλων.

[2] ὡς τὸ πολύ, says Strabo. This probably was an accepted rule, and another was chosen for *archos* only when the assembler's father was dead or in some way incapacitated for the duties entailed by the office.

[3] ἐξάγειν ἐπὶ δρόμους (Strab. *l. c.*) means to take them out for cross-country runs, not to the δρόμοι. Falconer's translation seems to have the right notion here; H. L. Jones' translation gives a similar rendering. The author interprets in the same way the use of δρόμους by Nicolaus of Damascus (*HGM* I. 151–2, from Stob. *Flor.* xliv. 41). This whole passage of Nicolaus should be compared, as it is a trifle earlier than the account of Strabo, though not so full.

[4] Ath. xiv. 28 οἱ δὲ Κρῆτες κυνηγετικοί, διὸ καὶ ποδώκεις.

certain days. To the strains of the lyre and martial flute, they clashed together and smote one another lustily with their fists, clubs of wood, and even more dangerous weapons. After three years or more of these battles they were as scarred as German student duelists, so earnest were they in their sport. Strabo tells us that they bore away from the mock battles marks, some inflicted by fists, some by weapons of iron. Apparently they used no buttons on their foils! They became inured to this rough treatment, for physical pain and hardship were their daily companions. In one sentence Strabo gives a good delineation of what they had to go through:[1] "With a view that courage, not fear, should predominate, they were accustomed from childhood to the use of arms, and to endure fatigue; hence they disregarded heat and cold, rugged and steep roads, blows received in gymnastic exercises and in set battles."[2] Still more compactly Cicero (*Tusc.* ii. 14. 34) summarizes the Cretan method of training their youth: *venando currendo, esuriendo sitiendo, algendo æstuando*.

Of instructors in addition to the *archos* we are told nothing. I think it highly improbable that there were any, since the Spartan analogy easily comes to mind, and especially since Josephus (*c. Apion.* ii. 172) says that the Cretans were not educated by the spoken word, but by custom and example. Besides, what the

[1] x. 4. 16 (480 Cas.) tr. Falconer.
[2] See the similar information in *Rerum Nat. Script. Gr. Min.* (Keller 1877) I. 115.

Cretans learned was simple, and they did not aim at cleverness and virtuosity in the exercises, wherefore no instructors except the *archos* would be needed. Such exercises as jumping, javelin throwing, and discus throwing are not specifically attested. Strabo records that the *agelaoi* practiced archery, and the dance in armor called the Pyrrhic. For both of these, certainly, they were famous. Athens in the days of the ephebia recruited most of the instructors in physical education from her own confines, but we find that once, at least, she procured an archery instructor (τοξότης) from Crete.[1]

An interesting feature of the Cretan system is the ephebic oath of citizenship taken by the *agelaoi* at the time when they left the *agela* and became *dromeis*.[2] The best preserved example of such an oath was found in Dreros in 1854 in an inscription dating from the close of the third century before Christ, but recording an oath of much greater antiquity.[3] The *agelaoi*, 180 in number, swore solemnly by a long list of gods and goddesses to be loyal to their city-state (φιλοδρήριοι), and to cherish everlasting enmity against Lyttos and its inhabitants, doing them as much harm as possible. From other Cretan cities, too, we have fragmentary records, mostly of the third and second centuries before Christ, showing that the *agelaoi* had to swear

---

[1] *IG* ii. 1². 665. Cf. Plat. *Legg.* viii. 834D τοξότης δ'ἀφ' ἵππων Κρὴς οὐκ ἄχρηστος.
[2] See Ziebarth (1914) 164 and n. 2.
[3] *SGDI* 4952.

to abide by the treaties made with neighboring cities: so at Gortyn,[1] Hierapytna,[2] Cnossus,[3] Latus,[4] and Malla.[5]

It is a matter of regret that our information about the educational system of Crete is so scanty. We can hardly give a general estimate of it, and little is known of its results. Plato[6] issued a protest against it, reminding us of Aristotle's criticism that the Spartan *agoge* made the boys brutal, like wild beasts: "Your military way of life is modelled after the camp, and is not like that of dwellers in cities; and you have your young men herding (ἐν ἀγέλῃ) and feeding together like young colts." The arrangements seem to have been less rigid than those of Sparta, and still simpler. We have not the least shred of evidence to show whether the girls were allowed to participate in the training with the boys. Since the circumstance would have been unusual enough to attract comment, if the girls had shared in the training, we may assume that they did not. The system seems to have had no influence on other states, as those of Sparta and especially Athens had. The writer can not improve on Freeman's conclusion (p. 38): "Of the practical results of Cretan education nothing can be said. From the day when Idomeneus sets sail from Troy, Crete almost disappears from Hellenic history."

[1] *SGDI* 5024.
[2] *Ibid.* 5044.
[3] *Ibid.* 5073.
[4] *Ibid.* 5075 (belongs to first century B. C.).
[5] *Ibid.* 5100.
[6] *Legg.* ii. 666E tr. Jowett.

CHAPTER IV

ATHENS BEFORE 335 B.C.

For a history of physical education at Athens we are better equipped than for any other city of the ancient world. The host of Athenian writers in the fifth and fourth centuries have furnished us with a wealth of detail; we are particularly indebted to Aristophanes, Plato, Xenophon, and Æschines. Among later writers, Lucian and Plutarch should be named as useful sources. The modern works of Grasberger and Girard merit high commendation, but are partly antiquated now by virtue of new discoveries and studies. Some points have been shuttle-cocks of dispute, as the difference between the *paidotribes* and *gymnastes*, the exact nature and relation of palæstra and gymnasium, and especially the date of the foundation of the ephebia. The discussion of the latter will be found in Chapter VI, but on the former questions as much light as possible will be shed in the present chapter.

It is in Athens that we can see physical education at its best, for there it grew up and flourished as an integral part of an admirable national life. Many modern histories of education, when treating of the Greek period, disregard the contributions of Crete and Sparta, not to mention other localities, and dwell exclusively on

Athens. Evidently the authors of these histories believe that Pericles spoke of his city with justice and truth, when he said in the famous Funeral Speech: Ξυνελών τε λέγω τήν τε πᾶσαν πόλιν τῆς Ἑλλάδος παίδευσιν εἶναι—"in short, I may say that our whole city is the school of Greece." As Delphi was thought to be the navel of the world in a geological sense, so was Athens in an educational sense. Here we find a scheme of instruction marked by perfect sanity and perfect balance, a scheme wisely formed to promote the wellbeing both of the individual and of the state. Neither were gymnastics overemphasized, as by the Dorians, nor literature and art, as by the Ionians. With an unerring judgment, Athens found the golden mean between these two asymmetrical viewpoints. A sound mind in a sound body was the goal for the individual, and with this goal attained there was sure to be soundness in the body politic. The specific ends of the physical education, as laid down by Aristotle,[1] were health, strength, agility, and beauty. The Athenians tried to make their bodies supple and alert; the Spartan style was heavier, aimed more to produce brute force and endurance.

The spirit in which the Athenians engaged in physical education was a serious one. In Homeric times the

---

[1] *Rhet.* i. 5 (p. 1361a 1–b3). *Pol.* viii. 2. 6 (p. 1338a 18f.). On beauty, see *Eth. N.* iii. 5. 15 (p. 1114a 23–5) τοῖς μὲν γὰρ διὰ φύσιν αἰσχροῖς οὐδεὶς ἐπιτιμᾷ, τοῖς δὲ δι' ἀγυμνασίαν καὶ ἀμέλειαν. "Though no one blames a man for being born ugly, we censure uncomeliness that is due to neglecting exercise and the care of the person" (tr. Rackham).

warriors had exercised mostly to amuse themselves, barely conscious of the ulterior purposes of keeping themselves fit and improving their efficiency in actual fighting. How different with the Athenians!

We read in Plato's *Laws:* [1] "For there ought to be no other secondary task to hinder the work of supplying the body with its proper exercise and nourishment, or the soul with learning and moral training: nay, every night and day is not sufficient for the man who is occupied therein to win from them their fruit in full and ample measure." A word the Athenians frequently used for gymnastic exercises was πόνοι, toils or hardships.[2] Plato classed physical education among the goods of life that are hardships and yet are beneficial to us; sometimes he referred to gymnastics as being engaged in perforce, and in the *Phædo* he spoke of gymnastics as physical punishment, or severe discipline, to say the least.[3] One thinks of the attitude of a man who does not really like vegetables, but eats them cheerfully because he knows they are good for him. I do not mean that the Athenians derived no enjoyment from their exercises, for they certainly did, but they regarded them in a business-like way, realizing fully the benefits they conferred, and discounting for the sake of these benefits the sweat and the weariness. Χαλεπὰ τὰ καλά was a characteristic saying: "All good things are hard."

[1] vii. 807D tr. Bury.
[2] Plat. *Polit.* 294E; Aristot. *Pol.* viii. 3. 3 (p. 1338b 13); Isoc. *ad Demon.* xii.; and scores of other passages.
[3] *Resp.* ii. 357C and vii. 536E. *Phædo* 94D.

In democratic Athens, physical education was the common privilege of all the male citizens. Only slaves, naturally, were debarred from taking part,[1] as they were in Crete and Sparta. Women were excluded from public life and obliged to stay at home in seclusion; hence no one thought of gymnastics for the girls. Athenian girls busied themselves with household tasks, and did not share with the boys in any part of the public education. No law defined how many years one must go to school, and those oppressed by poverty could and did give up their education at an early age.[2] The regular age for starting to school was six,[3] that is, when the boys were in their seventh year, and it seems to have been prescribed by law (see below, page 74) that none should enter at an earlier age. This is quite like Spartan usage, and corresponds to Aristotle's ideal.[4]

The usual school subjects were gymnastics and "music." The latter term embraced the studies presided over by the Muses, grammar and literature, as well as music in our sense of the word; in the following I shall use the word regularly in the Greek sense. When a boy first went to school, which of the two subjects was the earlier to be studied by him? This is a question that has been debated back and forth, but one can not find in any of the half-dozen or more schol-

---

[1] Æschin. *c. Timarch.* 138. Plut. *Sol.* i.
[2] Plat. *Protag.* 326C. Freeman 54.
[3] Ps.-Plat. *Axioch.* 366D. Plaut. *Merc.* 292 and 303. Grasberger I. 237. Freeman 51.
[4] *Pol.* vii. 15. 6 (p. 1336a 41–b 2).

arly works which have presented the divergent views any one which refers to all the passages that furnish evidence. Krause in 1851 (p. 99) was uncertain, but indicated that a passage in the pseudo-Platonic *Axiochus* [1] and another in Lucian's *Anacharsis* [2] made it seem probable that both subjects were pursued simultaneously from the beginning. Grasberger fifteen years later came to the opposite decision.[3] Before the boys went to the music teacher, he said, they visited the instructor of physical education, the *paidotribes;* and he expressed himself as unable to believe that boys from the age of six on visited daily two different schools, each for an equal length of time. Referring to one of Solon's laws,[4] which forbade both the music teachers and the *paidotribai* to open their schools before sunrise, he queried why this regulation should include both schools, if it were true that pupils went to both on the same day at different times, in which case only one type of school would open in the morning, and the other not until afternoon. Ussing in 1885 [5] stated his belief that the usage varied in different periods and within the same period; according to principle, the physical education began earlier, but in actual practice, the musical instruction often, and in the later

[1] 366D–E ὁπόταν δὲ εἰς τὴν ἑπταετίαν ἀφίκηται, πολλοὺς πόνους διαντλῆσαν, ἐπέστησαν παιδαγωγοὶ καὶ γραμματισταὶ καὶ παιδοτρίβαι τυραννοῦντες.

[2] 20 ἀλλὰ μὲν τῆς ψυχῆς μαθήματα καὶ γυμνασίας προτιθέντες, ἄλλως δὲ πρὸς τοὺς πόνους καὶ τὰ σώματα ἐθίζοντες.

[3] I. 239–40.

[4] Æschin. *c. Timarch.* 9.

[5] 83; cf. the view of Bischof (1912) 42.

period usually, began simultaneously with it or even earlier. He referred to the passage in the *Axiochus* and to a fragment of Teles preserved by Stobæus [1] as indicating that instruction in both began at once. Girard a few years later,[2] without citing ancient authority, expressed his view as being that "up to the age of twelve or fourteen the child divided his time between literature and music," taking up gymnastics after that. Stadelmann (57–8) in the same year expressed the opposite view in defiance of the passage in Lucian, agreeing with the dictum of Grasberger that the first school years were devoted to the palæstra.[3] The fifth edition of Bernhardy's *Griechische Litteraturgeschichte* in 1892 (I. 93) cautiously stated that gymnastics were partly simultaneously with, or else followed soon after, the beginnings of mental training. Schömann-Lipsius (I. 549) held with Bernhardy, although noting that Plato and Aristotle recommended the precedence of gymnastics. Finally in 1907 Freeman (51) put forth as his view that children were trained in music and gymnastics from the very first, though the physical exercises before the age of twelve were of the easiest and most elementary. He used as proof a Xenophon passage,[4] which had not previously been adduced.

---

[1] *Flor.* xcviii. 72 εἰ δ'ἐκπέφευγε τὴν τιτθήν, παρέλαβε πάλιν ὁ παιδαγωγός, παιδοτρίβης, γραμματοδιδάσκαλος κτλ.

[2] (1891) 127–8, cf. 194.

[3] Stadelmann's book is well done, but is hardly more than a judicious condensation of Grasberger's great work.

[4] *Lac.* ii. 1 εὐθὺς δὲ πέμπουσιν εἰς διδασκάλων μαθησομένους καὶ γράμματα καὶ μουσικὴν καὶ τὰ ἐν παλαίστρᾳ.

The collective weight of the passages of pseudo-Plato, Teles, Lucian, and especially Xenophon, is decisive. There can be no mistaking Xenophon's meaning: "As soon as children reach the age of understanding, . . . *straightway* they are sent to the schools to learn grammar, music, and the exercises of the palæstra." Unquestionably, boys began to study both music and gymnastics at the age of six. The difficulty raised by Grasberger has always remained, however, unanswered, but it is not impossible of solution. In the first place, the very law of Solon which he quoted can be turned against him. In forbidding the schools and palæstræ to open before sunrise or close after sunset, Solon indicated a tendency toward a very long day devoted to studies. Surely the Athenians were too sane to allow young children to sit in a school-room at their lessons daily from sun-up until sun-down, to say nothing of exercising in a palæstra for any such length of time. If, on the other hand, the children visited on the same day two schools, palæstra and music-school, with a long intermission at noon for luncheon and a siesta, each teacher would be zealous to accomplish as much as possible in the half-day allotted to him, and so we could rationally explain the tendency to long school hours. As for the question, why should Solon have extended his prohibition of early-opening to both schools, if they kept at different times of the day, it can not be proved that there was any constant practice as to which one held its session in the morning and which in the afternoon. Grasberger tried to show that, in the later years of a boy's life, when (he granted) both music and gymnastics were studied at the same time, the forenoon was devoted to the music-school and the afternoon to the palæstra. A chorus of dissent has pointed out the weakness of Grasberger's argument here, and the details need not be rehearsed again.[1] Even had this been the undeviating usage of Solon's time, that great lawgiver would have been sufficiently foresighted to envisage possible changes; he knew that the Athenians were no sticklers for tradition, and wished to guard against any evasion of the law, with the consequent revival of the abuses against which it was directed. With Grasberger's objections surmounted, we may with a clear conscience agree with those who hold that physical and mental education were commenced simultaneously.[2]

Resting on the conclusion that systematic physical exercise was commenced by every Athenian at the age of six, we must nevertheless not picture children at that age as engaging in heavy and violent exercises. The Athenians divided the exercises into two classes, the lighter ($κουφότερα$) and the heavier ($βαρύτερα$). No one was required to perform such as were beyond his age and strength.[3] As Grasberger (I. 276) suggested,

[1] See e. g., Hermann-Blümner 331-2 and Rauschen 31.

[2] We ought, however, to grant to Ussing the possibility of variation from this rule in different periods, when the enthusiasm for one subject or the other was uncommonly great.

[3] Cf. the recommendation of Aristotle *Pol.* viii. 4. 1 (p. 1338b 40ff.) on the use of lighter exercises until puberty.

Plato's advice that the first instruction in the palæstra should be a continuation of the childhood games was doubtless a reflection of actual practice.[1] Krause gave a long discussion [2] to the gradation of the exercises to suit the various ages; ball playing he put first, then running, jumping, wrestling, the javelin throw, and the discus throw.[3] Somewhat later came boxing, for boys who were strong and verging on youth, and perhaps a taste of the pancratium. In swimming no instruction was given,[4] but the knowledge of it was widespread.[5] Neither was dancing a part of the organized physical education.[6] Riding was taught, but not in early times, and not all could afford to pay the fees demanded by the professor of equitation. The latter had his riding school entirely apart from that of the *paidotribes*,[7] and since we hear so little about it,[8] we are certain that it was frequented only by the aristocratic and well-to-do, quite as in our own day.

---

[1] See *Legg.* i. 643D; vii. 790A–D, 797B, 798C, 808D, 820D.

[2] (1841) I. 282–9.

[3] The younger boys had a smaller discus.

[4] Mehl 5 *"Keine Nachrichten über irgendwelchen planmässigen Unterricht im Schwimmen sind erhalten."* Here again Grasberger (I. 376ff.) was in error.

[5] Diogenian. vi. 56 (*Parœm. Gr.* Vol. I) μήτε νεῖν μήτε γράμματα· ἐπὶ τῶν ἀμαθῶν· ταῦτα γὰρ ἐκ παιδόθεν ἐν ταῖς ᾽Αθήναις ἐμάνθανον. Cf. Hdt. viii. 89 on the universal knowledge of swimming among the Greeks; Mehl *l. c.*

[6] Girard (1891) 215.

[7] *Ibid.* 212.

[8] Ps.-Lucian *Amores* 45. τὸ σῶμα ταῖς ἐλευθερίοις ἀσκήσεσιν ἐκπονεῖ· Θεσσαλοὶ γὰρ ἵπποι μέλουσιν αὐτῷ· καὶ βραχὺ τὴν νεότητα πωλοδαμνήσας, κτλ. Xen. Eph. i. 1–2. The riding teacher was called πωλοδάμνης (Teles ap. Stob. *Flor.* xcviii. 72), and his subject ἱππική (Dio Chr. xii. 37 Budé; *IG* ii. 1². 1042 b21) or ἱππασία (Xen. Eph. *l. c.*).

A little casual sketch of the riding school was given us by the comic poet Mnesimachus (II. 437 K): "the ripe pupils, whom Pheido practices in mounting and dismounting." The famous Cynic, Diogenes, taught the sons of his master Xeniades to ride, as well as to perform other physical exercises.[1] Still a further subject of organized instruction was hoplomachy, or fighting in heavy armor.

To teach these various subjects, Athens had several different kinds of instructors of physical education. Most important among them was, of course, the *paidotribes*. His name, "boy-rubber," shows that one of his duties was to give the boys a rub-down, for which purpose the ancients regularly used olive oil. His chief duty, however, was to give instruction in the various ordinary exercises. He not only gave instruction by word of mouth, but, as is natural and proper, by actual demonstration. "It is not enough for the *paidotribai* to tell about the exercises, but they must also demonstrate them to the learner," said Dio Chrysostom (lxviii. 21 Budé). Clement of Alexandria in an important passage records further details of the teaching methods used by the *paidotribes:*[2] "There are three methods of benefiting another person and transmitting one's knowledge to him: first, by imitation, as the *paidotribes* moulds the boy; second, by resemblance, as one who urges another on to progress by himself making progress first—he co-operates with the pupil,

[1] Diog. Laert. vi. 30. [2] *Strom.* vi. 17. 160, 4.

and the pupil in turn profits the one who took him in hand; third is the method by injunction, when the *paidotribes* no longer moulds the pupil, nor gives a personal demonstration of the fall for the boy to imitate, since the boy is now more skilled, but simply calls for the fall by name."

The technique used by the *paidotribes* in group instruction is described by Plato in the *Politicus*,[1] where a stranger is represented conversing with the younger Socrates.

Stranger. "Well, there are here in Athens, as in other cities, classes for practice in athletics to prepare for contests in running or the like, are there not?"

Younger Socrates. "Yes, a great many of them."

Stranger. "Now let us recall to mind the orders given by the professional trainers when they are in charge of such classes."

Younger Socrates. "What do you mean?"

Stranger. "They think they can not go into details in individual cases and order what is best for each person's physique; they think they must employ a rougher method and give a general rule which will be good for the physique of the majority. And therefore they nowadays assign equal exercise to whole classes; they make them begin at the same time and stop at the same time, whether they run or wrestle or practice any other kind of bodily exercise."

The *paidotribes* was credited with the ability to

[1] 294D–E tr. H. N. Fowler.

make the boys shapely,[1] and he took such pride in them that he could recognize his own pupils "even if he saw them at a distance carrying home meat from the market-place."[2] Since Athenian boys were not unlike those of the present, they were frequently in need of discipline, and we are made sure by numerous vase paintings which show a *paidotribes* holding a whip or a stick, that rigorous discipline was enforced. Literary testimonials to the same effect are not wanting: Basil the Great[3] spoke of people receiving many blows in the school of the *paidotribes*, and Dio Chrysostom (lxv. 19 Budé) said that the *paidotribes* beat those who did not obey him. Plautus suggestively remarked[4] that if boys did not get to the palæstra bright and early, they paid no slight penalty. A passage of Aristophanes[5] shows how careful the *paidotribes* was to guard the modesty of the boys entrusted to his care, and we are told that when boys first went to the palæstra, great stress was laid on their deportment (εὐκοσμία). Occasionally the *paidotribes* was tempted to make athletes and specialized performers out of his pupils, but generally he held to his true function of promoting a rounded physical development, firmly based on health and vigor.[6]

[1] Clem. Alex. *l. c.* ὁ παιδοτρίβης σχηματίζων τὸν παῖδα. Artemidor. *Oneirocrit.* iii. 17 ἀνθρώπους πλάττειν ἀγαθὸν παιδοτρίβαις.

[2] Plut. *Dio* i.

[3] *de Leg. Græcis* vi. πολλὰς πληγὰς ἐν παιδοτρίβου λαβόντες.

[4] *Bacch.* 424–5.

[5] *Nub.* 973–4.

[6] For the temptation to make "star" performers in individual exer-

The *paidotribes* normally owned the building in which he taught. In many allusions to palæstræ in ancient literature, we find a proper name in the genitive attached to the word. Girard [1] has satisfactorily disposed of the ingenious but ill-founded hypotheses that these names refer to benefactors or architects, and has established that they refer to the *paidotribai* who owned them and used them for schools. We know from various sources the names of nine of these *paidotribai:* Hippocrates, Hippomachus, Sibyrtius, Timagetus, Eupolemus, Taureas, Timeas, Antigenes, and Pheidostratus.[2] The palæstra of Taureas is mentioned in literature four times, more often than any of the others.[3] A passage of Plato's *Lysis* (204A) has

cises, see the story about Diogenes the Cynic in Diog. Laert. vi. 30. Εὐεξία is one of the most constantly named objects of physical education; on εὐτονία, "vigor," see Gal. *de San. Tuend.* ii. 9. 14 Koch καθάπερ ἐν παλαίστρᾳ γυμνάζουσι τοὺς παῖδας, εἰς εὐτονίαν παρασκευάζοντες; cf. *ibid.* ii. 9. 25.

[1] (1891) 29. Haase (361) wrongly thought the *paidotribai* did not own them, though he granted (381) that they did in later times.

[2] All these are listed by Girard ([1891] 28–9), except Eupolemus (Æschin. *c. Timarch.* 102) and Hippomachus (Ath. xiii. 47). The writer believes we should identify this Hippomachus with the one called by Plut. (*Dio* i.) an *aleiptes*, and by Æl. (*V. H.* ii. 6) a *gymnastes;* the confusion of the three terms will be taken up presently (see for the nonce Hesych. *s. v.* παιδοτρίβαι). Timeas (*IG* ii. 1². 957, 961) and Antigenes (*ibid.* 958) belong to a later period, the middle of the second century B. C., but are listed here for convenience. The author would feel little hesitation in adding to this list Aristo of Argos, the teacher of Plato. Diog. Laert. (iii. 4) called him a παλαιστής, because thinking of the παλαίστρα in which he taught. It would not be surprising that foreigners, like Aristo, were *paidotribai* in Athens.

[3] The only contemporary reference, however, is Plat. *Charm.* 153A. The others were made by readers of Plato: Lucian *Parasit.* 43.; Liban. *Or.* xviii. 155, *Decl.* xii. 23.

been interpreted [1] to mean that Miccus was another *paidotribes* to be added to this list, but Hermann-Blümner (339 n. 1) and Girard pointed out the fallacy of this, and showed that Miccus was a sophist. In rare cases, some one built a palæstra and did not teach in it himself; a casual reference in Plutarch [2] informs us of a palæstra built at Athens by Habron, but we know Habron did not teach in the school, for he was a state man. Known to us by name are several *paidotribai* of Delos and other places; they will be mentioned in a later chapter.

A question that has disturbed many is the relation between the *paidotribes* and the *gymnastes*. As long ago as 1844, K. F. Hermann established the distinction in the main, but some modern writers are still retailing misinformation. In 1896 Bussemaker wrote: [3] "The most ordinary way of entering the career of *gymnastes* doubtless consisted in buying a palæstra and giving lessons there for money." Barth in 1920 (106) declared: "The state-paid teachers in Athens were the *paidotribes* for the younger boys, the *aleiptes* for the older ones." Wright in 1925 (78) stated that the *paidotribai* were assisted by subordinates, the *gymnastai*, who were assigned to coach in some of the individual exercises.

To turn from these inaccuracies, let us see what was the differentiation established by Hermann.[4] It was

[1] By Grasberger I. 253 n. 2.
[2] *x Orat. Vit.* vii. (*Lycurg.*) p. 843F.
[3] Dar.-Sagl. II. 1698.
[4] (1844) 71–3.

simply this: the *paidotribes* was the teacher of general physical education, and always the superintendent of a palæstra,[1] while the *gymnastes* was the coach of those preparing for an agonistic career as professional athletes.[2] For training athletes to take part in keen competition, one needed technical knowledge and skill, as well as an understanding of physiology, anatomy, and dietetics. This we find was true of the *gymnastes:* in every one of the eight passages in Plato where he is mentioned, it is in connection with doctors and the art of healing;[3] Aristotle[4] refers to him as having superior knowledge, and Philostratus[5] represents him as versed in both theory and practice, and the *paidotribes* only in the latter.

The best way to come to an understanding of the *gymnastes* and his relation to the *paidotribes* is by a genetic study. This study has been well performed by J. B. Egger, a pupil of Jüthner. The following is a brief résumé of his conclusions, which are based on complete collections and a thorough knowledge. Hippocrates never used the word *gymnastes*, and named the *paidotribes* only twice,[6] both times as a practical

---

[1] Plat. *Protag.* 312B; Dio Chr. xii. 17 and xxxii. 13 Budé; Diog. Laert. vi. 30 and countless other passages.

[2] Galen *de Simp. Medic. Temp. ac Facult.* ii. 5 (XI. 476 Kühn) made the distinction with perfect clarity: διὰ τί τρίβουσιν ἐλαίῳ τοὺς ἀθλητὰς οἱ γυμνασταί; διὰ τί δὲ καὶ οἱ παιδοτρίβαι τοὺς παῖδας;

[3] J. B. Egger 52.

[4] *Pol.* viii. 3. 2 (p. 1338b 6-8).

[5] *Gym.* 14.

[6] *de Diæta* i. 13 (VI. 488 Littré, XXI. 641f. Kühn) and i. 24 (VI. 496 Littré, XXI. 646 Kühn).

teacher of gymnastics. Plato refers to the *paidotribes* repeatedly, but we begin to find the word *gymnastes* also. Galen's researches gave him a partially correct historical perspective on the matter. "The gymnastic trainer Plato calls *paidotribes* more often than *gymnastes*, for it was only a little before Plato's time that the technique ($\tau\acute{\epsilon}\chi\nu\eta$) of the *gymnastai* arose, simultaneously with the rise of the system of professional athletics."[1] Really it was only the name, and not the technique, which originated in the latter part of the fifth century, and Plato used hesitantly and infrequently the new, unfamiliar word. The references to the *paidotribes* as an instructor of athletes can be explained by assuming that this was actually the situation, until the pressure of double duties became too much for the *paidotribes*, whereupon the *gymnastes* was introduced (Egger 53-4). The consequence was that Plato did not sharply distinguish between the two, nor did his contemporary Isocrates.[2] As athletics grew in prominence, the *gymnastes* rose in favor; Aristotle rated him above the *paidotribes*, and five hundred years later Galen accounted the art of the *paidotribes* merely ancillary to that of the *gymnastes*.[3] Not essentially different was the attitude of Philostratus.[4]

With this explanation before us, we can see the error of Bussemaker; clearly it was the *paidotribes*,

[1] *Thras.* 33.
[2] *de Perm.* 181.
[3] *de San. Tuend.* ii. 9. 25; ii. 11. 42 Kock.
[4] *Gym.* 14.

not the *gymnastes*, who began his career by opening a boys' wrestling school and teaching there for money. Barth was wrong for the period about which he was writing, in saying that the *paidotribes* was paid by the state; this statement would hold true only for the *paidotribai* of the ephebia, which originated later. Neither is any justification found for Barth's assertion that the *aleiptes* was a state-paid teacher of the older boys. Wright was obviously mistaken in taking the *gymnastai* to be merely assistants to the *paidotribai*; the two worked at different tasks, one with the athletes, the other with the boys.

Next in importance to the *paidotribes* was the *hoplomachos*,[1] who also taught in the palæstra,[2] but had as his sphere military exercises and drill. Hoplomachy was as old as Homeric times (*Il.* xxiii. 811), but the idea of employing it in physical education is ascribed to Demeas of Mantinea.[3] When the art was introduced into Athens, it met with instant favor. The earliest author to mention hoplomachy as a part of the Athenian education is Plato. In the *Laches* there is a discussion of its merits, wherein the claim is made that it is not inferior to any exercise, and is befitting to a man of culture (182A); and in the *Laws*[4] Plato recommended that it supplant wrestling in his Utopian state, and be practiced by both sexes. Also

---

[1] Rare variations of his title were ὁπλομάχης and ὁπλοδιδάκτης.
[2] Plat. *Gorg.* 456D–E.
[3] Ephorus *FGrHist.* lxx. F54 (from Ath. iv. 41).
[4] viii. 833E–834A.

in the Gorgias (456D–E) there is casual mention of the *hoplomachos*. Only once did Plato actually use the word *hoplomachos*,[1] but he often referred to such a person by some circumlocution, as "the instructor in hoplomachy."[2] About 378 B.C. Xenophon (*Lac.* xi. 8) used the word, and in such a way as to show that the *hoplomachos* taught tactics and generalship, as well as fighting in heavy armor, and should therefore be identified with the teacher called the "tactician."[3] Again in the *Memorabilia* Xenophon (iii. 1. 1) referred to such a teacher of tactics, but this time without denominating him as *hoplomachos*. Theophrastus barely mentioned him in the *Characters* (7 Jebb-Sandys). Philopœmen, "last of the Greeks," denounced athletics, but was personally fond of hoplomachy,[4] and in very late times Libanius still speaks of a teacher of tactics.[5] His greatest prominence, however, was as an instructor of the ephebi, and in this rôle we shall meet him again in Chapter VI.

Teachers other than these in the period before the ephebia were rare. The riding master, or *polodamnes*, was known in the fifth and fourth centuries. Themistocles had his son Cleophantus taught horsemanship, and the lad became so proficient that he could even hurl javelins while standing erect on the back of a horse moving at a trot.[6] Paralus and Xanthippus, the son of Pericles, also received training in horseman-

[1] In its by-form ὁπλομάχης, *Euthyd.* 299C.   [2] *Gorg.* 456D–E.
[3] ὁ τακτικός Ps.-Plat. *Axioch.* 366E.   [4] Plut. *Philop.* iii.
[5] *Decl.* xxxiii. 17 and xlviii. 8.   [6] Plat. *Meno* 93D.

ship.¹ A special teacher of javelin throwing, called the *akontistikos* (ἀκοντιστικός), seems to be alluded to by Plato (*Theag.* 126B). In a large and popular palæstra it is possible that the *paidotribes* had assistants; such existed in the ephebia and were called *hypopaidotribai*. The abler pupils were sometimes induced to take a hand in coaching those who were backward, and vase paintings show these student-teachers proudly holding a long stick like that of the *paidotribes*, and directing one exercise or another (Freeman 128). The vases show slaves as assistants in the palæstra, and we have literary testimony for a "palæstra keeper" (παλαιστροφύλαξ),² who presumably cleaned the building and kept it in order.

State educational officials in Athens prior to the ephebia did not exist. The state for the most part saw fit not to interfere with the private individuals who earned their livelihood by educating the boys and young men of Athens. In cases where recourse to the law was necessary, or where some flagrant abuse was growing up, the Areopagus was empowered to take steps to set matters right.³ This scarcely amounted

---

¹ Plat. *op. cit.* 94B. Other passages proving the existence of the riding master in this period are Mnesimachus *Fr.* 4. (II. 437 Kock) and Plat. *Theag.* 126B.

² Æl. *V. H.* viii. 14. Homolle (1890) 488 notes that on Delos he was a slave, and (1896) 575 served as "*gardien du matériel.*" At Abdera, however, he seems to have served on occasion as a wrestling partner or possibly instructor: Hippoc. *Epidem.* vi. 8. 30 (V. 345 Littré, XXIII. 630 Kühn).

³ Isoc. *Areop.* 37.

to a regular oversight of education, and the interference of the Areopagus must have been rare.

There did exist at Athens certain educational laws, which it was the business of the Areopagus to enforce if occasion arose. Already from time to time we have alluded to one or another of these laws, but now let us bring together all that can possibly have any bearing on our subject, and thus complete our picture of the relation of the state to physical education in Athens. In the main, the laws were made, or at least codified, by Solon, and the principal source of our knowledge about them is Æschines' speech against Timarchus (9–12). These were not the sort of statutes that say what shall and what shall not be taught, nor did they disturb *Lern- und Lehrfreiheit;* rather their object was solely to preserve the authority of the schools and to protect the health and moral integrity of the students.[1]

First is the law concerning school hours, to the effect that neither the regular schoolmasters nor the *paidotribai* should open their schools before sunrise, or close them after sunset.[2] This regulation was directed against pæderasty, as Æschines said, but also against the tendency to keep school for unbearably long hours. If the children went to school from sunrise until sunset, with only a break at noon to eat and take a siesta,

[1] Van der Bach 8.

[2] Æschin. *c. Timarch.* 10. and 12. That Greek schools in other localities besides Athens opened at sunrise, is clear from Thuc. vii. 29, where a school at Mycalessus has just opened at daybreak.

they endured all that could be expected of them and more. Modern children have not the health nor the patience for such unremitting school work. Second is the law prescribing what children might be admitted to the schools, and what age they had to attain before being admitted.[1] Why Æschines did not say what these conditions were is not known; as it is, we are left to conclude that an exclusion clause was aimed against slaves and girls (see above, page 57), and that the entrance age was set at six, that is, after a boy had reached his sixth birthday and was in his seventh year. Third is the law for state supervision of the boys, their slave attendants ($\pi\alpha\iota\delta\alpha\gamma\omega\gamma o\iota$), and their school festivals (the Musea in the music-school, and the Hermæa in the palæstra). It was formerly thought that this law referred to the *sophronistes* ("superintendent of morals"), but it is now known that this official did not exist earlier than the organization of the ephebia;[2] rather it refers to the authority of the Areopagus. A fourth law forbade any adults, except the teachers and their close relatives[3] to enter the music-school or palæstra while the boys were there, under pain of death. This law, again, was meant to avert immorality. That it was later repealed, or at any rate disregarded, we may see from the freedom

[1] Æschin. *op. cit.* 10.
[2] Wilamowitz I. 192–3; Girard in Dar.-Sagl. IV. 1399–1400 (a recantation of his previous belief, which had been stated in his book p. 44 and his article in Dar.-Sagl. III. 865); Oehler *RE* (2te Reihe) III. 1105. For a recent restatement of the old heresy, see Barker (1918) 183.
[3] Specifically brothers, sons, or sons-in-law (Æschin. *op. cit.* 12.).

with which Socrates visited the palæstra [1] as well as from references in Aristophanes, Theophrastus, Theocritus, and Lucian.[2] A fifth law forbade men to attend the Hermæa along with the boys, but this like the previous one was abrogated or neglected.[3] A sixth regulated the size of the schools, to keep them from swelling to such proportions as to hinder unduly the *paidotribes* or music teacher from giving each individual the proper oversight and instruction.[4] Still a seventh law (Plat. *Crit.* 50D) commanded parents to have their sons educated in music and gymnastics. I believe this seventh law, as Exarchopulos (47–9) well argued, was only a firmly established custom. It is mentioned nowhere save in this solitary passage, whereas it seems certain that a regular law so highly important would be referred to frequently. Besides, it is flatly contradicted by Plato himself in *I Alcibiades* (122B), and by implication in the *Laws* (vii. 804D) and *Theages* (122E). Aristotle too, implied the contrary in more than one passage. [5]

[1] Plat. *Charm.* 153A, *Lysis* 206E. Dio Chr. 43. 10 Budé. Max. Tyr. 21. 8h.

[2] Ar. *Pax* 762–3, *Vesp.* 1025 and scholia on both passages; Theophr. *Char.* 8. and 19. (Jebb-Sandys); Theoc. ii. 96ff.; Ps.-Lucian *Amores* 9. (where Callicratidas is said to visit the palæstra διὰ τοὺς παιδικοὺς ἔρωτας); Lucian *Navig.* 4. *Parasit.* 51.

[3] Plat. *Lysis* 206D-E. The gymnasiarchs whom the bracketed passage in Æschines *c. Timarch.* 12. indicate as the officials to enforce this law are an anachronism for Solon's epoch, when only liturgical gymnasiarchs were known; see Boeckh (1886) I. 549.

[4] The law determined μετὰ πόσων παίδων εἰσιέναι. For the discussion of it, see Exarchopulos 45–6.

[5] *Pol.* viii. 1. 2 (p. 1337a 22–6) for example; see the discussion of Exarchopulos referred to above, and his references.

One more connection the state had with education at Athens in the period which we are now discussing. We do not hear that this was a law, but it was certainly the regular practice. If a citizen of Athens died fighting for his country, the state saw to it that any children whom his death made orphans should be educated, like the more fortunate ones whose fathers were alive to earn money and pay the bills for sending their sons to school.[1] Aristotle relates that a certain eccentric and attractive character of Miletus, Hippodamus, made this one of the provisions in his Utopia, but this Utopian ideal, Aristotle goes on to remark, was an actuality, both in Athens and in other cities.[2] The state did not, of course, erect schools and hire teachers for these orphans, but sent them to some of the existing palæstræ and music-schools, paying for them the fees asked by the *paidotribes* and other teachers. When they reached the age of manhood, the state gave the orphans its blessing and a full equipment of armor, and relinquished its care of them.[3]

From time to time the gymnasium and the palæstra have been mentioned, both of them as places where gymnastic exercises were performed. The question naturally arises, what was the difference between these

[1] Thuc. ii. 46; Cratinus *Fr.* 171 (I. 66 Kock); and especially Aristot. *Pol.* ii. 5. 4 (p. 1268a 8–11). The custom went back at least to the time of Solon: Diog. Laert. i. 55.

[2] *l. c.* We have this confirmed for Iasus, a town on a small island off the coast of Caria, by a fragment of Heraclides Lembos [Ponticus], *FHG* II. 224, based on Aristotle.

[3] Plat. *Menex.* 249A–B. Æschin. *c. Ctes.* 154. Cf. Isoc. viii. 82.

two places? The question has been much debated, and the truth is that no categorical answer, applying to all countries and centuries, can possibly be given. The first good analysis of the subject was given in 1837 by Haase (360), who yet stumbled into some pitfalls. According to his investigations, the word palæstra had, besides its metaphorical use, three meanings which were to be carefully distinguished: (1) a wrestling school for boys, and so contrasted with the gymnasium,[1] (2) a part of the gymnasium, used especially by athletes in training for the games,[2] and (3) a gymnasium, in the usage of the Greeks of Magna Græcia and of the Romans.[3] All this is true, but Haase fell into serious error when he went on to say that, although palæstræ were in late times occasionally founded by private individuals, those of Solon's time were public, as were most palæstræ at all periods. In our discussion of the *paidotribes* on earlier pages, it has been shown that this was by no means the case.

A few years after Haase's article appeared, Krause brought out his voluminous work on Greek gymnastics

[1] Xen. *Lac.* ii. 1. Theophr. *Char.* 19. Jebb-Sandys. Themist. *Or.* xx., p. 292 Dindf. Galen *Puer. Epilept.* 3., *de San. Tuend.* ii. 9. 14 ἐν παλαίστρᾳ γυμνάζουσι τοὺς παῖδας; Hesych. s. v. παλαίστρα: ὅπου οἱ παῖδες ἀλείφονται. See Grasberger I. 254; Hermann-Blümner 339; Schneider 30; Ziebarth (1914) 33.

[2] At Elis, Paus. v. 15. 8, vi. 23. 4; Olympia, Paus. vi. 21. 2; at Athens the orator Lycurgus built the palæstra which formed part of the Lyceum, Ps.-Plut. *x Orat. Vit.* vii. 1. See also Plut. *Quæst. Conv.* ii. 4. 1; Ath. x. 10; Galen *Parv. Pil.* 5.

[3] Vitruv. v. 11 described the architecture of a Greek gymnasium and called it a palæstra. Cic. *II Verr.* ii. 14. 36 called the public gymnasium of Syracuse a palæstra.

and athletic contests.[1] He distinguished the gymnasia as places of public instruction in physical culture from the palæstræ as private exercise places. This is only half right. The gymnasia at Athens in the period with which we are now concerned were public, but were not schools; while the palæstræ were not only places for exercise, but also schools for instruction. Krause correctly observed that in some cities the gymnasia were schools,[2] and were visited by boys,[3] as well as by youths and adults, and that in late times the two words gymnasium and palæstra were used interchangeably, with no perception of their original divergence in meaning.[4]

In 1858 Petersen (6) made an incisive statement on the matter that still holds good for Athens before 335 B.C. A palæstra, he said, was for the instruction of boys under the *paidotribes;* add to the palæstra a *dromos*, or running-track, and you had the nucleus of a gymnasium, an institution for the use of young men and men in quest of health and strength, and likewise for the athletes who were training to participate in the games. Two difficulties might be raised to impugn the accuracy of this distinction: (1) if youths and men were spoken of as being in a palæstra, (2) if boys were mentioned in connection with the

[1] The discussion of the gymnasium and palæstra is to be found in I. 89 and in great detail I. 107-27.

[2] E. g., at Iasus: *Br. Mus. Inscr.* 925b.

[3] E. g., at Miletus and Pergamum: Ziebarth (1914) 26-7.

[4] In support of this statement Krause adduced Æl. viii. 14 and a bewildering host of other passages: see I. 122.

word gymnasium (γυμνάσιον). The first of these obstacles Petersen explained away by pointing out that men and youths are never represented as exercising in a palæstra; they go merely as spectators,[1] or to enjoy a festival such as the Hermæa,[2] or to listen to a sophist.[3] If they ever do exercise in a palæstra, we must understand that what is meant is the part of a gymnasium called a palæstra.[4] The second difficulty is met by translating the Greek word γυμνάσιον (gymnasium) as "exercise," a common enough signification.[5] The latter explanation, unfortunately, is so simple that it arouses one's suspicions. Putting it to the test, it appears that while it solves many a crux, we still need a further explanation for some others. In Antiphon's second *Tetralogy* we find a *paidotribes* in the gymnasium, and at least two boys engaged in javelin practice under his direction. One of the boys was hurrying across the gymnasium in answer to a call from the *paidotribes*, when he stepped right in the path of a javelin thrown by his playmate, and was instantly killed. This case obviously can not be met by Petersen's rule of γυμνάσιον = "exercise;" how can it be explained? Out of the numerous views expressed by different writers, the most plausible is that of Freeman (125). The private citizens who constructed

---

[1] Theophr. *Char.* 8. Jebb-Sandys.
[2] Plat. *Lysis* 206D.
[3] *Ibid.* 204A and 206D.
[4] Ar. *Nub.* 1052–4. Plut. *Quæst. Conv.* ii. 4. 1. Becker-Göll II. 242.
[5] Plat. *Lach.* 181E. Xen. *Œc.* x. 11, *de Re Equest.* vii. 18.

palæstræ were too poor to erect large buildings, and we must think of a palæstra as too small for the exercises of throwing the javelin and discus. For these exercises, then, and for running in the *dromos*,[1] the *paidotribes* would sometimes take his pupils to the gymnasia. An alternative explanation [2] for the Antiphon passage is that the boys were in the gymnasium preparing to participate in contests at the public games.

An argument that has been advanced [3] against the definition of the gymnasium as public and the palæstra as private,[4] is a sentence in a treatise on the Athenian constitution, which was handed down among the works of Xenophon, but really was produced by an "Old Oligarch," as he is now commonly called, between 430 and 424 B. C. The sentence reads as follows [5]: "Some rich people in Athens have private gymnasia, baths, and dressing-rooms, but the people builds for itself many palæstræ, dressing-rooms, and baths." It has rarely been noticed [6] that the parallelism here makes it practically certain that by "palæstræ" the Old Oligarch meant gymnasia, or else the palæstræ which formed a part of all gymnasia. The opposite suggestion, that these were separate palæstræ intended

---

[1] Girard (1891) 188.
[2] Offered by Becker-Göll II. 244–5.
[3] By Haase 360.
[4] Barth (1920) 106 flatly says: "*Beide waren Eigentum des Staates.*"
[5] Ps.-Xen. *Ath.* ii. 10.
[6] But see Ziebarth (1914) 33 n. 1. Girard (1891) 26–7, without remarking the parallelism, came to the same conclusion; so also Oehler *RE* VII. 2010.

for the instruction of boys, and were open to any *paidotribes* who was too poor to have a palæstra of his own, the author regards as improbable and contrary to what we know of Athens' educational policy. The natural course for a young *paidotribes*, who was too poor to build or purchase a palæstra, was to serve an apprenticeship to some older man who had a palæstra. Although there is no passage in Greek literature which uses the word *hypopaidotribes*, we know from epigraphical records that such assistant *paidotribai* were common in a later period.[1] If they existed then, there is no reason to believe that they did not exist earlier.[2] By saving as much as possible from his share of the pupils' fees, the assistant *paidotribes* could soon obtain a palæstra for himself. With this method in vogue for entering the career of *paidotribes*, there would have been no need for the state to furnish palæstræ to be used by those who were poor. All our testimony shows that nothing of the sort was ever done. How completely Athens kept her hands off education and everything pertaining thereto is proved by many statements in Greek literature. Socrates once told Alcibiades:[3] "No one cares about your

[1] The writer has in his collections over thirty inscriptional references to the *hypopaidotribes*.

[2] Freeman (128) says: "There were generally several under-masters in the palæstra."

[3] Plat. *I Alcib.* 122B tr. Jowett. A half-dozen or more other references in Plato and Xenophon, all leading to the same conclusion, are quoted by Bryant (80 n. 3). Burk (34) says categorically and, as the author believes, correctly: "*Alle Schulen waren Privatschulen ohne staatliche Aufsicht and ohne staatliche Unterstützung.*"

birth, or nurture, or education, or, I may say, about that of any other Athenian, unless he has a lover who takes care of him." If Athens had provided public palæstræ for educational purposes, Socrates could not have said that no one cared about the education of any Athenian. The author reverts, therefore, to his conclusion that the public palæstræ attested by the Old Oligarch were really the public gymnasia, or parts of them, and were used by athletes in training and by other adults, not by boys and their teachers. With this interpretation, the passage is in perfect harmony with our view that palæstræ which were used as wrestling schools for boys were without exception private, while the gymnasia were large, public edifices, which did not serve as schools, but as grounds for the continued practice, without instruction, of the exercises learned in the palæstra, and for the training of professional athletes under the coaching of the *gymnastes* and *aleiptes*.

The age at which the education of the palæstra terminated we can not fix. Had education at Athens been public, surely this age would have been set by law, and we should certainly hear in some author what it was. Fourteen or sixteen seems to have been common,[1] but we know from Plato [2] that there was no uniformity. Poor boys could not afford to stay in school as long as their richer playmates, and nothing hindered them from leaving when they pleased. On quitting the palæstra, the poor boys would be obliged

[1] Cf. Aristot. *Pol.* vii. 15. 11 (p. 1336b 37ff.).   [2] *Protag.* 326C.

ATHENS BEFORE 335 B.C.

to go to work in order to earn a living, but the richer ones could and did frequent the gymnasia. There they continued the exercises which kept them well and strong, exercises to which they were now devoted. Even into old age they retained the habit of going to the gymnasia for exercise; Plato speaks [1] of the "old men in the gymnasia, wrinkled and unpleasant to look upon, but still fond of their exercises." In the gymnasia, too, men found the social life with their fellows which compensated for the lack of home life. There were three of these gymnasia in Athens in the period before 335 B.C., the Lyceum, Academy, and Cynosarges.[2] The Cynosarges was originally for the use only of illegitimate children,[3] born to Athenians of alien women, but this distinction was apparently abolished early in the fifth century by a trick of the bold Themistocles, himself a child of a foreign woman. The future statesman lured some of those who were of full Athenian blood (γνήσιοι) down to the Cynosarges to exercise with him, and after that no one adhered any longer to the old regulation which had segregated the sheep from the goats.[4]

---

[1] *Resp.* v. 452B.

[2] These all existed as early as the time of Solon, if we may believe Demosth. *c. Timocr.* 114, who says that one of Solon's laws forbade stealing a cloak, oil-flask, or any of the equipment of the Lyceum, Academy, or Cynosarges; if the value of the stolen articles was over ten drachmas, the penalty was death. Others said the Lyceum was built by Pericles or the orator Lycurgus.

[3] Demosth. *c. Aristocl.* 213; Dio Chr. lxv. 3 Budé.

[4] The story is in Plut. *Them.* i. and Liban. *Decl.* x. 11. Socrates was wont to go out to the Cynosarges (Ps.-Plat. *Axioch.* 364A) without any comment or explanation, proving that this gymnasium was no longer scorned as the exercise grounds of νόθοι only.

The principal official of whom we hear in connection with these public gymnasia is the gymnasiarch. The gymnasiarchy was a service performed in behalf of the state by the rich at their own expense; the Greeks called it a "liturgy." The duty of the gymnasiarch was the preparation of the torch-race, and he was often called a *lampadarch*,[1] from *lampas*, the word for torch. Annually a gymnasiarch was chosen from each tribe, and he represented his tribe in the torch-race. His preparations included the choice of the runners from his tribe, paying to have them coached, supporting them while in training for the race, and providing the torches.[2] It was due to his necessary presence in the gymnasium while making ready for the race, and to his authority as an elected official, that he was granted some powers in the gymnasium, and in maintaining the discipline (εὐκοσμία) of those who were in his charge. How great these powers were, it would be over-bold to say, for our knowledge about the gymnasiarch is scanty and conflicting.[3] Another gymnasium official was the overseer, called *epistates*[4] or *epimeletes*.[5] His charge was apparently over the buildings and grounds,

---

[1] Boeckh (1886) I. 550. Haase 388. Cf. *Lex. Seguer. s. v.* γυμνασίαρχοι (Bekker *Anecd. Gr.* I. 228).

[2] Anon. arg. in Demosth. *Mid.* (p. 510).

[3] "*La question de la gymnasiarchie est une des plus obscures que soulève l'histoire des institutions grecques*," said Gustave Glotz (Dar.-Sagl. II. 1675), whose capable sketch the author has partly followed in the above.

[4] Over the Academy: Hyperid. *c. Demosth.* 22 Jensen.

[5] Over the Lyceum: Hesych. *s. v.* ἀρχέλας, and IG iii. 1. 89; over the Hadrian gymnasium in the second century of our era: *IG* iv. 1474.

and he was not concerned with the youths and their exercises.[1]

In studying physical education at Athens, we find that the enthusiasm for it and the zeal which was devoted to it, varied in different periods. At Sparta we observed the same circumstance; in the time just prior to the reforms of Agis and Cleomenes, the boys were not exercising so vigorously as they previously had done, while the Roman imperial age saw a revival of the old interest in educational gymnastics. At Athens the greatest furore over physical education was in the sixth century and the first half of the fifth. After the Persian wars had been fought, the Greeks realized what a part physical fitness had played in winning this momentous conquest for Western civilization, and their ardor for the exercises of the gymnasium and palæstra knew no bounds. In the latter half of the fifth century, however, there are distinct signs of a falling-off in interest. The sophists were turning the minds of youths and men into new and absorbing channels. This is written out plainly for all to read in the *Clouds* of Aristophanes (1002ff.) and so important is the whole passage for the condition of Athenian education in this epoch that I transcribe it here *in toto* from the inimitable version of Rogers:

"But then you'll excel in the games you love well, all blooming, athletic and fair:
Not learning to prate as your idlers debate with marvellous prickly dispute,

---

[1] Oehler *RE* VII. 2024 thought his sole duty that of treasurer.

Nor dragged into Court day by day to make sport in some
  small disagreeable suit:
But you will below to the Academe go, and under the olives
  contend
With your chaplet of reed, in a contest of speed, with some
  excellent rival and friend:
All fragrant with woodbine and peaceful content, and the
  leaf which the lime blossoms fling,
When the plane whispers love to the elm in the grove in
  the beautiful season of Spring.
  If then you'll obey and do what I say,
  And follow with me the more excellent way,
  Your chest shall be white, your skin shall be bright,
  Your arms shall be tight, your tongue shall be slight,
  And everything else shall be proper and right.
  But if you pursue what men nowadays do,
  You will have, to begin, a cold pallid skin,
  Arms small and chest weak, tongue practised to speak,
  Special laws very long, and the symptoms all strong
  Which show that your life is licentious and wrong."

The allusion to the sophists is plain in the idlers who "debate with marvellous prickly dispute," and the description of the results of neglecting physical education "nowadays" tells us a whole story. Later in the play, after some sophistic arguments from Wrong Reason, Right Reason cries out in disgust: "This, yes, this is the nonsense that our youths babble always, all day long, filling the bath house and leaving the palæstræ deserted." [1] Still in the same play, Aris-

[1] 1052–54. Aristophanes was no friend of the warm baths which played such a part in the new-fangled *Heilgymnastik* of his day (see below, pp. 91–92.)

tophanes ridiculed the new passion for riding which was affected by the rich and aristocratic youth; this exercise was exclusive and far too costly for the ordinary Athenian boy, and it demanded less physical exertion than the exercises of the palæstra. It was part and parcel of the laziness and foppery that Aristophanes lamented in the rising generation. In the *Frogs*, too, the same conditions are described: sophistry has engaged the whole attention of Athens and emptied the palæstræ (1069–71); the youths now by reason of not exercising (ἀγυμνασία) are unable to bear a torch in the torch-race (1087–8); they are pale and fat, in the worst of physical condition (1092).

Not from one author alone do we learn of this state of affairs: pseudo-Andocides [1] declared that the youths spent their time in the law-courts instead of in the gymnasia, and they stayed in Athens while their elders went off soldiering. The blame for this was fastened by pseudo-Andocides on the shoulders of Alcibiades, but the writer is sure that the sophists, exponents of the New Education, were the principal cause in this unwonted neglect of physical education. The Old Oligarch [2] was another who recorded these conditions, and he ascribed the change, as one would expect from an Old Oligarch, to the *demos*, the people. His words are as follows in the translation by Dakyns: "Citizens devoting their time to gymnastics and to the cultivation of music are not to be found in Athens; the sov-

---

[1] c. *Alcib.* 22. and 39. [2] Ps.-Xen. *Ath.* i. 13.

ereign People has disestablished them, not from any disbelief in the beauty and honor of such training, but recognizing the fact that these are things the cultivation of which is beyond its power." According to the Old Oligarch, then, it was through envy of the rich, who had more time to exercise and more money to pay for the privilege, that the people of Athens had "abolished" gymnastics. The poor were absolutely unable to afford either money or time for much physical education; they had no money, and their time was fully occupied in looking after their own affairs and those of the state. There was more and more of the tendency, described by Isocrates (*Areop.* 45), for the rich to engage in riding, gymnastics, hunting, and philosophy, while the poor busied themselves with agriculture and business.

Xenophon is still another author who gives evidence on the neglect of physical education in the period of the sophists. Under the new financial scheme which he set forth in the *Vectigalia*, he promised [1] that those "who are under orders to go through gymnastic training will devote themselves with a new zeal to the details of the training-school," implying that the zeal when he wrote was but feeble. In the *Memorabilia* [2] Xenophon represented Socrates as exclaiming that the Athenians "not only neglect to make themselves fit but mock at those who take the trouble to do so." On another occasion [3] Socrates noticed the poor physical

[1] iv. 52. tr. Dakyns.   [2] iii 5. 15 tr. Marchant.
[3] *Mem.* iii. 12. 1.

condition of the young Epigenes, and spoke to him about it: "You look as if you need exercise, Epigenes." "Well," he replied, "I'm not an athlete, Socrates." Epigenes represented the sentiment of his time; only a professional athlete was expected to keep in good trim. Plato devoted scores of pages to a new scheme of education, partly because he felt that the influence of the sophists was ruining the harmony between mind and body, which had been preserved by the earlier Athenians. Archæology gives confirmatory evidence on the point in question; the fondness of vase-painters for representing scenes of the gymnasium and palæstra changed about 440 B.C. From that time on we find far fewer paintings of youths at their exercises; if the scene is in the exercise grounds at all, the youths are not jumping or throwing the javelin, but are lounging about and talking with one another.[1]

Ere closing this chapter on physical education at Athens prior to 335 B.C., there are two related developments which deserve our attention. These are the rise of athleticism and the discovery of health gymnastics.

Even as early as the seventh century before Christ, voices of protest against athletics began to be heard. The first note sounds from Sparta, whose martial folk early learned that the training for the games was the reverse of salutary for those who were to be soldiers. Their spokesman was Tyrtæus, and it is only by

[1] Jüthner *RE* VII. 2053–4.

chance that we have his words preserved; if there were a Spartan literature, perhaps we should hear more of their attitude.[1] Tyrtæus' words were these:[2] "I should not mention nor count as aught a man for excellence either in running or in wrestling, even if he had the size and the strength of the Cyclops, and should conquer in running Thracian Boreas, . . . even if he had all honor except martial valor." In the sixth century the progressive thinker, Xenophanes, issued a famous denunciation,[3] on the ground that athletes were from every point of view useless to a city; with this attitude Solon agreed, at least in part.[4] In the *Epinician Odes* of Pindar we see signs of the rise of professionalism.[5] Later on, a heavy diet of meat was prescribed for the athletes, and they became notorious for their gluttony, their surfeited sleep, and brutish stupidity. They were made to train ten months for the Olympic games, the last month being spent at Olympia. Men began to choose athletics as a profession and a means of earning a livelihood. When athletes were too old to enter the games, they turned to the instruction of the younger generation. At first these ex-athletes, when they became instructors, called

[1] One bit of evidence is the growing infrequency of Spartan names in the victory lists of this and the following century.

[2] *Fr.* 9 Diehl. The author uses the translation by Manning (see the bibliography) p. 75.

[3] *Fr.* 2 Diehl. An English translation will be found in Manning's article.

[4] *Fr.* 44 Bergk⁴. Solon cut down the public rewards of victors in the games: Plut. *Sol.* xxiii, Diog. Laert. i. 55.

[5] Manning 75.

themselves *paidotribai*, on the analogy of the instructors of the boys in physical education, but when the new term *gymnastes* came into use, shortly before Plato's time, they seized on it, and soon every athletic coach was calling himself a *gymnastes*. Since one of his chief functions was rubbing the bodies of the athletes with oil, the name *aleiptes* ("anointer") was invented, and is in frequent use as a synonym for *gymnastes* from the fourth century on.[1] Professionalism was now at its height, and men took more pleasure in sitting at their ease, watching the performances of the athletes, than in themselves toiling at the exercises. Against this malignant bane of athleticism Euripides took up the cudgels:[2] "Of the myriad evils that press on Hellas, there is no greater evil than the athlete folk." Epaminondas revived the Spartan complaint that athleticism was a force incompatible with the making of good soldiers.[3] Socrates,[4] Plato,[5] and Aristotle[6] swelled the chorus of condemnation. Universally, then, among thinking people, professional athletics were in disrepute.

Only toward the close of the fifth century before Christ did the new conception arise that gymnastics could be used as a handmaid of medicine. A *paidotribes* of Selymbria, named Herodicus, hit on the idea, and inasmuch as he was a valetudinarian, he

---

[1] Reisch *RE* I. 1360-1. [2] *Fr.* 282N.
[3] Nepos. *Epam.* ii. 4 and v. 4. [4] Xen. *Symp.* ii. 17, *Mem.* i. 2. 4.
[5] *Resp.* iii. 404A, 410B-D.
[6] *Pol.* vii. 14. 8 (p. 1335b 5-11), viii. 3. 3 (p. 1338b 10-11).

tested out his new scheme on himself, and found that it prolonged his years.¹ Plato, cherishing the Spartan ideal of the survival of the fittest, believed that valetudinarians should not be encouraged to live, and he made fun of Herodicus, as having prolonged, not his life, but his death. Herodicus, however, had written a book explaining his new science, which he called simply "gymnastics," ² and it was not to be killed by Plato's mockery. Bathing was an important part of the héalth gymnastics, and since the system did not necessitate strenuous efforts, it became very popular. The rich people of Athens had small private gymnasia with baths connected, and the common people flocked to the public gymnasia.³ The tendency toward bathing eventually resulted in the metamorphosis of the gymnasium into the huge *thermæ*, or baths, of Roman times—but to trace that development would carry us too far afield.⁴

[1] Plat. *Resp.* iii. 406A–B.
[2] γυμναστική. It was later called "diet" (δίαιτα), then "hygiene" (ὑγιεινή). See Jüthner (1909) 50.
[3] Ps.-Xen. *Ath.* ii. 10.
[4] An enlightening sketch of health gymnastics, or *Heilgymnastik*, is given by Jüthner *RE* VII. 2054–7.

CHAPTER V

THEORIES OF THE PHILOSOPHERS

Three Athenian philosophers of the fourth century before Christ left to us in their works ideal and theoretical schemes of physical education. These men are Xenophon, Plato, and Aristotle. Their discussions of the theory are so full and copious as to out-bulk all the information that can be gathered from all sources on the actual practice of Athenian education at the time. Their theories are of importance, partly because they reflect certain existing conditions, partly because they were influential in modifying the educational practices of the following generations, and partly because they mean something to our own age.

Xenophon, though an Athenian by birth, was out of sympathy with the democracy of his native city, and cherished a warm admiration for the aristocratic Sparta. He wrote a treatise *On the Spartan Polity*, in which he described at some length the educational arrangements established by the Spartan state. So strongly did he believe in the *agoge* of Sparta that he joined the small number of men who sent their sons there to undergo the training. Through his children, Diodorus and Gryllus, he obtained a first-hand knowledge of the *agoge*. Their reaction to it must have been favorable, for Xenophon never swerved in his allegiance.

In his later years Xenophon wrote the *Cyropædia*, a work which we might fairly call a historical novel. The title, "the education of Cyrus," does not indicate the range of the book's contents, for it is a complete, though imaginary and unhistorical, biography of the great Cyrus. The title might be compared to *The Education of Henry Adams*, which is likewise a complete biography, in this case an autobiography. The description which Xenophon gives of the Persian education of Cyrus fills only one chapter (the second) of book one. Any reader of this chapter will recognize easily that it is just as unhistorical as the rest of the *Cyropædia;* as a source book on Persian education it is absolutely valueless. The reader also perceives readily that, while it is an ideal scheme, Xenophon certainly had a definite model in mind, and that model was Sparta. The "education of Cyrus" is no more than a slightly altered and idealized sketch of Spartan education.

Like the *agoge*, the system which Xenophon describes is public in nature and military in purpose. The majority of states, said Xenophon (with Athens especially in mind), have the unwise policy of allowing the individual parents to rear their children with whatever education they please. These states trust to luck that the children will grow up to be good citizens in spite of this haphazard method. No such laissez-faire policy is pursued in Persia. The state there exercises complete control over the education of the young and over the daily life of the grown men. It effects this by the following procedure.

In the capital city there is a sort of Government Square, where are situated the king's palace and various public buildings. The square is divided into four parts, one for the boys, one for the ephebi, a third for the mature men, and a fourth for the elders. Every day at dawn the boys and mature men must present themselves in their respective quarters. The elders are not so stringently bound, and may come late or not at all, except on certain special days. The strictest régime is reserved for the ephebi, who, like the Spartan *eirens*, are kept away from home altogether. The ephebi are given light arms, and are made to spend their nights sleeping about the public buildings. The married ones may slip off occasionally, but it is improper for them to be gone too often. Exactly so at Sparta, the married young men visited their wives only infrequently and by stealth.

Each of the four groups is commanded by twelve officers, corresponding to the twelve tribes of Persia. These officers are not chosen on the ground of birth, rank, or wealth, but on the basis of the single consideration of fitness for the duties which they must perform.

In the class of boys the officers do not put much stress on physical education, but they send the boys to school chiefly to learn justice. Self-control and abstemiousness in eating and drinking are inculcated in the boys both by precept and by the example of the elders. The only physical exercises that Xenophon mentions for this age class are the use of the bow and arrow and practice with the javelin.

At sixteen or seventeen the boys are promoted to the class of ephebi. One of their principal functions now is to guard the buildings in Government Square, around which they pass the nights. Their days are spent in whatever service the state requires. Many times every month the king goes hunting, and each time he takes half of the ephebi with him. The expenses of the hunting expeditions are borne by the state treasury, for it was believed that hunting wild game was the very best training for war. Hence the king in person leads the chase, and hunting is regarded as the favorite and most important exercise. Xenophon himself was particularly fond of hunting, and once wrote a treatise on hunting with dogs (the *Cynegeticus*). He takes occasion at this point in the *Cyropædia* to expatiate on the merits of hunting: it teaches one to rise early, to endure extremes of temperature, to walk and run long distances, to be courageous and alert. The lad who is a good hunter is sure to prove a good soldier.

Meanwhile, the half of the ephebi who stayed behind in Government Square practice with the bow and arrow and javelin, or else perform garrison duty.

Sometimes they serve as police and do tasks like those of the Spartan youths of the secret service. This ephebic training, partly in the city, and partly out on active service, lasts for ten years, and is completed when the lads are twenty-six or twenty-seven years old.

The Persians belong to the class of adults for twenty-five years, during which time they hold magistracies, serve in the army, and serve the state in any other capacity suited to their years and ability. Then passing into the last class, that of the elders, they act as judges in the courts, advisers to the king, and instructors of the boys.

Xenophon makes this system of education restricted to the well-to-do, and here again it resembles the aristocratic model of Sparta rather than the democratic one of Athens. Only those who complete the first stage (the boys') under the public teachers may enter the ephebi, and the same rule holds for admission to each successive group. Like Plato's, this scheme is for public education, with the military end always kept in view, but it lacks the originality and boldness which characterized the theory of the genius of the Academy.

Plato wrote copiously on the topic of education, because he realized its vast importance in human life. In the *Republic*, the *Laws*, and occasionally in other dialogues he revealed his conception of what physical education should be, and what part it should play in the ideal state. The system which he outlined in the

Laws is much more detailed and elaborate than that of the *Republic;* the later, however, does not contradict the earlier sketch in any fundamental point, only modifying and altering details, and confirming the scheme of the *Republic* in its general lines.[1]

Satisfied with some features of the Athenian education in which he was reared, Plato was unfavorable to others. He observed that the Athenians were left in this matter to their individual initiative; no one had authority to determine at what age a boy should enter or leave school, or what and how he should study while there. Yet surely the happiness and success of one's whole life, and the supreme welfare of the state, hinged upon those crucial years of education. No state could afford to neglect a matter which concerned it so vitally. The very foundations of Sparta, as Plato well understood, rested on the uniform and rigid scheme of education; once abolish this, and the formidable structure of Spartan power would fall in cataclysmic ruin. In Plato's ideal "republic" (which was the farthest remove from being a republic), the state did not exist for the individual, but the individual for the state. As in Sparta, the state interposed its will everywhere, and the education of the young was public as a matter of course.[2]

Still having his eyes fixed on Sparta, Plato recommended for his ideal state another change from Athenian practice. The girls must be made equal with the

---

[1] Dantu p. viii.   [2] *Legg.* vi. 764 C-766B.

boys, both in other respects, and in sharing the public education.[1] In our modern era, when women enjoy such a degree of freedom and equality, it is not easy to realize how revolutionary and radical such a proposal was. The women of Athens were disregarded and slighted; they were made to be neither seen nor heard; and that they should be educated, or in any way allowed to participate in the life and affairs of the men was incredible and taboo. The Athenians would have approved, or at least sympathized with, the proverb of India: "Educating a woman is like putting a knife in the hands of a monkey." How they must have gasped and gaped when they read in the *Republic* the recommendation of such a piece of heresy! But Plato was not to be deterred by the scoffers, and refused to retract this part of his plan when he wrote the *Laws*.

In a third respect the educational practices of Athens in the fourth century failed to win Plato's approval. Socrates shared with the sophists the blame of getting the Athenian youth so enthusiastic over philosophical thought and the world of the intellect and reason, that they forgot everything else, gymnastics included. Socrates himself was the first to complain of this undesired neglect of gymnastics,[2] and Plato reacted against it with all his might. He was insistent that a balance be found and preserved be-

---

[1] *Resp.* v. 451E–452A. *Legg.* vii. 804D–E, 813E–814A.
[2] See Xen. *Mem.* iii. 12. 1ff. Dantu 5.

tween mental and physical education; the soul and
the body, he declared, must have a parallel development.[1]

The program for developing sound bodies Plato
worked out systematically from the very beginning,
just as the Spartans had done. No one can fail to
remark that Plato's scheme of physical education
bears to the Spartan *agoge* a resemblance too close to
be accidental. Evidently the *agoge*, except for its
neglect of mental education, impressed him almost as
favorably as it did Xenophon. Had he known it as
intimately as he knew the Athenian education, he
would not, I suspect, have esteemed it so highly. Regarding it from a distance, he was enchanted. The
Spartans demanded physical fitness on the part of
parents, and Plato likewise insisted on eugenics.[2] Expectant mothers, he prescribed, should take regular
exercise,[3] by this means improving their chances for
bearing strong, healthy children. In the years of
infancy, the children should have plenty of exercise by
proxy—that is, the nurses should keep carrying them
around, out in the pleasant fields, to the temples, or
perhaps to visit relatives.[4] Up to the age of three,
then, children were to be left entirely to the care of
the family. From three to six they have the games
that are natural to childhood, but in these they are
under regulation by the state. Their playgrounds or

[1] Dantu 18.   [2] *Legg.* vi. 773C–774A.
[3] *Ibid.* vii. 789A–E.   [4] *Ibid.* 789E.

kindergartens are by the village temples, and there they are to be supervised by their nurses and by a responsible woman as playground director.[1] At the age of six systematic physical education under teachers of riding, archery, javelin throwing, and slinging begins. In the *Republic* Plato has the boys and girls, the men and women, exercise together without regard to sex, but in the *Laws* he abandoned this point, although he still demanded that the girls have full participation in the physical exercises.[2]

All physical exercises Plato included under the two heads of wrestling and dancing. With this broad use of the word "wrestling" ($\pi\acute{a}\lambda\eta$), we may compare the use of "wrestling school" or "palæstra" to mean a school for physical education in general. Military dances in armor, performed by both boys and girls, Plato recommended especially. Trickery in wrestling he frowned upon, indicating that the purpose of wrestling should not be to win a contest, but to promote suppleness, strength, and health. Hunting he favored for its mental and physical value [3]; here again Sparta was hovering in his thoughts, for we have seen that the Spartan lads were zealous for the chase.

The gymnasia and schools Plato wanted to have in three places in the center of the city, and in three places outside the city limits.[4] The latter were to be spacious, providing plenty of room for horse-racing,

---

[1] *Legg.* vii. 794A–B. [2] Compare *Resp.* v. 452A–B with *Legg.* vii. 794C.
[3] *Ibid.* 824A–B. Bischof 55. [4] *Ibid.* 804C.

archery, and hurling the javelin. The teaching was to be done by salaried foreigners, who were to live in the school buildings, where they taught. Attendance should be compulsory for all, with no regard to sex.[1] School was to open at daybreak,[2] as was the ordinary custom in Greece.

The state should appoint officials to oversee music and gymnastics, each branch having two such officials.[3] One of the ministers would superintend the instruction and the schools, the other the various contests and competitions. Over them would be the supreme leader of the entire educational system, the *epimeletes* or Minister of Education.[4] It must be clearly understood that his position is the most important one in the whole state, for everything else is secondary to education, and no effort should be spared in the endeavor to find the best possible incumbent for this office. He should be a man of mature years and judgment, at least fifty years old, and himself keenly interested in education because of having children of his own. His term of service should be five years.

Plato's conception of the aims of physical education differed somewhat from the ideas both of his own day and of ours. He emphasized to the Athenians that gymnastic exercises not only fostered a sturdy citizenry, but formed the best training for soldiery. War Plato

---

[1] *Legg.* vii. 804D. [2] *Ibid.* 808C. [3] *Ibid.* vi. 764C–D.
[4] *Ibid.* 765D. Cf. 751D, 753D; vii. 801D, 809C, 813C. Dreinhöfer 9.

regarded as inevitable, and he proposed to make due preparations against its coming. Dances and gymnastics were to be the daily training of future warriors, and at least once a month heavy military drill and sham battles were to be held.[1] The children should be taken out to see actual battles, and both boys and girls should be trained in the military arts. Then if the enemy came, as he surely would, he would be crushed by the strong, fearless army of men, and Amazons fighting beside the men.

In addition to the military goal, Plato emphasized the moral goal of physical education. For him the moral value of the exercises and sports far outweighed the physical value. Vice, he declared, was due to bad education and an unhealthy physical condition;[2] gymnastics served both as a preventive and a remedy of the latter, and so contributed to the extirpation of vice. We moderns generally regard physical education as an end in itself, but Plato regarded it as a means toward moral perfection. He consequently had no desire to train the body to the utmost degree possible, and there was no danger of athleticism in his ideal state.[3] He really debarred permanently any chance of such evils, by ruling that no changes in his system of gymnastics should ever be permitted.[4] Yet, while gymnastic training should never be carried to excess, it should never cease, but should last ἐκ παίδων διὰ βίου,

[1] *Legg.* viii. 830D.
[2] *Tim.* 86E.
[3] Dantu 65.
[4] *Resp.* iv. 424B.

from boyhood on through life.[1] Too high commendation can not be given to such sane ideals, and they should surely convey some message to our own generation.

Another point, and not the least interesting one, in Plato's educational prescriptions is the discussion in the *Laws* (vi. 760B–763C) of a police and guard service, performed by young men from twenty-five to thirty years old, and lasting for a period of two years. These guards are to go about from place to place, getting thoroughly acquainted with their country's topography; they are to have common meals, and are to sleep together. Much more discussion is to be found in the passage, but some of the points have been singled out that are of most significance to establish the contention that here we have some suggestions which Athens employed later in the creation of the ephebia. Not all the details are the same, nor should we expect them to be. The actual age of the ephebi was from eighteen to twenty, not from twenty-five to thirty;[2] but the guard duty, the periodical shifting from place to place in the country, the common life, and particularly the fact that this was part of a scheme for public education, all point in the same direction. Wilamowitz (I. 194) was surely right: "*Platons Gesetze*

---

[1] *Resp.* iii. 403C.
[2] In the *Republic* vii. 537B Plato made recommendations which in this respect more closely coincide with the later actuality: a training period of two or three years devoted wholly to gymnastics, beginning at about the age of eighteen.

haben die ephebie erzeugt." We must not get ahead of the story, however, and further discussion of the ephebia is postponed until the next chapter.

Aristotle set forth his educational ideals at the end of the seventh and beginning of the eighth books of his *Politics*. Like Plato and Xenophon, he stressed the military aspect of education, and proposed that all the training of the young should be under state control. All three of these theorizers, Xenophon, Plato, and Aristotle, were at one in their demand for public education, and this demand bore fruit in the Athenian ephebia and the compulsory state education of many Greek cities. In one point, however, Aristotle differed seriously with his master, and this was the question of throwing open education, both physical and mental, to girls as well as to boys. The desire to regenerate the female sex from its humble and lowly position at Athens had fired Plato's enthusiasm, but the idea left Aristotle cold. The nature of women is different from and inferior to that of men, he asserted in direct contradiction of Plato;[1] hence they could have no part in education and public affairs. With this remark he summarily dismissed the question.

Physical education Aristotle accounted important, but he ranked it after literary-musical studies. He did, however, recommend that instruction in physical exercises should last for a longer period of years than the instruction in all other subjects. He agreed with

[1] *Pol.* i. 13. 9 (p. 1260a 21ff.).

Plato in not considering physical education an end in itself, but he favored it from the belief that a beautiful, strong, healthy body is conducive to a sound mind. Furthermore, it builds soldiers, and all the ancients, whether philosophers or not, deemed this desirable.

Eugenics as a means of fostering a sturdy race played a part in Aristotle's as well as Plato's state. The proper age for entering upon matrimony is suggested (eighteen for women, thirty-seven for men), and the ideal physical condition of the parents is described. Athletes make just as poor fathers as weak, anemic men; the mean between these extremes is the desirable constitution.[1] Aristotle wished to apply his doctrine of the mean to gymnastic exercises as much as to anything else; if such exercises are taken either in excess or in deficiency, he declared, they are ruinous to the physical powers.[2] Athleticism encountered no mercy at the hands of Aristotle. Prospective mothers he admonished to have a care of themselves, taking exercise daily and adopting a suitable diet. If, in spite of all these precautions, a deformed child should be born, he ordered that it should be exposed to die.

In the earliest years of infancy, particular attention should be given to diet, and every effort should be exerted to make children active and hardy. Aristotle's whole philosophy demanded activity, instead of Stoic passivity or Epicurean dawdling, and this influenced his attitude toward physical education. Up to the

[1] *Pol.* vii. 16. 12 (p. 1335b 5ff.). [2] *Eth. N.* ii. 2. 6 (p. 1104a 15–16).

age of five, no study or regulated exercise should be expected of children, but the natural instinct for play will keep them from being sluggish or inactive. Even so early in life the children, although left at home until they are seven, are under the general supervision of the directors of education (*paidonomoi*). From the age of five to the age of seven, boys should be spectators and listeners in the schools and palæstræ, making a preliminary acquaintance with the subjects of study and with the gymnastic exercises.

Beginning at seven, regular school instruction should be given to the boys in gymnastics. The body should be trained before the mind, Aristotle contended, and he wished instruction in grammar, music, and drawing to begin at a later age. Light exercises, of such a character as not to stunt the boys' growth, should be taken until the age of fourteen or fifteen, and then stopped altogether for a period of three years. These three years should be devoted to mental education, but after they are over, at the age of eighteen or thereabouts, stiffer exercises should be commenced. These arrangements Aristotle justifies by saying:[1] "Men ought not to labor at the same time with their minds and with their bodies; for the two kinds of labor are opposed to one another; the labor of the body impedes the mind, and the labor of the mind the body." Apparently Aristotle had no thought that men would fail to continue moderate exercises throughout life, for he

[1] *Pol.* viii. 4. 2 (p. 1339a 7–10) tr. Jowett.

casually mentions that it would be a "charming" thing to have the older men (πρεσβύτεροι) perform their gymnastics in the "freemen's square."[1] Further details are wanting, however, for the end of the *Politics* is lost.

Thirteen years before Aristotle's death, a great change was wrought in Athenian education, a transformation of spirit and practice. The new force in education, which Aristotle himself described in the *Constitution of Athens*, was destined to be of major significance for Athens and the whole Greek world. In the next chapter we shall see what was the character, and what the history, of this new institution, the Athenian ephebia.

[1] *Pol.* vii. 12. 2 (p. 1331a 35ff.). Plato, too, wished to have part of the gymnasia in the center of the city, perhaps by the ἀγορά (*Legg.* vii. 804C). The Athenian gymnasia were outside the walls.

CHAPTER VI

THE ATHENIAN EPHEBIA

The ephebia at Athens was an organization of the youths from the age of eighteen to twenty. Prior to its foundation, Athenian education had only two stages, primary and secondary, but the ephebia furnished an additional stage, the higher or tertiary.[1] The principal purpose in its creation was to give cadet training as a preparation for more efficient service in warfare. The state had complete control of the ephebia, through a hierarchy of officials, and thus the tertiary education differed from the two lower stages by being public and compulsory. The training given in the ephebia was originally military and gymnastic, but later literary and philosophical education were included, and caused the warlike nature of the institution gradually to fall into abeyance. Since the Athenians thought highly of the cadets, their position in the state was one of honor and esteem; the importance of their rôle in Greek history may be better comprehended if we state from the very outset that it was at

[1] The three stages of education in the late fourth century before Christ were clearly described by Teles ap. Stob. *Flor.* xcviii. 72 and Ps.-Plat. *Axioch.* 366D-367A. See Walden 18-19; Girard (1891) 237-8. Zimmern (297 n.) observed that even the secondary stage was unknown until about a century before 335. Freeman's book does not sufficiently emphasize these changes.

least six centuries and perhaps even longer, that the ephebia endured. Few indeed were the Athenian institutions that lasted half as long. The importance of the ephebia is further vouched for by its wide and persistent influence in the remainder of Greece, and in all the parts of the Mediterranean basin which came under Greek sway or were affected by Greece's far-flung colonies. Unfortunately, its existence covers centuries from which the remains of Greek literature are pitifully meager, with the consequence that our information about it is incomplete and in some points uncertain. In 1860 a great boon for the historian of the ephebia came, in the discovery at Athens of a long series of inscriptions relating to the ephebi and their instructors.[1] These epigraphical finds, supplementing some previously made, enlarged appreciably the compass and certainty of our knowledge. In 1891 occurred another event which deserves mention here, one which greatly extended our knowledge of Athenian history and did not fail to revise materially our previous conceptions about the ephebia. The writer refers to the publication from an Egyptian papyrus belonging to the British Museum of Aristotle's *Constitution of Athens*.

It will not be amiss to chronicle here some of the more important work that has been done, and progress that has been made, by the studies of modern scholars on the ephebia.[2] The oldest discussion to which the

[1] See Dumont *Introd.* pp. iii–v.
[2] For the titles of the works referred to and other data, see the bibliography.

author has had reference, but not access, is that of the Dutch scholar, van Dale, published in 1702. Half a century later, the Italian Corsini devoted some attention to the ephebi; his work the author has not seen, either, but seemingly it was respectable for his time, as Boeckh [1] gave it a measure of commendation: *Pleraque non male persequitur*. Boeckh's own work on the subject, though most accessible in the fourth volume of his *Kleine Schriften*,[2] dated 1874, was first published in 1819. He determined correctly the ephebic age as eighteen to twenty (138), but represented the ephebi as taking oath on entering the college. It will serve to illustrate the blunders made before the discovery of Aristotle's *Constitution of Athens*, to mention that Boeckh considered inaccurate a statement quoted from this very work of Aristotle's by the lexicographer Harpocration.[3] The statement was that the ephebi had their arms presented to them at a public assembly in the theater; Boeckh said this applied only to the orphans who were reared and educated at state expense, and not to the ephebi. After the discovery of the ephebic inscriptions in 1860, the first ensemble study based on the new material as well as the old was the doctoral dissertation of the famous epigrapher, Wilhelm Dittenberger. This was a piece of work wrought with care, skill, and judgment;

[1] (1874) 141 n. 1.
[2] Reference to his work will be made by the pagination in this volume of the *Kleine Schriften*.
[3] s. v. περίπολος.

after sixty-odd years it still deserves to be consulted. Dumont's work in the next decade is the largest and most comprehensive that has ever been written on the subject of the ephebi. The second volume, published one year before the first, contains the text of nearly all the ephebic inscriptions which had been published up to that time, and a study of their chronology in relation to that of the Athenian archons; thus it is a source book for the elaborate description and history of the ephebia which fills the first volume. Dumont still represented the ephebia as existing early in the fifth century; and he fell into Boeckh's error of disregarding the plain testimony of Aristotle, as quoted by Harpocration, concluding, as even Dittenberger had, that the youths received spear and shield and took their oath at the age of eighteen, when they entered the ephebic ranks. In 1881 Grasberger issued the closing volume of his comprehensive work on ancient education. Nearly the whole of this third volume was devoted to the ephebia, and, while the sources were not reprinted, as they were by Dumont, the treatment was even more detailed and thorough than that of the French scholar. Grasberger repeated once more the venerable heresies that the arming and taking oath occurred at the time of entrance to the college, and that the institution existed in the fifth century. Being no weakling thinker, he boldly took issue with Dittenberger on the question of the duration of ephebic service in the second century before Christ and later, declaring his belief that it was always two years, the standard originally adopted. This belief was properly rejected by Girard in 1891; yet Girard, both in his book and in his 1892 article on the ephebi in Daremberg-Saglio, insisted on the fifth century origin of the ephebia.

The new and, as we believe, correct view of the date when the organization of the ephebi originated, was half discerned by E. Egger and Selchau, but first clearly perceived by the acute mind of Wilamowitz in 1893. The date which he established, 335/4, has been accepted by Beloch (1905), Bryant, Bury, Dittenberger,[1] Kirchner,[2] and Brenot; some have ignored his work, Chapot wavered, and Lofberg was unconvinced. Busolt-Swoboda (II. 577) were not sure of the exact date, but thought Wilamowitz probably right, and would not by any means allow that the ephebia existed prior to 355/4. Such is the present status of the question:[3] now to consider the arguments that may properly be adduced, and to find if we can determine from them the truth of the matter.

The *argumentum ex silentio* was well employed by Wilamowitz.[4] He pointed out that Plato and Isocrates could not have known any such institution as the ephebia, where education was public and the teachers were chosen and salaried by the state. This was just

[1] On *SIG*³ 957.   [2] On *IG* ii. 1². 1156.
[3] The author has passed over in this brief survey some of the minor contributions: Ahrens, Beutler, Østbye.
[4] I. 191–3.

what Plato insisted on for his ideal state,[1] but he never uttered a word that would permit us to believe that anything of the sort was true in Athens when he was writing the *Laws*, in the middle of the fourth century.[2] His description of the guard system for his state [3] can not be modelled on an ephebia already existing, as some have thought,[4] for his suggestion was that the guards be chosen by election,[5] from the number of those whose age was anywhere between twenty-five and thirty,[6] and that they perform the service of guarding for two entire years.[7] Now in the actual ephebia all the lads of nineteen and twenty were obliged to submit to a course of military training, in which most of the guarding and patrolling of the land came during the second year. Plato's recommendations, in these points and many others, were so incompatible with reality that he can have had no existing model in mind.[8] It is natural, on the other hand, that if Athens created the ephebia with Plato's *Laws* in mind, it should adapt the philosopher's recommendations to make them more feasible from a practical point of view. It occurred to the Athenians that they might as well combine the good of the individual with

---

[1] *Legg.* vii. 613E on state-paid teachers.

[2] Plato was working on the *Laws* at least as late as 352 (see Oldfather in *AJP* XLIV. [1923] 275-6), and they were not yet published at the time of his death in 347.

[3] *Legg.* vi. 760A-763C. Cf. above, pages 104-105.

[4] Lofberg 332.

[5] *l. c.* 760B.

[6] *l. c.* 760C.

[7] *Ibid.*

[8] Such is the argument of Brenot 27-8.

that of the state, by so arranging the guard duty that it would be educational to those who performed it, while at the same time it was a measure of protection to the state. Practical motives led to a one-year preparatory period of military and gymnastic training, and to the fixation of the ages between eighteen and twenty, in order to link this period closely with the previous stages of education. The compulsion to enter the ephebia was occasioned by the desire to train as many soldiers as possible to fight for Athens in the period of her military decline. In this way all the divergences of actuality from Plato's scheme may be explained. The argument [1] most conclusive in proving that Plato was not using any already existing ephebia as a model, is that nowhere in the passage referred to above did he use the word "ephebi" or *peripoloi* ("patrols", the name given to the ephebi in the second year, when they patrolled the frontiers), and he even admitted that he was at a loss to know what he should call these guards.[2] Neither did he speak of a *kosmetes* or *sophronistes*, in this passage or in the seventh book of the *Laws*, where education is treated in minute detail.[3] In the second book of the *Laws* (666E), the Athenian stranger speaks of the Spartans as herding together like colts; he could not have uttered this reproach, had there been Athenian ephebi living in common barracks, else it would have

[1] Brenot 28.
[2] *Legg.* vi. 763B εἴτε τις κρυπτοὺς εἴτε ἀγρονόμους εἴθ' ὅτι καλῶν χαίρει.
[3] Wilamowitz I. 192.

been cast in his teeth by the Spartan with whom he was conversing. At another point in the conversation,[1] the Spartan grants that the virtue of the Athenians was a matter of choice, not of compulsion; the ephebia, however, made it compulsory.[2]

The other writings of Plato lead to the same conclusion. Socrates talked either at length or incidentally *de omnibus rebus et quibusdam aliis*, but never so much as alluded to an institution so striking and important as the ephebia surely was. In the *Laches* (179E) we have a father inquiring from Socrates whether or no he had better have instruction in hoplomachy given to his sons; but if the ephebia had existed, with its compulsory training in hoplomachy, this conversation could never have taken place.[3] Crito in the *Euthydemus* (306D) expresses doubt as to what he should do with his son Critobulus, who was about the ephebic age; could there have been any doubt if the ephebic training had then existed?[4] The impatient Alcibiades was after political office before he was twenty years old,[5] an impossibility if all his time had been taken up by service as an ephebus.

Isocrates also gives testimony that seems incontro-

---

[1] *Legg.* i. 642C–D.

[2] Bryant 84. The state kept the ephebi *"streng von der corruption des lebens entfernt"* (Wilamowitz I. 191). See Artemidor. *Oneirocrit.* i. 54 Hercher σχεδὸν γὰρ ἡ ἐφηβεία κανών ἐστιν ὀρθοῦ βίου καὶ ὑγιοῦς.

[3] Bryant 80 n. 2. See Aristot. *Ath.* xlii. 3 on required hoplomachy in the ephebia.

[4] Bryant 81 and n. 1.

[5] Plat. *I Alcib.* 123D and the other citations given by Bryant 81 n. 3.

vertible. In the first place, he did not mention the ephebia in the *Areopagiticus*, where we should expect it if any such thing existed. He extolled the good discipline of former days, which surely leads us to infer that there were no discipline-masters, *sophronistai*, in Athens when he wrote.[1] In the second place, his oration *On the Peace*, written in 356 or 355,[2] tells as definitely as one possibly could that no ephebia was in existence then:[3] "We are unwilling to take the field, and while we undertake war, I may almost say, against the whole world, are at no pains to train ourselves for it, but fill our army with men partly homeless, partly deserters, and with others who have gathered here in consequence of other vicious propensities, and who, if others were to offer them higher pay, would follow them against us."

A study of other authors yields yet more substantiating evidence. In the *Memorabilia*[4] Xenophon represented Socrates as having some misgivings about Bœotia, and as recommending that the young men in light arms should guard the passes that led over the mountains to that hostile country. This is exactly what the ephebi did later on, but apparently not even the sort of *peripoloi* who were known prior to the ephebia,[5] were performing such a service in this period,

[1] Wilamowitz I. 192.
[2] Blass *Att. Beredsamkeit*² II. 300.
[3] *de Pace* 44 tr. Freese. This passage was duly stressed by Busolt-Swoboda II. 1189.
[4] iii. 5. 25–7; for the value of this passage see Selchau 212.
[5] Foucart 265f.

which was after 371.[1] In the *Hellenica* there is not a word that could be interpreted to refer to the ephebi.[2] Glaucon, when just under twenty years of age, was questioned by Socrates, and revealed that he was totally ignorant of military affairs, and had never gone to the frontiers.[3] It is impossible to think that any ephebia existed in the time of Socrates, when we read another passage in the *Memorabilia*[4]: "Military training is not publicly recognized by the state." Antiphon tells[5] of a young man reaching his majority and immediately hurrying off to Abydos for a good time, obviously without a thought of any such thing as ephebic duties.[6] In Demosthenes, Æschines, and Aristotle's *Politics* we do not hear of ephebic officials, such as the *sophronistai*.[7] Wilamowitz declared that

[1] Of course Socrates was dead long before 371, but it was easy for Xenophon to put his own thoughts into the mouth of his master. Wilamowitz, Brenot, and others have observed that Xenophon surely had in mind the situation of Athens after the battle of Leuctra in 371, when he wrote about the advisability of guarding the passes to Bœotia. True, Bœotia had been an enemy country during most of the latter half of the fifth century, but the situation pictured by Xenophon resembles that after 371 best of all.

[2] Brenot 21.

[3] Xen. *Mem.* iii. 6. 1ff. See Bryant 82; Selchau 211.

[4] iii. 12. 5 (a passage whose bearing on this question has hitherto remained unnoticed) ἡ πόλις οὐκ ἀσκεῖ δημοσίᾳ τὰ πρὸς τὸν πόλεμον. Marchant's translation is given.

[5] *Fr.* 69 Thalheim (from Ath. xii. 28).

[6] Bryant 82.

[7] Wilamowitz (I. 192) remarks that Æschines would surely have mentioned *sophronistai*, had they existed, in the speech against Timarchus, where he tried to gather all the evidence he could for the discipline and restraint of the young. No one argues that the use of the word *sophronistai* by Demosth. xix. 285 proves the existence of such officials in Athens: see Schömann-Lipsius I. 553 n. 4.

the sixth book of Aristotle's *Politics* was written after 338, but when it gives a list of educational magistrates,[1] not one of those pertaining to the ephebia is included. In short, the evidence [2] heaped up by Selchau, Wilamowitz, Bryant, Brenot, and Busolt-Swoboda is enough to convince even the most prejudiced person that there was no ephebia prior to 335. Even the paternalistic spirit of the ephebia is so inharmonious with the liberty and freedom of life which Athens cherished in the fifth and early fourth centuries that this alone should serve to prove the non-existence of any such institution in that period.[3]

As I have already indicated, the date of 335 for the origin of the ephebia has not gone unchallenged. No one assigns a later date, for the oldest ephebic decree (*IG* ii. 1². 1156) is of the year 334/3, and relates to the second year ephebi, who were enrolled in 335/4. Many, however, have thought of the ephebia as existing in the fifth century; let us turn to their arguments and see how they may be refuted.

Much of the argument levelled against the date we have set was due to the repeated mention of *peripoloi* in earlier literature, some of it even belonging to the fifth century. Foucart (265f.) did the pioneer work in establishing the distinction between these *peripoloi* and the second-year ephebi who were called by the same title; he showed that the fifth century *peripoloi*

[1] vi. 5. 13 (p. 1322b 38ff.).
[2] To only part of which the author has referred.
[3] See the eloquent words of Wilamowitz I. 191.

were not of the ephebic age,[1] and were foreign mercenaries,[2] led by *peripolarchs*.[3] Lofberg (330) thinks that not all were mercenaries, but it is improbable that noble and wealthy Athenian ephebi would consent to do police service in company with hired soldiers from abroad. Furthermore, these fifth-century *peripoloi* could cross the frontier,[4] which the ephebi or cadet soldiers were not permitted to do.[5] Lofberg sees in the "youngest soldiers" (νεώτατοι) of Thucydides (ii. 13. 7) the ephebi, explaining that the failure to call them ephebi is due to the circumstance that Athenian writers are "notoriously careless of technicalities." The author is willing to grant that these lads may have been aged eighteen to twenty, and even [6] yield to Girard [7] the point that in the fifth cen-

---

[1] Thuc. viii. 92 uses the word ἀνήρ of one of the περίπολοι.

[2] The foreign extraction of some of the *peripoloi* engaged in the plot described by Thuc. (*l. c.*) is proved by Lysias (*c. Agorat.* 71). Ar. (*Av.* 1172ff.) mentions περίπολοι and ἱπποτοξόται in one breath as being police; it would seem natural, as Selchau (214) says, that the former, like the latter, should be foreigners.

[3] *IG.* ii. 1². 204 and 1193.

[4] Thuc. i. 105. 4; iv. 67. 2.

[5] Aristotle's careful account and the detailed inscriptions have given us a complete panorama of the ephebic activities, but we never hear of the ephebi venturing over the border. Lofberg (331) thinks the ephebi might have crossed the border in the exciting days of the Peloponnesian War, especially to relieve their tenseness by a change in routine. Sparta, however, was not threatening Attica's frontier when the *peripoloi* made their trip beyond the border (Lofberg grants this), and therefore we doubt if there was much tenseness. Besides, getting accustomed to routine is essential for soldiers, and surely there should be no relaxation in time of war. Lofberg is forced to make many assumptions of this sort in defending the early origin of the ephebia; the date of 335 obviates the necessity for these assumptions.

[6] With Bryant 79 n. 5. [7] Dar.-Sagl. II. 621f.

tury the youths of this age formed a separate military class; yet there is no shred of evidence to prove that they had special ephebic officials or any organized military or gymnastic training whatsoever. In fact, as has already been shown, there is everything to prove that this was not the case. Another fact, which makes Lofberg uncertain of his ground, is that the "youngest soldiers" of Thucydides were hoplites, whereas the ephebi were always light-armed.

Lofberg finds another argument in Xenophon [1] for ephebic *peripoloi*. The resemblance of the language used by Xenophon to that of Aristotle, in describing the ephebi, makes him certain that these *peripoloi* of Xenophon were not mercenaries. A mere resemblance of language proves nothing, and one who argues from it is grasping at a straw. Lofberg notes, too, that Xenophon suggested that the patrols would do their work better when "maintenance is duly supplied for the work done;" now foreigners, says Lofberg, would not work simply for their maintenance, but would demand more pay. The passage, however, may simply mean that the *peripoloi* had been paid irregularly in the past,[2] and I do not feel as sure as does Lofberg, that the foreigners would expect more than a maintenance (τροφή). As for the Xenophon passage already referred to,[3] where Socrates advised garrisons

---

[1] *Vect.* iv. 47 and 52.

[2] This explanation occurred to the writer independently; he later discovered that Wilamowitz I. 199 gave the same interpretation.

[3] *Mem.* iii. 5. 25–7; above, page 117.

on the Bœotian frontier, Lofberg thinks that Socrates was urging offense as well as defense,[1] wherefore the defensive ephebi might have existed when that was written. The two phrases which he quotes in substantiation of this are widely separated, and an unbiased comparison of the passage will force any one to admit that the thought uppermost in the mind of Socrates was certainly defense, not aggression, against the growing Bœotian power. Another author mentioning the *peripoloi* is Æschines, who says [2] that he himself had been a *peripolos* for two years about 372 B.C. Lofberg thinks this proof positive that the ephebia existed then, but I can not agree with him in this. It merely suggests the possibility that the police service performed by mercenaries in the fifth century may have been entrusted now, under economic pressure, to the lads eighteen and nineteen years of age.[3] If this be true, and it is most uncertain, it did not constitute an ephebic training, and the only leaders were the *peripolarchs;* Æschines did not account his service as *peripolos* as part of his education, any more than such patrol duty was a phase of education when performed by mercenaries. It certainly was not compulsory for any one, and perhaps did not absorb all the time of those who did it.[4] It is a long step from

[1] *l. c.* 27 βλαβερούς μὲν τοῖς πολεμίοις εἶναι; iii. 5.4 πορθοῦντες τὴν Βοιωτίαν.
[2] *F. L.* 167.
[3] Busolt-Swoboda II. 1195.
[4] Bryant 80. If the *peripoloi* of the first half of the fourth century were Athenian lads, there is not the least difficulty over their unsatisfactory pay (Xen. *Vect.* iv. 52, and see above).

patrol service of this sort to an ephebia requiring all the time of every Athenian between the ages of eighteen and twenty.

Another stumbling block has been the ephebic oath, with its apparent antiquity and one notice of it in literature prior to 335.[1] It was about ten years before 335 when Demosthenes alluded unmistakably to the oath, and it should be added that Plutarch [2] mentions the oath as existing in the days of Alcibiades. With this I have no quarrel. The oath of allegiance on entering the rights and privileges of citizenship is quite natural, but does it prove that there was an ephebic training? The word ephebus was, as every classical scholar knows, used loosely for centuries, referring to a youth who had recently attained the age of puberty; if the Athenian ephebi in this sense of the word took an oath of allegiance in the fifth century or earlier, we are not therefore bound to think that there was an ephebic organization. Of course, the oath was taken in the ephebia from 335 on, but its existence even as early as Solon, if one pleases,[3] does not presuppose any sort of military training or organization.[4] Lofberg's crowning argument, that the ephebia must be ancient

[1] Demosth. *F. L.* 303.

[2] *Alc.* xv. 7.

[3] Grasberger III. 29–32. On its antiquity see Lycurg. *c. Leoc.* 75–6, where it is said to be among οἱ παλαιοὶ νόμοι καὶ τὰ ἔθη τῶν ἐξ ἀρχῆς ταῦτα κατασκευασάντων.

[4] See Brenot 29. Busolt-Swoboda (II. 1188–9) argued for the late origin of the ephebia, but had no qualms over admitting the antiquity of the ephebic oath (II. 1190). Before 335 the oath was taken at the time of enrolment on the catalog of hoplites.

because a vase [1] representing the ephebic oath dates back at least a century before 335, therefore falls to the ground. The fact that Æschines [2] called his fellows in the service of the *peripoloi* "synephebi," or "fellow ephebi," signifies nothing, for this term, like that of *ephebi* was employed non-technically before the rise of the ephebia.[3] Girard argued [4] that the ephebi merely served a military apprenticeship, having no connection with education until a late epoch. Even a cursory reading of Aristotle's chapter on the ephebi, in the *Constitution of Athens*, will prove the absurdity of such a suggestion; neither Lofberg nor any one else, so far as I know, ever adopted this argument for the early origin of the ephebic organization.[5]

With the date of 335 established, still further insight into the genesis of the ephebia is possible: we can name its founder, we can find the germs of suggestion that lay behind its arrangements, and we can detect the general and specific causes that led to its creation soon after 338. If we will reread the selection from Isocrates which is quoted above on page 117, we shall understand the military situation of Athens in 356/5.

---

[1] Conze *Annali* XL. (1868) 266 Plate H (wrongly referred to in Conze's text and Lofberg's article as Plate I). The armor of this "ephebus" is not identical with that employed in the ephebia; the ephebi had only shield and spear, while this "ephebus" has a helmet. The πέτασος (broad-brimmed, soft hat) was the headgear of the ephebi (Poll. viii. 164). Lofberg failed to notice this discrepancy.

[2] *c. Timarch.* 49, *F. L.* 168.

[3] Busolt-Swoboda II. 1189.

[4] Dar.-Sagl. II. 621.

[5] Girard was well refuted by Bryant (80).

The martial spirit of the people was at a low ebb,[1] and mercenaries were being used in large numbers to fill up the gaps in the army. Now citizens who fought only occasionally, and who were no longer animated by the splendid heroism which had overcome the Persian hosts, made a poor showing beside the hardy and efficient professional soldiers. The need to give the citizen soldiery some training became increasingly apparent, but Athens still cherished enough of her old ideals of personal liberty to shudder at the thought of compulsory military training. A cruel lesson was needed in order to bring her to the point of action in the matter, and the lesson came in the disaster of Chæronea, 338 B.C. In this battle, whereby Greece became subject to the hegemony of King Philip, Athens' military inferiority was painfully manifest. The hour for reform had struck.

That the suggestion for the ephebia lay in Plato's *Laws* has already been emphasized. The customs of educating and arming the orphans at the expense of the state [2] furnished further precedents on which Athens could draw. It was decided that the state should finance the military and gymnastic education of the ephebi, and give them their armor at a public assembly in the theater,[3] as had been done for the orphans.[4] From 335 on, no more mention is made of special provision for the orphans; they were enrolled

---

[1] στρατεύεσθαι δ'οὐκ ἐθέλομεν.
[2] See above, page 76.
[3] Aristot. *Ath.* xlii. 4.
[4] See Bryant 87.

in the public education with their fellows of ephebic age, and received their equipment of armor with no more ceremony and display than was accorded to the rest of the ephebi. A third suggestion which may have come to the minds of the Athenians when they were ready to create the ephebic organization, was that of Socrates, or rather Xenophon,[1] for guard service in the passes to Bœotia.

The founder of the ephebia was named Epicrates. Our sole source of knowledge about him is a fragment of the orator Lycurgus, preserved by Harpocration.[2] Here we learn that a statue of this man was set up in bronze, "because of his law concerning the ephebi." That this law was the one which established the ephebia is generally recognized.[3] It is probable that his patriotic zeal impelled him to make a generous contribution toward the expenses of founding and maintaining the ephebia. Such donations in behalf of public education were fairly common in antiquity, as Ziebarth has shown.[4] Epicrates was well able to do this, for he had amassed, Harpocration says, the enormous fortune of six hundred talents; the circumstance that Harpocration mentions this in connection with his ephebic law, leads to the inference that he

[1] *Mem.* iii. 5. 25-7.

[2] s. v. Ἐπικράτης.

[3] Ussing 131. Wilamowitz I. 194. Mahaffy 75. Dittenberger on *SIG*³ 957. Kirchner on *IG* ii. 1². 1156. Brenot 30 and 49. Busolt-Swoboda II. 1189.

[4] Pages 45-78 in his book *Aus dem gr. Schulwesen* are devoted to school endowments and endowed schools.

expended some of the money for an ephebic endowment.

The general purpose of the ephebic college is well put in one of the inscriptions:[1] "The people, being ever most zealous for the training and discipline of the ephebi, and desiring to have those who are leaving boyhood and entering manhood, become worthy successors of their fathers in the duties of citizens, enjoined by law that they should become acquainted with the land, the fortresses, and the borders of Attica, and that they should perform in arms the exercises appertaining to war. On account of the aforesaid training, the people has adorned the city with trophies most beautiful and august; for which cause, likewise, it chooses the *kosmetes* from the men who have led the noblest lives." Now let us proceed to investigate the organization under which the college, headed by the *kosmetes*, functioned, and see how the purpose stated in the decree was fulfilled.

Even before the discovery of Aristotle's *Constitution of Athens* scholars were generally agreed that eighteen was the age for entering the ephebic college at Athens. There is no necessity for arguing this now, and the confused testimony of late authors and lexicographers may be disregarded. Aristotle has made it perfectly plain that the enrolment in the ephebic lists took place after the termination of the eighteenth year and the attainment of the eighteenth birthday,[2] hence

[1] *IG* ii. 1². 1106 l. 52ff.
[2] *Ath.* xlii. 1. Cf. Bryant 76 and n. 4. Thalheim *RE* V. 2737. Busolt-Swoboda II. 1189.

the ephebic service occupied the nineteenth and twentieth years of one's life. The enrolment took place only once a year, and all, including the thetes,[1] who had reached eighteen since the last previous registration, were enrolled at one time.[2] The lads were strictly examined by their fellow-demesmen as to their age, legitimacy, and parentage. If any one was not yet of the proper age, he was sent back into the ranks of the boys; a further examination by the Senate of Five Hundred caught any who eluded the vigilance of their demesmen. To be an ephebus, one had to be the son of a father and mother who were both citizens; if one who was born of a foreign mother, for example, tried to enter the ephebi, he was, if detected, sold as a slave by order of the state.[3] Athens was at first meticulous in her demand that absolutely all her citizen youth, and no others, should become ephebi, and that at a definite time. Somewhat later, the stringency of these regulations was wholly abandoned, as we shall see.

Once the ephebi were enrolled, the next concern of the people was the selection of the highest ephebic officials, the *kosmetes*, or president, and the *sophron-*

---

[1] Aristotle says nothing to indicate that the thetes were not included in the obligatory ephebic service. See Beloch (1905) 351 and Reinach (1913) 210 n. 1 against Girard in Dar.-Sagl. II. 622.

[2] Bryant 76.

[3] From the ephebia at Athens, as from physical education generally, there and elsewhere, slaves were excluded. See the interesting observation of the dream interpreter, Artemidorus (*Oneirocrit.* i. 54 Hercher): ἐφηβεύειν δοῦλος ἐὰν δόξῃ, ἐλεύθερος ἔσται, ἐπειδὴ μόνοις ἐλευθέροις ἐφίησιν ὁ νόμος.

THE ATHENIAN EPHEBIA

istai,[1] or discipline masters. There was to be one *sophronistes* from each tribe,[2] and the fathers of the ephebi chose three nominees from the tribesmen. Thus there were thirty nominees each year, and ten to be elected. The whole people in assembly chose the ten. The responsibility over Athens' youth that rested on the shoulders of the *sophronistai* caused the rule to be made that all the nominees should be over forty years of age.[3] Aristotle reports that the candidates were such as were considered the best men in character, and the most suitable to take care of the ephebi. Their salary was one drachma daily.

The duties of the *sophronistai* were enough to keep them busy. At the beginning of their year's magistracy, they aided the *kosmetes* in leading the ephebi. "They take them in charge, and after first visiting with them all the temples, march down to Piræus, where they garrison the north and south harbors, Munychia and Acte."[4] The pay that was apportioned to the ephebi by the state was turned over to the

---

[1] That *sophronistai* existed in the time of Solon (Freeman 70) or prior to 335 (Dumont I. 200) is an utterly unjustifiable assumption. Wilamowitz I. 194 proved the contrary and converted Girard: see the latter's retraction in Dar.-Sagl. IV. 1399–1400.

[2] Aristot. *Ath.* xlii. 2, on which passage were based the statements of Phot. *Lex. s. v.*, *Lex. Seguer. s. v.* (in Bekker *Anecd. Gr.* I. 301), *Etym. Mag. s. v.*

[3] The conjecture of Grasberger III. 473–4 that sixty was the required age for *sophronistai* was ingenious, but on this, as on a host of other matters, we are set at rights by Aristotle's *Constitution of Athens*.

[4] Aristot. *Ath.* xlii. 3. tr. Poste.

sophronistai, and each *sophronistes* purchased the food supplies for the cadets of his tribe. While Aristotle, with his customary brevity, gives no more details on the duties of this official, he does add the significant remark: "And he takes care of everything else."[1] Apparently the title, "discipline master," by no means indicated the full scope of the activities of the *sophronistes*. He looked after the meals as well as the morals[2] of the ephebi. He supplied the clothing and other necessaries for the lads of his tribe, and exercised a general superintendence over their military and gymnastic training. It is no wonder that the author of the pseudo-Platonic *Axiochus* (367A) remarked: "And *all* the toil of the young men is subject to the *sophronistai*." If the *sophronistes* performed his duties well, the tribe which he had represented gave him an honorary decree. Such is the oldest ephebic inscription in existence,[3] the one set up in 334/3 by the Cecropid tribe in honor of their ephebi and the *sophronistes* Adeistus. The tribe praised Adeistus and gave him a golden crown "because he took care of the ephebi of the Cecropid tribe well and diligently." Other decrees[4] are similarly lavish of praise. Like other state officials, the *sophronistes* was obliged to render

[1] καὶ τῶν ἄλλων ἐπιμελεῖται πάντων.

[2] *Lex. Seguer. s. v. σωφρονισταί* (Bekker *Anecd. Gr.* I. 301).

[3] *IG* ii. 1². 1156.

[4] *Ibid.* 1189 (334/3) and 1159 (303/2). Cf. the fragmentary decrees 478 (305/4) and 556 (*ca.* 305). These four with 1156 and a new one published in 1918 ('Αρχ. 'Εφ. 1918, 76 no. 96) are the only inscriptions before Hadrian's reign that mention the *sophronistai*.

account of his conduct in office at the end of the year.[1] He was responsible to his superior, the *kosmetes*, and to the senate.[2] One or two points on the history of the *sophronistai* are in order before we leave them for the present. In 306/5, two new tribes were created in Attica, the Antigonid and Demetriad.[3] This enlarged the number of *sophronistai* to twelve, and twelve were actually listed in the sadly fragmentary decree of 305/4.[4] It seems, however, that with certain changes in the ephebia (see below, pages 152–153) which greatly reduced the numbers enrolled, it was realized, soon after 305/4, that there was no more need of the *sophronistai*. The last decree in which they are mentioned [5] is of the year 303/2, and in 282/1 they had disappeared.[6] After four centuries, the office of *sophronistes* was revived in the time of Hadrian, and on a later page will be recorded what is known of the *sophronistai* of that period.

More important even than the *sophronistai* was the *kosmetes*, the president of the ephebic college. The date when his office originated was for a long time disputed. Krause did not have the benefit of the older ephebic inscriptions, and referred the origin of the *kosmetes* to the period of the Roman Empire.[7]

---

[1] *IG* ii. 1². 1156 l. 42–3 ἐπειδὰν τὰς εὐθύνας δῶι. As we begin to quote inscriptions, attention is called to the fact that letters are not bracketed which have been supplied by editors, except in cases of doubt. As for iota subscript or adscript, the different editors are followed and uniformity is not attempted.

[2] *IG l. c.* l. 38.
[3] Lécrivain in Dar.-Sagl. IV. 453.
[4] *IG* ii. 1². 478.
[5] *Ibid.* 1159.
[6] *Ibid.* 665.
[7] (1841) I. 214.

Dittenberger (31) disagreed with Krause, and thought the time soon after Alexander's death (323 B.C.) more reasonable. Dumont, with his theory of the ancient origin of the ephebia, desired to assign the origin of the *kosmetes* to early times, but, unfortunately, the solitary piece of real evidence which he thought he had is now proved worthless.[1] Grasberger [2] believed the *kosmetes* originated in the early part of the third century. Let these serve as examples of the bewildering divergence of results arrived at by learned men working with inadequate evidence. The *Constitution of Athens* and one inscription [3] have irrefutably proved that the *kosmetes* originated in 335 with the rest of the ephebic organization.

Like the *sophronistai*, the *kosmetes* was chosen by election, not by lot.[4] He was elected annually [5] from the whole body of Athenians, and so might come from any tribe. A salary for the *kosmetes* is not mentioned by Aristotle nor the inscriptions: he probably served for glory and not for pay. Oehler states [6] that he, like

---

[1] His argument is given I. 169–70, and his evidence he reprints II. 207 no. 23 from Benndorf *Gr. u. Sicil. Vasenbilder* Plate X. This vase inscription may be of the early fourth century, as Dumont says, but the supplementing [κοσμη]τεύοντος Εὐρυκλείδου (accepted also by Cecil Smith *BSA* III. 198–9) has been proved incorrect by Adolf Wilhelm *Beitr. zur gr. Inschriftenkunde* 81–2. The true reading is [ταμ]ιεύοντος. Those who believe that the ephebia started before 335 must expect to see their props thus knocked from under them.

[2] III. 475.

[3] *IG* ii. 5. 1571b. See Girard Dar.-Sagl. III. 865; Oehler *RE* XI. 1490.

[4] Aristot. *Ath.* xlii. 2. *IG* ii. 1². 1009, 1028, 1042.

[5] *IG* ii. 1². 1009, 1028.

[6] *RE* XI. 1491.

the *sophronistai*, was obliged to be forty years of age or over, but, while this is plausible, the passages cited by Oehler [1] do not really prove his point. He was subject only to the senate and the decrees of the people,[2] but was required to give account of the conduct of his magistracy at the end of the year.[3] No case of malfeasance is known, and it is evident that the people adhered to the practice of choosing the *kosmetes* "from the men who had led the noblest lives." [4] Honors were regularly bestowed on the *kosmetai* at the end of their term of office by the senate and people,[5] often by the ephebi,[6] and once by the grateful fathers of the ephebi.[7]

The duties entailed by the office of *kosmetes* were multifarious. In the words of Dumont: [8] "He was a high director watching over all the important affairs of the college, head of the whole faculty of teachers, direct delegate of the people, predestined for the offices of *strategos* and archon. The ephebi do not perform a single act with which the *kosmetes* is not associated; in all circumstances, the spokesmen of the senate say,

[1] They are these: Aristot. *Ath.* xlii. 2; Æschin. *c. Timarch.* 11.; Plat. *Legg.* vi. 764E.

[2] *IG* ii. 1². 1008, 1009, 1028.

[3] *Ibid.* 1006, 1008, 1009, 1011, 1022.

[4] See above, page 127. Malfeasance was not proved against Philocles (Dinarch. *c. Philocl.* 15.), but his character was, or was believed to be, such that the people thought best to take his magistracy away before his term was up. The ephebi, nevertheless, gave him the usual honors: 'Αρχ. 'Εφ. 1918, 76, no. 97. On Philocles as *kosmetes*, see below, page 144, n. 7.

[5] *IG* ii. 1². 478, 556, 665, 681, 900, and often.   [7] *Ibid.* 1042.

[6] *Ibid.* 1006, 1008, 1009, 1011, 1028.   [8] I. 166–7.

he accompanied and led them, he was responsible for them." The ephebic inscriptions of the fourth and third centuries before Christ furnish almost no details on the labors of the *kosmetes*, but from the second and first centuries we have long and verbose decrees, some of them well preserved, that are rich in information. In these latter centuries the ephebia was intimately concerned with festivals and religion; accordingly we find the *kosmetes* offering numberless sacrifices on all occasions in behalf of the college,[1] sometimes at his own expense.[2] Education in literature, rhetoric, and philosophy was by now playing an important part in the ephebia, and over this phase of the ephebic life the *kosmetes* had governance.[3] In the parades, when the cadet corps made a proud showing, the *kosmetes* marched at their head,[4] as he did in their marches to the Piræus,[5] the border forts, and various parts of the countryside.[6] When they marched to the gymnasia daily for their exercises,[7] and when they came before the senate to be reviewed,[8] it was always the *kosmetes* who led them. He assumed the responsi-

---

[1] See for example *IG* ii. 1². 1006, 1008, 1009.
[2] *Ibid.* 1009 l. 37; 1039 l. 25.
[3] *Ibid.* 1006, 1039, 1042, 1043.
[4] *Ibid.* 930, 1006 l. 74 συνετέλεσεν δὲ τάς τε πομπάς. For the Pythaid processions to Delphi, see *SIG*³ 696, 697, 711, 728.
[5] Aristot. *Ath.* xlii. 3.
[6] *IG* ii. 1². 1006 l. 65–6 ἐποιήσατο δὲ καὶ τὰς ἐξόδους αὐτῶν ἐν ὅπλοις ἐπί τε τὰ φρούρια καὶ τὰ ὅρια τῆς ᾿Αττικῆς; cf. l. 69–70 and 1028 l. 85–6 (where it is said that they made these trips πλεονάκις).
[7] *Ibid.* 1006, 1028, 1029, 1030.
[8] *Ibid.* 1006, 1008, 1011, 1028, 1030, 1039.

bility for their health, studiousness, discipline, and general virtue [1]—a heavy burden indeed, as every modern college president and dean will testify. What we are most interested in for our purpose is his connection with the military-gymnastic education. One of the inscriptions [2] tells us that the *kosmetes* Dionysius conducted the running in the gymnasia, and was zealous for artillery training; he renewed the abandoned instruction in the use of the catapult, fixing up one of the old ones for this purpose. Other *kosmetai* were lauded for their diligence in regard to the physical exercises, drill in arms, and equestrian training of the ephebi.[3] As early as 107/6, the *kosmetes* was empowered to select his own staff of instructors,[4] whereas in earlier times these had been chosen by the popular assembly. So far as we are informed, the office of *kosmetes* endured throughout the history of the ephebic college, the last datable inscription which names a *kosmetes* being of 262/3 or 266/7 after Christ.[5]

In the fourth century before Christ, very likely in

[1] ὑγίεια 1006, 1028.
παιδεία 1006, 1008, 1011.
φιλοτιμία 1006.
περὶ τὰ μαθήματα φιλοτιμία 1008, 1011.
εὐταξία 1006, 1008, 1009, 1011, 1027 (and cf. Erotianus *Lex. Hippoc.* s. v. κόσμοι: κοσμηταὶ οἱ τῶν ἐφήβων εὐταξίας προνοοῦντες).
ἀνδρεία 1006.
εὐπείθεια 1006, 1008, 1011.
σωφροσύνη 1006.
φιλία 1006, 1009, 1028.
ὁμόνοια 1006, 1008, 1009, 1011, 1027, 1028.
πατρικὴ εὔνοια 1006.

[2] *IG* ii. 1². 1006.
[3] *Ibid.* 1039, 1042, 1043.
[4] *Ibid.* 1011 l. 21.
[5] *IG* iii. 1202.

the third and second as well, the whole corps of instructors in the gymnastic and military exercises was chosen by the people. Aristotle [1] has named them over for us: two *paidotribai*, *hoplomachos*, *toxotes* (archery instructor), *akontistes* (javelin instructor), and *katapaltaphetes* or simply *aphetes* (catapult instructor). The proportion of teachers of military exercises to those of strictly gymnastic exercises (the *paidotribai*) is instructive: it is two to one. The ephebia in its origin had a strongly military character. The collective title for all the teachers was *didaskaloi*,[2] but about the end of the second and beginning of the first centuries before Christ the more high-sounding term *paideutai* ("educators") was gaining a foothold,[3] and from 80 B.C. on the latter term was regularly used.[4] Under the Empire, the inscriptions occasionally named the *paidotribes* and *hoplomachos* apart from the rest of the *paideutai*;[5] this was done, probably, *honoris causa*.

The two *paidotribai* mentioned by Aristotle were

[1] *Ath.* xlii. 3.
[2] Found between 305/4 (*IG* ii. 1². 478) and the beginning of the first century B.C. (*Ibid.* 1030).
[3] In 106/5: *BCH* XXX. (1906) 229; in 97/6: Michel (Suppl.) 1524.
[4] The author disagrees with Colin (235–6), who assumed that the *paideutai* and *didaskaloi* were different, the former perhaps supplanting the *sophronistai*. Colin was unable to cite any inscription containing both terms, and his argument that the *paideutai* could never hold office more than once (so being differentiated from *didaskaloi*) was grounded on only two inscriptions, nine years apart, which record totally different sets of *paideutai*. It is not surprising that none should be the same after nine years.
[5] *IG* iii. 1094, 1098. The former also names the *hegemon* separately.

soon diminished to one, as the number of ephebi dwindled. In 305/4 [1] and thereafter, the inscriptions named only one. This ephebic *paidotribes* is to be distinguished from the one who taught boys in the palæstra; the latter was still existing in the third century before Christ, as we are assured by Teles,[2] and in the middle of the second century, as the inscriptions show.[3] Whether the ephebic *paidotribes* gave instruction in publicly owned palæstræ, or in the great gymnasia which were used by the ephebi, can only be a matter for conjecture; at least we do not hear of any such palæstræ for the ephebi, whereas the *kosmetes* was often lauded for taking his cadet corps to the gymnasia regularly the whole year through.[4] After the disappearance of the *sophronistai*, the *paidotribes* ranked next to the *kosmetes*, and was regularly listed first among the teachers; Teles (*l. c.*) named him directly after the *kosmetes* and before the *hoplomachos*. While the *kosmetes* was never re-elected, the *paidotribes* who was recognized for efficiency was often appointed again and again. So we find that Hermodorus was *paidotribes* about 282/1, again in 275/4, a third time in an undetermined year, and still a fourth time a little after 260.[5] Since the decrees of the intervening years are lost, he may have been *paidotribes* for the whole

[1] *IG* ii. 1². 478.

[2] ap. Stob. *Flor.* xcviii. 72.

[3] *IG* ii. 1². 957 col. 1, l. 46ff. Dexiphon won the torch-race τῶν παίδων ἐκ τῆς Τιμέου παλαίστρας. Cf. *ibid.* 958 and 961.

[4] E. g., *IG* ii. 1². 1006 l. 60. See above, page 134.

[5] *Ibid.* 655, 681, 700, 766.

period of twenty to twenty-five years. I might add that the tradition ran in Hermodorus' family, for a descendant of his was an ephebic *paidotribes* a century later.[1] Only in 1906 did we learn that foreign incumbents were permitted, but rarely, we may be sure, to hold the office of ephebic *paidotribes*; one of the valuable Pythaid inscriptions informs us that the *paidotribes* of 128/7 was Nico, son of Alexis, from Berytus.[2] While the custom of having only one *paidotribes* for the ephebi was closely observed, an assistant, known as the *hypopaidotribes*, was sometimes appointed; we have proof of this practice as early as 60 B.C.,[3] and later it was an invariable custom to have such an assistant.

Under the Empire the usage was established of appointing meritorious *paidotribai*, as well as other instructors, for life. Two are especially well known to us because of their long term of service: Aristo and Abascantus. Aristo and another *paidotribes* named Demetrius began serving, either both in the same year or one succeeding the other, about the year 111 of our era; after Aristo's death, in 127 or thereabouts, Demetrius carried on until 138.[4] In that year Abascantus was appointed *paidotribes* for life, and his term of service was at least thirty-four years.[5] The date

---

[1] *IG* ii. 1². 900, with Kirchner's comment.

[2] *BCH* XXX. (1906) 226ff. = Michel (Suppl.) 1523. Nico appears also in the non-Pythaid ephebic inscription of the same year, fragments of which were published by Graindor *Rev. Belge* III. (1924) 13ff.

[3] *IG* iii. 104, and cf. 105 and 106, which date only a few years later.

[4] Neubauer 150.

[5] Graindor (1915) 381ff.

of our last epigraphical information about the *paidotribes* is the same as for the *kosmetes*.[1]

The *hoplomachos*, who instructed in heavy-armed fighting, was esteemed highly, as we should expect in an institute for military education. In rare instances,[2] he was placed in the hierarchy even above the *paidotribes*.[3] He trained the ephebi, not merely in heavy-armed fighting, but in all phases of warfare except the use of the javelin, bow, and catapult; under the Empire he taught even the latter exercises, if they were taught at all. An assistant for him was sometimes found necessary, and he was called by the awkward designation of *hypohoplomachos;* the only one still known to us[4] was a foreigner, coming to Athens from Tarsus. We have no record of a *hoplomachos* being reappointed so early in the history of the ephebia as the *paidotribes* was, but at the end of the second century before Christ, a certain Herodotus was reappointed at least twice.[5] In the reign of Claudius, Nicias was *hoplomachos* under two archons,[6] and later the same was true of Asclepiades[7] and Onesimus.[8] About the beginning of the third century of our era Dionysius, son of Nicostratus, was chosen

[1] See above, page 135.

[2] *IG* ii. 1². 900.

[3] Rarely the *hegemon* or the secretary, in the time of the Empire, was placed above the *hoplomachos:* Dumont I. 189.

[4] *BCH* XXX. (1906) 226ff. = Michel (Suppl.) 1523.

[5] *IG* ii. 1². 1009 (117/6), 1011 (108/7), 1028 (101/0).

[6] *IG* iii. 1081, 1082.

[7] *Ibid.* 1104, 1106.

[8] *Ibid.* 1122, 1132.

to the office for life, and his name recurs in many inscriptions.[1]

The *akontistes* in Aristotle's list follows the *toxotes*, but in the inscriptions regularly precedes him. The most famous javelin teacher was Nicander.[2] With the decay of military spirit in the ephebia, it was eventually decided that the *hoplomachos* was the only military instructor needed, and as early as 39/8 B.C.[3] the *akontistes* was dropped. The *toxotes* belonged fifth in the hierarchy, and exception was made to this rule only once, when a foreigner, Sondros of Crete, held the office.[4] Archery was never, it seems, a favored exercise at Athens, and it does not surprise us that the *toxotes* disappeared at the same time that the *akontistes* did. The *aphetes* (or *katapaltaphetes*) taught the use of the catapult, an engine of war which was important in the siege warfare of Alexander's epoch. The *aphetes* was very likely some seasoned veteran, a *miles gloriosus* who had beleaguered and captured cities. Once he obtained the position as teacher of the ephebi, he held it for year after year.[5] One of the inscriptions [6] tells us that instruction in the use of the catapult had not been given for several years prior to

---

[1] *IG* iii. 1171, 1176, 1177, 1184, 1186, 1188.

[2] He served in 128/7, Michel (Suppl.) 1523; 123/2, *IG* ii. 1². 1006; and 117/6, *IG* ii . 1². 1009.

[3] *IG* ii. 1². 1043 of that year no longer mentions an *akontistes* among the teachers.

[4] *Ibid*. 665. On this Cretan *toxotes* see above, page 52.

[5] Calchedon *IG* ii. 1². 1006, 1008; Nicias *ibid*. 1009, 1011, 1028.

[6] *IG* ii. 1². 1006.

THE ATHENIAN EPHEBIA

123/2.[1] The *kosmetes* Dionysius revived the exercise in that year and appointed Calchedon instructor. We can trace the *aphetes* from then on to 99 B.C., but not after that. Two other functionaries connected with the ephebic college in the time before the Empire complete the list.[2] These were the secretary (γραμματεύς), who kept the records, and the servant ὑπηρέτης), whose duties were not told, but are not hard to conjecture.

In addition to all these functionaries, from the *kosmetes* to the lowly servant or man-of-all-work, the state exercised a general supervision over the ephebia through the senate, the Areopagus, the *strategoi*, and the gymnasiarchs.

If the ephebi wished to have some change made in the regulations pertaining to them, it was to the senate that they presented their arguments.[3] Before the senate they held a review, displaying the proficiency they had acquired during the year,[4] and before the

---

[1] The truth of this may be tested by consulting the complete list of ephebic functionaries for 128/7 (Michel [Suppl.] 1523); no *aphetes* is among them.

[2] As for the "Pythian explainer" (ἐξηγητὴς Πυθόχρηστος), he is mentioned only once, in 128/7, in connection with the Pythaid procession to Delphi, and his relations with the ephebi may be presumed to have lasted only a few days. The same important inscription of 128/7, Michel (Suppl.) 1523, mentions two *tarantinarchs*, teachers of a mode of cavalry fighting, which consisted in harassing the foe by hurling javelins at him from a distance and keeping out of his reach. The *tarantinarchs* also occur in a victor list of the Thesea, about 155 B.C. (*IG* ii. 1². 958 col. 1, l. 57–9), but the writer does not think they should be included in the list of the regular ephebic instructors.

[3] *IG* ii. 1². 1039, 1043. The formula is πρόσοδον ποιησάμενοι πρὸς τὴν βουλήν.

[4] *Ibid.* 700, 1011, 1028.

senate the *kosmetes* rendered account of his stewardship and of "every thing that had happened to the ephebi during the year."[1]

As for the Areopagus, its oversight of education had been abolished in the first half of the fifth century by Ephialtes, but it came back into its own about a score of years after the ephebia was founded,[2] through the good offices of Demetrius of Phalerum. In the Roman imperial age, we see the Areopagus, either with or without the senate and people, honoring *kosmetai*,[3] and once we find that the august Areopagus sat and patiently listened to a youthful declamation delivered by an ephebus.[4]

The authority of the *strategoi* ("generals") over the ephebi [5] is amply proved by the decrees, until the period when the original military object of the ephebia was totally obliterated. It was inevitable that the cadets should begin to come into contact with the state's military officers, as well as with their own in-

---

[1] *IG* ii. 1². 1028 l. 89–91.

[2] Schömann-Lipsius I. 553. Its "commission over the young men" is mentioned in Ps.-Plat. *Axioch.* 367A.

[3] *IG* iii. 1102 (between 98/9 and 110/1); *ibid.* 752 (before 157/8).

[4] *Ibid.* 53. Unfortunately, the speech is so fragmentarily preserved that we can barely make out its general drift. It had something to do with Theseus, an athletic Athenian hero, in whom ephebi would naturally be interested.

[5] With the education of boys, too, before the establishment of the ephebia, the *strategos* Dercylus had some unexplained connection. About 350 B.C. the deme of Eleusis honored him highly because of his care ὅπως οἱ παῖδες παιδεύωνται οἱ ἐν τῶι δήμωι: *IG* ii. 1². 1187. See Girard (1891) 52. Ziebarth ([1914] 34) noted that these deme schools were certainly private, but also observed that this is the oldest certain testimony to the care of state magistrates for the education of children.

structors; modern cadets have the same experience. Especially when they were guarding the forts of Attica, their relation with the *strategoi* must have been close; for example, in 282/1 or thereabouts a decree praised the ephebi for carrying out all the orders of the *strategos* in guarding the Museum (a fortress).[1] Apparently this had been a special task of the ephebi during that year, when some petty war, not recorded by the historians, was causing a little trouble; it is, by the way, the only record we have of the ephebi performing actual service in warfare. In the earliest period of the ephebia, as Aristotle described it, the first-year ephebi who guarded Munychia and Acte were in charge of the *strategoi* who were assigned to those two forts.[2] The only conceivable reason for delegating two *strategoi* to the Piræus is that hundreds of ephebi were sent there annually, and divided between two forts.[3] The *strategos* ἐπὶ τὴν χώραν ("over the land") had command of the ephebi in the second year when they patrolled the countryside.[4] In the period of the long and detailed ephebic inscriptions, at the end of the second and beginning of the first centuries before Christ, we regularly hear that the ephebi were obedient to the orders of the *strategoi*, as well as to those of the *kosmetes*

[1] *IG* ii. 1². 665.
[2] 'Αρχ. 'Εφ. 1918, 76 no. 97; the *strategoi* of Piræus and Acte were crowned by the ephebi of 324/3 B.C. Cf. also Schömann-Lipsius I. 553.
[3] Ferguson 9 n. 2.
[4] 'Αρχ. 'Εφ. 1918, 76 no. 96. Østbye (38) conjectured in 1893 that this was true, and this new inscription, published in 1918 by Leonardos, has given him full confirmation.

and teachers.[1] In 128/7 no less than five *strategoi* had relations with the ephebi, to wit those over the hoplites, the navy, the cavalry, the Piræus, and Eleusis.[2] The *strategos* at Eleusis commanded the forts of Eleusis, Phyle, and Panactum, to which the ephebi went to do guard duty. The relation of the ephebi to the naval *strategos* is presumably referred to by another inscription,[3] which has it that the ephebi "performed the launchings and beachings of boats, obedient to the commands of the *strategoi*." That the ephebi practiced riding in this period is proved by the mention of the cavalry *strategos*. The relation of the hoplite *strategos* to the ephebi was particularly close under the Empire.[4] In the gymnasia, too, as well as in the forts and the field, the *strategos* had unquestioned authority over the ephebi,[5] and in the time of Plutarch he was brought into relation with the ephebic studies of literature, geometry, rhetoric, and music, in all of which subjects he held examinations in the Diogeneum.[6] Altogether, then, the *strategoi* were linked with the ephebi almost as closely as the *kosmetes* and the other college officials were.[7]

[1] *IG* ii. 1². 1006, 1008, 1011, 1028, 1030, 1039. Cf. Hauvette-Besnault 147.

[2] *BCH* XXX. (1906) 226 f. = Michel (Suppl.) 1523.

[3] *IG* ii. 1². 1028 l. 37–8.

[4] In fact, the hoplite *strategos* was the only one connected with the ephebi of the imperial age.

[5] Artemidor. *Oneirocrit.* v. 36 Hercher.

[6] Plut. *Quæst. Conv.* ix. 1. 1.

[7] On the question of the capacity in which Philocles had charge of the ephebi (Dinarch. *c. Philocl.* 15), there used to be three views, all ardently

One of the changes instituted by Demetrius of Phalerum at the end of the fourth century before Christ, was the abolition of the liturgical gymnasiarchy, along with the rest of the liturgies. The gymnasiarch at Athens henceforth was a magistrate,[1] but one whose duties and powers we are ill able to define. He offered prizes at the Thesea and Epitaphia (two of the annual festivals), according to one inscription;[2] Oehler has deduced from this that he had some connection with the celebration of games and festivals. He had disciplinary powers over the youth who exercised in the gymnasia,[3] and even over any visitors to the gymnasia, such as the philosophers.[4] As a symbol of his authority he carried a staff. Indications of his activity further than these have not been vouchsafed to us.

Now we turn to the ephebi themselves and their

supported. Philocles had been a *strategos* repeatedly, and this led Hauvette-Besnault (147), Girard ([1891] 43), Schömann-Lipsius (I. 553), and Wilamowitz (I. 193 n. 11), to believe that he was a *strategos* when he was removed from the command of the ephebi; Foucart (261), Sandys on Aristot. *Ath.* (xlii. 2 [2nd ed.]), Brenot (2 n.), and Busolt-Swoboda (II. 1865 n. 5), considered that he was a *sophronistes;* while Dumont (I. 169–70) (followed by Grasberger [III.475] and Oehler [*RE* XI. 1490]) argued well enough to convince the author that he was a *kosmetes*. Some time later, the author was happy to find his conclusion, or rather Dumont's, verified by the inscription which Leonardos published in 'Αρχ. 'Εφ. 1918, 76 no. 97; this inscription names Philocles as the *kosmetes* in 324/3 and settles the matter. Brenot and Busolt-Swoboda overlooked this new record, which takes its place among the most ancient ephebic inscriptions.

[1] Oehler *RE* VII. 1988–9; Busolt-Swoboda II. 930 n. 2 and 976–7.

[2] *IG* ii. 1². 1009 l. 4–6.

[3] Plut. *Ant.* xxxiii.; Ps.-Plut. *Axioch.* 366E–367A ἔπειτα Λύκειον καὶ 'Ακαδήμεια καὶ γυμνασιαρχία καὶ ῥάβδοι καὶ κακῶν ἀμετρίαι.

[4] Ps.-Plat. *Eryx.* 399A; Diog. Laert. iv. 63; Plut. *de Garr.* xxi.

activities. Attention is called at the outset to their resemblance, partly to the cadets at West Point, partly to the Reserve Officers Training Corps in American colleges, and partly to the Boy Scouts. The resemblance to the R. O. T. C. was confirmed in 1918 by the disclosure that the cadets had student officers, called *lochagoi* ("captains"). Eleven of these commanded the seventy-odd cadets of the Leontid tribe; if we may assume eleven for each tribe, there were 110 *lochagoi* every year.[1] Under the leadership of the *kosmetes* and *sophronistai*, Aristotle tells us, the first official act of the ephebi was to make the round of the temples and pay their respects to the gods. Athens knew the value of a religious spirit in her sons, and found the period of ephebic service useful for inculcating an attitude of reverence toward the gods. One is amazed on perusing the long list of festivals, sacred processions, sacrifices, and other religious ceremonials in which the ephebi participated.[2] After this preliminary religious duty was terminated, the ephebi marched down to the Piræus, and began performing guard duty at Munychia and Acte. There they led a barracks life, and the ephebi of each tribe had a commons.[3] Their time was occupied with various gym-

[1] The inscription is the one repeatedly referred to already: ’Aρχ. ’Eφ. 1918, 75 no. 95; on the *lochagoi*, see the comments of Leonardos *ad loc.* p. 84.

[2] *IG* ii. 1². 1006 l. 6–16 and *passim* will serve as an example. This aspect of life in the ephebia is not pertinent to the subject; any who are interested are referred to Dumont I. 249–305.

[3] Aristot. *Ath.* xlii. 3 συσσιτοῦσι γὰρ κατὰ φύλας. Dittenberger (21),

nastic exercises, more strenuous than they had hitherto known, and with military drill in all the arts that a soldier needs to know. Their pay was four obols, or about eleven cents, daily. At the end of their first year, they were reviewed and put through their paces before a public assembly in the theater. When the review was over, they were ceremoniously presented with their armor, a shield and spear, and were required to take the ephebic oath.

The arguments that have been raised over the ephebic oath make it necessary to dwell on it briefly here. As has been said earlier in this chapter,[1] there is no reason to doubt what the evident antiquity of the oath would lead us to believe, that it was a prerequisite to citizenship from very early times. Neither is there reason to disbelieve that the oath was taken at the time of enrolment on the citizen lists, when one reached one's eighteenth birthday and became liable to military service. After the creation of the ephebia, however, armor was not given to the young men until they had completed their first year of training: the express testimony of Aristotle leaves no doubt on that point. Now since the oath begins with the words: "I will not put to shame my sacred arms", we have no choice but to believe that the taking of the oath, after the foundation of the ephebia, was postponed until the end of the

with his customary acumen, had already, in 1863, come to the conclusion that this was true from the mention of συντρίκλεινοι in a single inscription, *IG* iii. 1105.

[1] Above, page 123.

first year of service.¹ The passage of Pollux (viii. 105) which records the oath says it was taken "in the twentieth year;" if we take this to mean, at the beginning of the twentieth year, it harmonizes with our conclusion. The oft-quoted statement of Lycurgus ² that the oath was taken at the time of enrolment on the citizen lists, is quite correct, but refers to the time before 335 when Leocrates took (or evaded taking) the oath. Dittenberger ³ refers to a scholium of Ulpian on Demosthenes,⁴ which says that the oath was taken by those "passing out from the boys into the ephebic ranks," as proving that the oath was taken on entering the ephebia; but Ulpian was referring to the earlier lifetime of Demosthenes, when there was no ephebia, and the oath was taken at eighteen. That Ulpian's statement can not hold for the period after 335 is plain, for he says that the ephebi took oath in full armor (μετὰ πανοπλιῶν ὤμνυον); after 335 they did not get their armor until one year after they had "passed

---

[1] The first to see the light in this matter was, probably, Iwan von Müller (189); it was more clearly set forth by Thalheim (*RE* V. 2738); with this view Taylor (496–7) and Busolt-Swoboda (II. 1190) agreed implicitly. It was not strange that, before the publication of Aristotle's *Constitution of Athens*, scholars should have been in error on this point, e. g., Grasberger (III. 27–8) and Hermann-Blümner (322); but even after 1891 the error was repeated by Schömann-Lipsius (I. 379) and others. Thalheim's article appeared in 1905 and still many persisted in the old error: Bryant (77), Walden (35), Sandys on Aristot. *Ath.* (xlii. 3 [2nd ed.]), Ziebarth ([1914] 163), Dittenberger on *SIG*³ 527, Brenot (37).

[2] *c. Leoc.* 76.

[3] On *SIG*³ 527.

[4] *F. L.* 303. The scholium is printed in Dindorf's edition of Demosthenes, Vol. 8, p. 447.

out from the boys into the ephebic ranks." The Ulpian passage, therefore, does not prove what Dittenberger thought it did;[1] nor should our beliefs be greatly swayed by it, anyway, for Ulpian was an untrustworthy scholiast.

The text of the ephebic oath is handed down to us by Pollux and Stobæus,[2] both giving it in substantially the same form. A critical text may be found on page 488 of Taylor's article (see Bibliography, page 286) together with the following translation:[3] "I will never bring reproach upon my hallowed arms, nor will I desert the comrade at whose side I stand, but I will defend our altars and our hearths, single-handed or supported by many. My native land I will not leave a diminished heritage but greater and better than when I received it. I will obey whoever is in authority and submit to the established laws and all others which the people shall harmoniously enact. If anyone tries to overthrow the constitution or disobeys it, I will not permit him, but will come to its defense single-handed or with the support of all. I will honor the religion of my fathers. Let the gods be my witnesses, Agraulus, Enyalius, Ares, Zeus, Thallo, Auxo, Hegemone."[4]

---

[1] Its true import was seen by Taylor (496–7).
[2] Poll. viii. 105. Stob. *Flor*. xliii. 48. Cf. Lycurg. *c. Leoc.* 76.
[3] Another translation will be found in Van Hook (170–1), apparently the version which graces the hall of the Chicago Y.M.C.A.
[4] The additional clause given by Plut. *Alc.* (xv. 8) ὀμνύουσι γὰρ ὅροις χρήσασθαι τῆς Ἀττικῆς πυροῖς, κριθαῖς, ἀμπέλοις, σύκαις, ἐλαίαις, οἰκείαν ποιεῖσθαι διδασκόμενοι τὴν ἥμερον καὶ καρποφόρον, and alluded to by Cic.

After taking this oath, the ephebi spent their second year as patrols and as guards in the frontier forts. Their guarding of Eleusis is mentioned by one of the two oldest ephebic inscriptions.[1] Their dress in both years was a soft, broad-brimmed hat, called a *petasos*, and a black cloak or *chlamys*.[2] Herodes Atticus in the second century of our era defrayed the expenses of discarding the black cloaks for new white ones;[3] for in that period the ephebi were no longer called on for rough and strenuous work, and so could wear white cloaks without getting them dirty.

The number of ephebi in the years immediately after 335 was large. Beloch and Sundwall have studied painstakingly the fragments of the earliest lists, the former being aided by his unrivalled knowledge of population statistics. It would be superfluous to go over their reckonings, especially as, while working independently and simultaneously, they arrived at practically the same conclusion,[4] namely that 450 or 500 ephebi entered the college each year. Such a large number proves that the ephebic training was obliga-

---

Rep. (iii. 9) is accepted by Taylor (497 n. 2) for the period of Athens' great power, but he thinks it was dropped after the Peloponnesian War. Grasberger III. 30 flatly says that this clause is *unpassend*.

[1] *IG* ii. 1². 1189.

[2] Poll. x. 164. Philost. *Vit. Soph.* ii. 5 (p. 550 Olearius).

[3] Philost. *l. c. IG* iii. 1132 gives a documentary record.

[4] Beloch (1905) 351–3. Sundwall 22. Girard ([1891] 288) was not well-grounded in his statistics, which led him to think that 900 or 1000 ephebi annually entered on the period of training; Beloch's figures show that such a number would have been totally out of proportion to the population of Attica.

tory, even for thetes.¹ Still more ephebi, to the number perhaps of 150 annually, were sent in by Athens' cleruchies, which at this time numbered only five: Samos, Lemnos, Imbros, Scyros, and Salamis.² In the reticence of literary sources and the paucity of the oldest ephebic inscriptions, we can name only one son of a cleruch who came to Athens for his ephebic duties: Epicurus.³ Epicurus, as Beloch remarks, would naturally have served as an ephebus in Samos, where his father lived, had it not been a law that the cleruchs' sons should come to Athens for this duty.

The case of Epicurus is important from another aspect. Strabo says that a companion of his in the ephebia was Menander. Now Menander was born in 343/2,⁴ hence entered the ephebia in 325/4.⁵ Epicurus, born in 341, came to Athens in 324/3 to enter the ephebia. Thus we may conclude with certainty that the duration of ephebic service at this time was still two years, for otherwise Menander could not have been a fellow-ephebus of Epicurus.⁶ Certainly the obligation to enter the ephebia still held even for

---

¹ Beloch *l. c.* Busolt-Swoboda II. 1188 n. 7.
² Beloch 354.
³ Strab. xiv. 1. 18 (638 Cas.).
⁴ The author uses the dates given by Christ-Schmid *Gr. Litteraturgesch.*⁶ II. 38–9 and 95.
⁵ He gave his first play in this year, while he was an ephebus: Anon. *de Com.* 17. (*CGF* p. 9, line 71), where the name of the archon has been emended by Legrand from Διοκλέους to Ἀντικλέους. See Christ-Schmid 39 n. 2.
⁶ The whole argument here is based on Girard ([1891] 294), whose dates, however, are at fault.

thetes, in 324/3, the year when Menander and Epicurus were *synephebi*. A list of ephebi for that year from the Leontid tribe gives 63 names, although three demes were lacking in the record.[1] Leonardos estimated by the average number from each deme that the three lacking ones must have contributed eleven or twelve more, making 74 or 75 from a single tribe. Multiplying by ten, we arrive at the number of 740 or 750 for the whole body of citizenry, but this number may be too high.

Directly after this, in 322, a timocratic government was imposed on Athens by Antipater, and all whose wealth fell short of 2000 drachmas were excluded from the state education; after Antipater's government was overthrown, this rating still remained,[2] with the result that in 306/5 there were about 100 fewer ephebi annually eligible than there were before 322.[3]

The inscription of 305/4,[4] giving the data for 306/5, is instructive in many ways. In studying the fragmentary list of names, Köhler (333) observed that in two cases brothers were listed.[5] The implication is obvious, that the age of eighteen for entrance to the ephebia was no longer adhered to strictly. With this in mind, we are no longer obliged to follow Boeckh in

---

[1] ’Αρχ. ’Εφ. 1918, 75 no. 95.
[2] de Sanctis 4–5.
[3] Busolt-Swoboda II. 1190–1. Cf. Ferguson 22.
[4] *IG* ii.1². 478.
[5] Col. 2, l. 35–6 and col. 3, l. 81–2. Deme and patronymic correspond. Dumont (I. 41f.) thinks all such cases coincidence, but they happen more frequently than twins do.

casting doubts on the accuracy of Terence, who represents a sixteen-year-old boy as an ephebus doing guard duty at the Piræus.[1] Terence probably was following Menander to the letter. The same inscription teaches us that the period of ephebic training was now reduced to one year, for the archon under whom they were enrolled was the one just preceding the one under whom they were honored at their "commencement."[2] It may be that even in this year the compulsion to enter the ephebia was already completely abandoned: Beloch (352) estimated only 400 ephebi for this year, and Girard[3] has observed that some demes furnished only one or two. Still another important change occurring only a few years after this was the disappearance of the *sophronistai*.[4]

These many changes justify us in making the assertion that the ephebic college passed through a major transformation at the end of the fourth century. Bad financial conditions made Athens unable longer to bear the burden of supporting and educating her young men for two years,[5] and she decided to do it for one year only. Discouraged by the Macedonian overlordship and the state of the treasury, weakened in military spirit and morale, she relaxed the obligation formerly compelling all citizens' sons (or, since 322,

[1] The boy was Chærea, in the *Eunuchus*. See lines 290, 693, and 824. See also Østbye 30.
[2] Girard (1891) 295.
[3] (1891) 292.
[4] There is no record of *sophronistai* after 303/2. See above, page 131.
[5] Busolt-Swoboda II. 1191.

all who possessed the proper census rating) to enter the ephebia, and allowed those who did enter to help meet the financial exigencies by liturgies and personal contributions. Thus the ephebia began to change into an aristocratic institution for the instruction of the few who were wealthy and could pay the price.

When we turn the page and ponder the inscriptions of the next century, the third before Christ, we are amazed at the pitifully small number of ephebi. In 283/2 there were 33, in 275/4 only 29.[1] Shortly after the ill-omened Chremonidean War, which resulted in the capture of Athens by Antigonus in 263, the ephebi numbered but 23.[2] This drop in the enrolment to a fraction of what it was in the fourth century makes us feel certain that it had worked a hardship on the poorer classes, and they dropped out with a sigh of relief when the obligation to service was annulled. They needed the two years from eighteen to twenty for work as wage-earners.[3] Even at the end of the previous century, when the number enrolled was already contracted, two tribes had furnished more ephebi than all twelve did in any year, so far as we are informed, of the next half century.[4] For 125 years after 250 B.C., the paucity of inscriptions leaves us almost no data on the history and number of the ephebi, but we will hardly be wrong in saying that the

[1] *IG* ii. 1². 665, 681.
[2] *Ibid.* 766.
[3] Ferguson 48.
[4] Köhler 332.

institution barely survived at all, and the numbers enrolled were insignificant.[1]

On the gymnastic and military exercises one of the few inscriptions made before 250 B.C. gives us some fragmentary information.[2] The ephebi took cross-country runs, and in all their activities displayed zeal and ambition. At their graduation, they held the customary review before the senate. While tantalized by the lack of further details, we are sure, from the repeated mention of the *paidotribes* and military instructors all through the period, that the exercises were all carried on. The Ptolemæum and Diogeneum are the gymnasia most commonly named in the ephebic inscriptions,[3] but before these were erected, the three old gymnasia must have been used by the ephebi as well as by the other youths. Later the youths (νεανίσκοι) of the Lyceum were named as a group wholly distinct from the ephebi,[4] and we know of a club of men who used the Lyceum for an exercise place at about the same period;[5] it is probable, therefore, that the Ly-

---

[1] There were about thirty-one ephebi in an uncertain year not far from 236/5: *IG* ii. 1². 787.

[2] *IG* ii. 1². 700 (date not determinable).

[3] The γυμνάσιον τῶν ἐφήβων, which Oehler (*RE* VII. 2012), referring to *IG* ii. 1². 478 l. 30, suspects as not identical with any of the gymnasia which are otherwise known, the author would identify with the Lyceum, a gymnasium especially frequented by the ephebi before 275 B.C. when the Ptolemæum was built. The reading of the inscription, besides, is only conjectural, and we are not justified in assuming from such a slender thread of evidence a gymnasium not known from any other source.

[4] *IG* ii. 1². 956 l. 67 (161/0 B.C.), 958 l. 65, 961 l. 31–2.

[5] *Ibid.* 957, l. 51.

ceum was not then used by the ephebi. The victor lists [1] of the Thesea in 161/0 and later show that the ephebi took part in torch-races, and in various gymnastic contests, such as hoplomachy and the javelin throw. Moreover, the alumni of the ephebic college, that is, those who had just graduated and were nineteen years old, were organized to carry on their gymnastic sports. In 161/0 the alumni team won from the ephebi in the torch-race,[2] and about 155/4 the alumni had a torch-race of their individual members.[3] The boys from various palæstræ, also, took part in these contests of the Thesea, as did teams of young men from the Lyceum, boys "of the first age" (14–15), and boys "of the second age" (16–17).

In 146 B.C. Athens came under Roman sway and began to enjoy an era of greater prosperity. Despite the decline of military spirit, the original purpose of the ephebia had not hitherto been forgotten or wholly disregarded, but from now on it was increasingly slighted. There was obviously nothing to be gained any longer by training up a body of citizen soldiery, since offensive war was out of the question, and the Romans could be depended on for adequate defense. Hence the ephebia changed gradually until it bore more resemblance to a modern state university, which has a branch of the R.O.T.C., but naturally does not esteem it the most important part of the univer-

[1] *IG* ii. 1². 956–65.
[2] *Ibid.* 956 col. 1, l. 64.
[3] *Ibid.* 958 col. 1, l. 63–4.

sity education. The ephebia, however, put much more stress on gymnastic education than does a modern university. Philosophical and literary studies came in at first as extras, under tolerance, but before long they had a firm foothold, and occupied a large part of the time and attention of the ephebi. Foreigners were admitted and came in large numbers from Asia Minor, Syria, and Rome. The ephebia gained fresh strength and started on an entirely new epoch. These facts we know from the abundance of long inscriptions made between 138/7 and 38/7—inscriptions which allow us to give a more detailed analysis of the history of the ephebi in this century.

From 138/7 we have a partial list [1] of the ephebi who marched in the first Pythaid procession to Delphi. The number listed is fifty-eight, and we understand at once that the enrolment in the college was much larger than it had been during the past century and a half. The list is incomplete, and not all the ephebi went in the procession anyway, as will be shown directly. Hence fifty-eight may have been only one half or less of the total number of ephebi in 138/7. Exactly ten years later, the record of the second Pythaid [2] lists sixty-nine Attic ephebi; but in a fragmentary non-Pythaid inscription [3] of the same year, also listing the ephebi, there are fifteen names not among the sixty-nine. This proves that by no means

[1] *BCH* XXX. (1906) 225f.
[2] Michel (Suppl.) 1523.
[3] *Rev. Belge* III. (1924) 13ff.

all the ephebi went in the processions to Delphi, and shows that there were at the very least eighty-four ephebi in 128/7.

About the ephebi of 123/2, five years later, we have some satisfying information from a lengthy and reasonably well-preserved inscription.[1] The list of names at the end is the most fragmentary part of the record, but Dumont (I. 53), by getting averages from the lists of the tribes that are most fully preserved, has been able to estimate that there were 120 ephebi in this year. The ephebic activities which are enumerated were multifarious; quite as in modern college life, there was something to keep one busy every day and every minute. As for their physical education, it is stated that they went to the gymnasia the whole year through. As we read on in the inscription, we learn that the gymnasia were now used for philosophical as well as gymnastic instruction (l. 19ff.): "All the year through the ephebi were faithful in attending the lectures of Zenodotus in the Ptolemæum and Lyceum, likewise of all the other philosophers in the Lyceum and Academy." They also held a race in armor at the Epitaphia, and raced on other occasions as well. At the Epitaphia and Thesea, they gave a military drill for the edification of the spectators. Their military training was not neglected, for they marched under arms out to the borders and the fortresses of Attica, getting acquainted with the roads and the topography

[1] *IG* ii. 1². 1006.

of the country. This was the year in which the use of the catapult in ephebic training was revived, and we are told about this repeatedly in the same inscription. Garrison duty was no longer required of them. They were given a little acquaintance with the sea, sailing around to various places near by, and twice during the year they had a boat-race. At the close of the year they passed in review, and yielded to a new group of ephebi, who were headed by an almost wholly new faculty.

The contents of this inscription are duplicated, for the most part, by the others of the same period. In 119/8,[1] however, the list of ephebi reveals for the first time [2] the presence of foreigners, only seventeen of them among 141 ephebi. After this foreigners were admitted freely. So far as we can tell, they were treated just as well as were the sons of Attic citizens.[3] They came from other cities of Greece, as Sicyon and Thespiæ, from the islands, as Paros, and from Asia Minor. In 119/8, one was from Berytus, three from

---

[1] *IG* ii. 1². 1008.

[2] An apocryphal decree of the Athenians, printed in the Littré edition of Hippocrates (IX. 400–2), after recounting the many and great services the famous physician of Cos had rendered to Athens, listed as one of the privileges and honors accorded to him in recompense: καὶ ἐξεῖναι πᾶσι Κώων παισὶν ἐφηβεύειν ἐν ᾿Αθήναις καθάπερ παισὶν ᾿Αθηναίων, ἐπειδή περ ἡ πατρὶς αὐτῶν τοιοῦτον ἄνδρα ἐγέννησεν. Littré recognized that this document was spurious, though ancient; whether there is any particle of truth concealed in it is unknown. As for the date 119/8, Girard ([1891] 289) said the oldest inscription listing foreign ephebi was *IG* ii. 1². 1009 (117/6). This seems clearly to have been an oversight on his part.

[3] For details on this point the writer refers to Dumont I. 98.

Antioch, one from Rome. Some, of course, may have been metics. Their provenience in 119/8 is typical for the later history of the ephebia: the largest percentage, six out of the seventeen, came from Asia Minor, and Syria sent three. Rome in this period contributed a large number of young men to the ephebia.[1]

In 117/6 [2] there was a record number of ephebi, 162 Athenians and twelve foreigners. Ten years later [3] we find fewer Athenians, 116, but twice as many foreigners, twenty-four.

The inscription for this year gives one or two other interesting bits of information. It mentions the ephebic alumni (l. 9–10): "And the ephebi ran the torch-race at the Epitaphia against last year's ephebi, whom also they beat." When the excursions of the ephebi out over the countryside and to the borders are recounted, it is said that they made them "several times" ($\pi\lambda\epsilon o\nu\acute{a}\kappa\iota s$). How different from the earlier days when they were always out at the forts or about the countryside, and rarely in Athens! In this epoch they are regularly to be found in Athens, and they go out on expeditions "several times" only.

The best way to get a clear concept of the number of ephebi in this century from 138/7 to 38/7 will be a table which is given on the following page.

---

[1] By actual count, more came from Rome than from any other city save Miletus. Dumont I. 117–8 and Capes 27 incorrectly assert that Rome sent few ephebi to Athens.
[2] *IG* ii. 1². 1009.
[3] *Ibid.* 1011.

THE ATHENIAN EPHEBIA

Date	Remarks	Total	Source
138/7	At least 58 in 1st Pythaid	58+	*BCH* XXX (1906) 225f.
128/7	69 in 2nd Pythaid. 15 others in ephebic inscription	84+	Michel (Suppl.) 1523 and *Rev. Belge* III. (1924) 13ff.
123/2	About 120 (see Dumont I. 53)	120±	*IG* ii. 1², 1006
119/8	124 Athenians and 17 foreigners	141	*IG* ii. 1², 1008
117/6	162 Athenians and 12 foreigners	174	*IG* ii. 1², 1009
108/7	116 Athenians and 24 foreigners	140	*IG* ii. 1², 1011
107/6	97 in 3rd Pythaid		*BCH* XXX (1906) 228ff.
	2 others in ephebic inscription	99+	*IG* ii. 5, 1226d
?	112 Athenians and no foreigners	112	*IG* ii. 1², 1027
101/0	102 Athenians and 36 foreigners	138	*IG* ii. 1², 1028
97/6	66 in 4th Pythaid	66+	Michel (Suppl.) 1524
90–80	Fragmentary record: 3 Athenians, 14 foreigners	?	*IG* ii. 1², 1031
83–73	Incomplete; 105 Athenians, 5 foreigners	110+	*IG* ii. 1², 1039
39/8	52 Athenians and 67 foreigners	119	*IG* ii. 1², 1043

A study of the table shows that Dumont (I. 58) was certainly not overestimating in placing the average number of ephebi in this period at about 125. Those of the records which are complete show a pretty steady increase in the number of foreigners, from seventeen in the year when we first find them recorded, to sixty-seven exactly eighty years later. In the latter year they even outnumbered the Athenians; the Athenian youth had been decimated by the Roman wars.[1]

In this epoch and perhaps earlier as well, riding was one of the favorite exercises of the ephebi.[2] Of course, it is one more sign of how aristocratic the institution had become Another sign was the foundation of a library in the Ptolemæum in 119/8 and the enforced contribution to it of one hundred books annually at the expense of the ephebi.[3] The religious expenses mount and mount. As early as 73 B.C.,[4] the ephebic gymnasiarchy was known. This type of gymnasiarchy should not be confounded, as it was by Boeckh and Dittenberger, with the state gymnasiarchies, either the liturgy of the early time or the magistracy of the third century before Christ and later. It was of a liturgical nature, but was held principally by the ephebi themselves. Glotz [5] explains its origin as follows: All special expenses of the ephebia had to be met from some source other than the Athenian treasury. If the funds of the ephebic treasury were inadequate, a generous *kosmetes* would make a donation or induce some of his richer students to offer a contribu-

---

[1] Dumont *l. c.*
[2] *IG* ii. 1². 1040 l. 29f.; 1042 frg. a, l. 21, frg. c, l. 9; 1043 l. 21.
[3] *Ibid.* 1009, l. 7ff.
[4] *Ibid.* 1039, l. 29f.
[5] Dar.-Sagl. II. 1676.

tion.[1] This custom became regularized, and the ephebus, *kosmetes*, or teacher who purchased oil or defrayed any of the expense for the gymnasia was called a gymnasiarch.

From the first century before Christ we have unsatisfying references to *mellephebi*. The word *mellephebi* means "those about to be ephebi," and Censorinus[2] defines their age as fifteen. This statement of Censorinus is hardly based on conditions in Attica, for he goes on to set the regular age of ephebi as sixteen. It is possible that the Athenians were called *mellephebi* at the age of fifteen or sixteen, but quite certain that they were so called at seventeen. The *mellephebi* had their preparatory school at the Piræus. The attendance at the school was usually small, eight or ten annually,[3] and the fees were probably as high as in modern preparatory schools. Foreigners were admitted freely, and we know of one each from Miletus and Antioch, two cities which sent relatively large numbers to Athens for the ephebia. Normally one teacher was ample for the small number of students, and he was probably a teacher of "music." This follows because the *mellephebi* made their dedications to the Muses

[1] This is well illustrated by *IG* ii. 1². 1039 l. 29f. "Those who were willing and ambitious in spending money, the *kosmetes* urged to the gymnasiarchy, relieving of this expense those whose funds were but moderate." In 39/8 an ephebus named Sosis made a marked impression by his generosity in this matter: the details may be read in *IG* ii. 1². 1043 l. 62ff.

[2] *de Die Nat.* xiv. 8.

[3] In one year, however, the attendance was about sixty: Ἐφ. Ἀρχ. 1884, 187ff. This is surprising.

instead of to Hermes. Physical education was not apt to be slighted at the mellephebic age, but the trio of inscriptions [1] which give us all our information say nothing on that score. What was the nature of the *epimeletai* or "guardians," who were honored by the Senate in the longest of the three inscriptions is uncertain; they existed in a year when there were about sixty pupils (see n. 3 on page 163), and the term may be intended to include a faculty of several members.

In the ephebia under the Empire much was changed from the earlier time. One of the most striking features is the greater complexity of the organization. As many as twenty-five instructors and functionaries of one sort and another were sometimes set over the ephebi. At the head of the college was still put the *kosmetes*, always some man of good family and one who was prominent in the state.[2] The military instructors formerly known had disappeared, with the exception of the *hoplomachos*, and only one new one had come into existence, the *kestrophylax*. The latter taught the use of a sort of artillery engine, called the *kestrosphendone*, which hurled sharp missiles with considerable effect. In general, he was one of the humblest members of the faculty, and was listed at or near the bottom of the annual record.[3] Frequently

[1] All three were found at the Piræus; two were published by Foucart *BCH* VII. (1883) 75ff. no. 3, the third by Dragatses 'Εφ. 'Αρχ. *l. c.* The word [με]λλεφήβων with no comprehensible context appears at the end of *IG* ii. 5. 952b.

[2] Ahrens 55. Dittenberger 31ff. Dumont I. 171.

[3] For examples see *IG* iii. 1094 l. 32; 1104 col. 3, l. 15.

the same man was *kestrophylax* for several years,[1] and one Pythicus was given a life-long appointment about the year 125.[2] The existence of the *kestrophylax* is attested by inscriptions from the reign of Titus to the end of the ephebia.[3]

Assistants to the leading functionaries of the college were numerous. They bore the title of the man they assisted, with the prefix of *anti-* or *hypo-*. The *kosmetes* acquired a helper called the *hypokosmetes* about the year 125. In the year 124/5, in fact, there were two such helpers, but another inscription of about the same time names only one.[4] Aside from this pair of references, the *hypokosmetes* is never found; the term *antikosmetes*, "vice-president", was adopted and retained until the end of the ephebic organization. The precise sphere of activity assigned to the *antikosmetes* is not determinable. A *kosmetes* named Alcamenes, who held his office A.D. 200 or thereabouts, left us an interesting footnote on the *antikosmetes;*[5] "An *antikosmetes* I did not have, because there is nothing written in the law about this, but in a way I did use my son Marcus Aurelius Alcamenes for this service." The assistant *paidotribes* was always called *hypopaidotribes*. His office had originated be-

---

[1] So Syntrophus, *IG* iii. 1094, 1095, 1096.

[2] *IG* iii. 1106. For the whole period of the Roman empire, the author uses the dates established by Graindor *Chronol. des archontes ath. sous l'Empire* (1922).

[3] *IG* iii. 1086 to 1202.

[4] Two: *IG* iii. 1104; one: *IG* iii. 1108.

[5] *IG* iii. 1165 col. 4, l. 9ff.

fore the Empire, and it continued as long as the records last. A Milesian named Telesphorus held the position in 166/7 and 172/3.[1] A little later life-long appointees were common.[2] The ephebic secretary, too, often had an assistant in this age; he was originally called the *antigrammateus*,[3] but this term was abandoned for *hypogrammateus*.

The *hegemon* was a novelty in the ephebic faculty, attested for the year 44/5 and thereafter.[4] His function was presumably, as the derivation of his title would indicate, to lead the ephebi when they took part in parades and ceremonies, or when they went out on marches and expeditions.[5] Whether he was charged with any part of their instruction, we can not ascertain. The inscriptions accord the *hegemon* a large measure of honor, by placing him high among the ephebic officials, frequently next to the *kosmetes*. Another newcomer in the ephebic faculty was the *prostates*, or "head man." We are at a loss to say what his duties were, for the inscriptions of this epoch irritatingly give us lists and lists, with no explanations. Dumont[6] was led by the etymology of the word to believe that the *prostates'* task was to preside over some of the exercises. He was one of the latest inno-

---

[1] *IG* iii. 1128, 1133.
[2] Nicostratus: *IG* iii. 1145; Eutychianus: 1156, 1158, etc. The latter served a long time and is named in ten inscriptions.
[3] *IG* iii. 1121.
[4] *Ibid.* 1079 is the earliest datable inscription to mention him.
[5] Dittenberger 36.
[6] I. 196–7.

vations in the corps of ephebic functionaries, as we find no trace of him before the year 175 or thereabouts.[1] A little earlier,[2] we find another newcomer, who was called *didaskalos*, or "teacher," in a special sense. In the early history of the ephebia, it will be recalled, all the teachers had been collectively called *didaskaloi*, while under the Empire they were called *paideutai*. The new *didaskalos* was a teacher of music, and at one period, at any rate, he taught especially hymns in praise of the deified emperor, Hadrian.[3]

Some of the servants and attendants who figure in the ephebic records will be mentioned summarily. The *lentiarios*, first found in 172/3,[4] had charge of the ephebic wardrobe. The *kapsarios* was a bath servant who guarded the clothes and possessions of the ephebi while they bathed.[5] In the third century, a doctor was appointed annually to guard the health of the youths;[6] of course it may be that his services were required only for part of his time. The *thyroros* ("doorkeeper") was, the writer judges, a concierge; he was looked down upon, and almost always was named at the end of the collegiate personnel.[7] The *hypozakoros*

[1] *IG* iii. 1137.

[2] In 158/9: *IG* iii. 1122.

[3] *IG* iii. 1128, dated 166/7, or nearly thirty years after Hadrian's death.

[4] *Ibid.* 1133. Cf. Dumont I. 198.

[5] *Ibid.* 1171, 1184, 1202, 1242. Cf. Dumont I. 198–9; Graindor (1922) 228 n. 2.

[6] *IG* iii. 1191, 1193, 1199, 1202.

[7] The *thyroros* was added earlier than most of the supernumeraries, about 44/5: *IG* iii. 1080.

was a subordinate priest delegated to the ephebi in order to direct them in their manifold relations with religion.[1] The *hypotaktes*, finally, is an unsolved mystery.[2]

In addition to all these, there were some special officers for the gymnasium called the Diogeneum. Most commonly named of these was the caretaker,[3] but in one catalog [4] there are listed no less than eight others: *hypopaidotribes, hoplomachos,* secretary, undersecretary, *kestrophylax, didaskalos, hegemon,* and *thyroros*. The reason for this separate corps in the Diogeneum will be explained later in this chapter.

Far more important than any of these new officials were the *sophronistai*, who were revived under the Empire. First mentioned in the reign of Hadrian, between 120 and 130,[5] they recur constantly thenceforth to the end of the ephebia. As might be expected, not all the same statements would hold good for these *sophronistai*, that held for those of the fourth century before Christ. They were six in number now, and there was a corresponding number of *hyposophronistai*.[6]

[1] *IG* iii. 1193, 1199, 1202. The ephebi had no *hypozakoros* before the third century.

[2] Not even the form of his title is quite sure, for *IG* iii. 1113 reads ὑβοτάκτῃ. The word recurs in only one other inscription (*SEG*. iii. 262), one which has but recently come to light. The dates of the two inscriptions are, respectively, *ca*. 135 and 143/4.

[3] *IG* iii. 1133 and often. His Greek title was ὁ ἐπὶ Διογενείου. See Graindor (1922) 228 on the nature of his office.

[4] *IG* iii. 1184 (dated *ca*. 220).

[5] *Ibid*. 1108.

[6] The *sophronistai* are alluded to, without their number being given, in *IG* iii. 1108, 1117, 1218, 1222.

No longer was one chosen from each tribe, and in one case a man was *sophronistes* and his son *hyposophronistes* in the same year.[1] Almost the only distinction between the *sophronistai* and *hyposophronistai* was in age, so that promotion from the lower to the higher grade was easy. In 166/7 some of the *sophronistai* resigned during the year, whereupon three *hyposophronistai* were immediately promoted to their places, the rest of the vacancies being filled by new men.[2] The specific duty of the twelve *sophronistai* and *hyposophronistai* was to take charge of the ephebic divisions, which were called *systremmata*, and were sometimes, but seemingly not always, twelve in number.[3] Each *systremma* was led by one of its members, who was called the *systremmatarch*;[4] the latter must have been under the orders of the *sophronistes* who was assigned to his *systremma*. One other point concerning the *sophronistai* that merits passing mention, is that they were sometimes munificent in furnishing oil for the exercises, when there were too few ephebic gymnasiarchs to bear the expense for the entire year; in one year they bore this expense, in conjunction with the *kosmetes*, for six months.[5]

Among all these officials, so many that even to enumerate them is tedious, there was an understanding

[1] *IG* iii. 1116. See Dumont I. 201.
[2] Cf. *Ibid.* 1028 with 1029.
[3] Dittenberger on *IG* iii. 758.
[4] That the *systremmatarchs* were themselves ephebi is proved by *IG* iii. 1164, where they dedicate a list of their *synephebi*.
[5] *IG* iii. 1199.

as to rank and degree of importance. There was, therefore, always chance for advancement. One who, like the *kestrophylax*, taught some specialized subject, could not, of course, change to another special subject that was more highly esteemed; he might possibly, however, become a *sophronistes* or even *kosmetes*. An under-secretary could become a secretary, a *hypopaidotribes* a *paidotribes*, an *antikosmetes* a *kosmetes*. Even the servants and attendants could be promoted, from the humbler tasks to such as were more dignified. Dumont [1] has drawn up lists, for various periods, of the officials in their order of importance. On account of the discontinuance of certain sorts of teachers, and the introduction of new ones, no single list holds good for all periods; and besides, some officials, such as the secretary, were very differently rated at different times. At all times, we may be sure, the ephebic teacher who was meritorious could win promotion.

The activities of the ephebi under the Empire were no longer military in nature. Gymnastic and mental education had almost wholly driven out military training. There was more attention paid to fine appearance, to parades, and to festivals. The ephebia had become a school of politics and citizenship rather than of war. The lads organized among themselves every year a miniature state, with archons, generals, heralds, and other high state officials. They called themselves "citizens" (πολῖται), and even had an

[1] I. 204ff.

Areopagus council of their own. With so many things to occupy their minds and consume their energies, the ephebi gave less attention to physical exercises than had been their wont.[1] Torch-races and ship-battles were prominent.[2] Hoplomachy and the use of the *kestrosphendone* were the only military exercises still in use. Races of different lengths,[3] wrestling, and the pancratium complete the list of the exercises attested in this period.[4] Small wonder that Philostratus mourned the decadence of gymnastics, and wrote his treatise in a vain endeavor to stem the tide that was setting away from physical education. Athletics, however, were flourishing, and more and more physical training was being left to the professionals.

The numbers enrolled in the ephebia under the Empire were large. Doubtless it was a matter of pride for all the aristocrats to spend a year in the college, and the foreigners who came to enrol were more numerous than ever. The earliest records we have from this period do not mention foreigners, but that does not justify us in assuming that there were none. The inscriptions were no longer official records made by the order of the state, but were made at the expense of the *kosmetes* or some wealthy ephebus; if they wished to

---

[1] This trend became noticeable even a little before the Empire. Cf. Cic. *Rep.* iv. 4. *Iuventutis vero exercitatio quam absurda in gymnasiis! quam levis epheborum illa militia!* See Barth (1920) 137.

[2] Dumont I. 234; the inscriptions *passim*.

[3] The δόλιχος or long race, δίαυλος or race of two laps, and στάδιον or race of one lap.

[4] *IG* iii. 1129, 1147.

save money by having the stone-cutter omit the list of foreigners, there was nothing to hinder. When foreigners were listed at all, it was often without the patronymic, always without the ethnic. The earliest inscription from this period is of 13/2 B.C.,[1] and gives a list of about sixty-five Athenians for six tribes, from which we may estimate 130 for the twelve. In the reign of Claudius, there were only ninety-six in one year,[2] but 102 or more in 44/5;[3] in the reign of Domitian the number was eighty.[4] At this point we come upon a stumbling-block, for with the eighty Athenians are listed 151 "Milesians." Is it possible that Miletus, which, it is true, sent many ephebi to Athens, could have sent such an enormous number in a single year? Obviously the answer is no. Disregarding the old theories that were constructed to explain this phenomenon, let us give at once the theory of Thalheim,[5] which seems to me almost certainly the true one: All the foreigners were grouped under the name of "Milesians;" that is why there are no lists of other foreigners in the catalogs which have the "Milesians."[6] Of course there had to be many real Milesians in the college, as there certainly were, to occasion the practice of calling all the foreigners "Milesians." Later on, the

[1] *IG* iii. 1076.
[2] *Ibid.* 1081.
[3] *Ibid.* 1079 and 1080.
[4] *Ibid.* 1091.
[5] *RE* V. 2739.
[6] *IG* 1096 and 1098. The latter is supplemented by a new fragment published by Graindor *BCH* XXXVIII. (1914) 422f. no. 25.

foreigners were called *epengraphoi*, or "those enrolled in addition,"[1] as it was felt that this was more appropriate than the arbitrary designation of "Milesians."

In 111/2, of one hundred ephebi nearly four-fifths were foreigners; a few years later, for some inexplicable reason, there were only fifty-two ephebi in all, and only four of these were Athenians.[2] A record of from five to fifteen years after that tells us positively that there were 202 ephebi; how many were foreigners it does not say.[3] With such fluctuations, we can set up no average number. For the most part the number ranges between 100 and 200; the foreigners numbered from thirty or forty to 154. The following table will give the details:

Date	Remarks	Total	Source (*IG* iii.)
13/2 B.C.	*Ca.* 65 in 6 tribes; hence *ca.* 130 in the twelve. Foreigners not mentioned	130±	1076
44/5	102+; no indication as to whether they were partly foreigners	102+	1079,[4] 1080
41–54	96 listed; no indication given as to whether they were partly foreigners	96	1081

[1] The term is found earliest *ca.* 100 after Christ, *IG* iii. 1092. In 111/2 and 115/6 (or 116/7) the term *Milesians* was used, but after that ἐπέγγραφοι was employed invariably. Thalheim *RE* V. 2740 wished to identify the ἐπέγγραφοι with οἱ περὶ τὸ Διογένειον (of whom more later), but this hypothesis was thoroughly refuted by Graindor (1922) 225–7.

[2] See the inscriptions mentioned in note 6 on the previous page, with Graindor's comments *l. c.*

[3] *IG* iii. 1109.

[4] Better edited by Merriam *AJP* VI. (1885) 5.

GREEK PHYSICAL EDUCATION

Date	Remarks	Total	Source (*IG* iii.)
81–96	80 Athenians and 151 "Milesians"	231	1091
111/2	21 Athenians and 79 "Milesians"	100	1096
115/6 or 116/7	4 Athenians and 48 "Milesians"	52	1098 [1]
121/2, 125/6, 128/9, or 129/30	202 in all; what portion were foreigners is unknown	202	1109
141/2	Incomplete; 79+ Athenians and 29+ foreigners	108+	1124
143/4	84 Athenians; foreigners not listed	84	1113
148/9	Incomplete; ca. 106 Athenians, and 4 names with no deme given: probably foreigners	110+	1114/1116
150/1	70 Athenians and 7+ foreigners	77+	1120
158/9	Incomplete; ca. 106+ Athenians and 109+ foreigners	215+	1122
164/5	Incomplete save for certain tribes; average of 11 for these tribes gives 143, a total which is too high: 19+ foreigners	162≑	1127
166/7	95 Athenians and 41 foreigners	136	1128
172/3	80 Athenians and 154 foreigners	234	1133

[1] As supplemented by Graindor *BCH* XXXVIII. (1914) 422f.

Date	Remarks	Total	Source (*IG* iii.)
175/6–177/8	106 Athenians and 109 foreigners	215	1138
180/1–192/3	*Ca.* 60 or 65 Athenians (Dumont I. 56) and 37 foreigners	100±	1147
186/7–191/2	76+ Athenians and 76+ foreigners	152+	1145
192/3	85 Athenians and 39 foreigners	124	1160
Ca. 200	94 Athenians and 104 foreigners	198	1163
Ca. 200	70 Athenians and 61 foreigners	131	1165
198/9–207/8	76 Athenians and 27 foreigners	103	1171
199/200–207/8	61 Athenians and 32 foreigners	93	1169
Before 212/3	*Ca.* 60 Athenians (Dumont I. 56) and 31+ foreigners	91+	1176
212/3 or soon after	57+ Athenians and 38+ foreigners	95+	1177 [1]
217/8 or soon after	42 Athenians in 8 tribes = *ca.* 65 for the 13 (Dumont I. 56) and ? foreigners	65+	1184
230–5	92+ Athenians and 44+ foreigners	136+	1192
230–5	78+ Athenians and 5+ foreigners	83+	1193
239/40 or 243/4	Ephebi and Diogeneum pupils together, 229		1197

[1] With a new fragment: Graindor *BCH* XXXIX. (1915) 262.

Date	Remarks	Total	Source
			(*IG* iii.)
247–60	Incomplete; ephebi and Diogeneum pupils together; probably about same number as in 1197		1199
262/3 or 266/7	Ephebi and Diogeneum pupils together, at least 313, and 52 foreigners		1202

A new development of the ephebia in the Christian era was connected with the Diogeneum. This gymnasium had been erected in the late third or early second century before Christ,[1] and after being repaired in 107/6 by the *kosmetes* Eudoxus,[2] it was still standing and in use as late as the third century of our era.[3] Originally used by the ephebi like the other gymnasia, in the second century of our era, the custom originated of reserving it for those who were preparing to enter the ephebia, the *mellephebi*.[4] The subjects the *mel-*

---

[1] Oehler *RE* VII. 2006; Graindor (1922) 220.

[2] *IG* ii. 1². 1011, l. 41.

[3] *IG* iii. 1202, of 262/3 or 266/7.

[4] Dumont I. 50. The earliest mention of οἱ περὶ τὸ Διογένειον, the regular designation for these *mellephebi*, is found in a letter of the emperor Hadrian, dated 131/2 (*IG* ii. 1². 1102 as supplemented by *SEG* iii. 111). Plut. *Quæst. Conv.* ix. 1. 1 refers to the Diogeneum as still used by the ephebi about thirty or forty years before that; the general Ammonius gave to the ephebi there an examination in literature (γράμματα), geometry, rhetoric, and music. Graindor ([1922] 225) seems to think Plutarch meant *mellephebi*, instead of what he said. The mention of γράμματα as a subject of study does not prove that the students were under the ephebic age, for the word can mean "literature" or "learning" as well as simply "reading:" see the new Liddell and Scott *s. v.* IV. Plutarch named only intellectual subjects as taught there, while the inscriptions of a later time, when *mellephebi* studied

lephebi studied may have been partly intellectual, as in the earlier preparatory school at the Piræus, but certainly physical education was not neglected. We are permitted to judge the subjects of instruction only by the list of teachers. These have already been named over (above, page 168): besides the secretary, under-secretary and concierge, they included the *hypopaidotribes, hoplomachos, kestrophylax, didaskalos*, and *hegemon*. More than half of the teachers, then, were for the gymnastic and military exercises. The secondary importance of the preparatory school is well brought out by the fact that only a *hypopaidotribes*, not a *paidotribes*, was assigned to it. The number annually enrolled in the school must remain doubtful, for in the three inscriptions where they were listed, they were mixed in with the ephebi.

Our last datable record of the ephebia was made in 262/3 or 266/7.[1] A glance at this extraordinarily long inscription reveals that there was still plenty of strength and vigor in the institution which had lasted so many centuries. As a reference to the table on page 176 shows, there were in this year fifty-two foreigners in attendance, and the combined number of Athenian *ephebi* and *mellephebi* reached the astonishing total of 313 or more. The teachers and func-

---

there, name principally teachers of gymnastic and military training. Besides, countless inscriptions bring the general or *strategos* into relation with the ephebi, but none with the *mellephebi* (with παῖδες only in *IG* ii. 1². 1187).

[1] *IG* iii. 1202.

tionaries number fifteen, in addition to six *sophronistai* and six *hyposophronistai*. The *paidotribes* and *hypopaidotribes*, the *hoplomachos* and *kestrophylax* are there to prove that gymnastic and military exercises were still in vogue. Surely, as the author's predecessors have observed,[1] the ephebia had enough momentum in 262/3 (or 266/7) to carry it on to the year 300, at least. But the inscriptions fail us abruptly; perhaps some day more will come to light, and let us finish this chapter on the Athenian ephebi. Out of the ephebia, at all events, grew the University of Athens. We have seen how the ephebic college was originally founded as a military institute, but gradually absorbed the higher intellectual education of the time. After completing the ephebic year, many students chose to go on with their study of literature, rhetoric, and philosophy. From this practice the beginnings were made; an organization of the philosophers and other teachers was effected, rules and regulations were established, and the University of Athens was an actuality.[2] Eventually, though at what precise time our documents do not permit us to say, the university crowded its forefather out of existence. Thus physical education at Athens was ended. So were Athens' glory and greatness ended, and that definitively.

[1] Dumont I. 3; Graindor (1922) 175.
[2] See Walden, especially pp. 39–40, on the genesis of the university.

CHAPTER VII

THE REMAINDER OF GREECE AND THE GREEK WORLD

Of physical education in those parts of Greece and the Greek world not already discussed, we have only piecemeal information. Without the inscriptions we should fare much worse, but happily they are rather numerous, and we may justly hope for many more. The literary sources are not wholly barren for this phase of our subject, and the papyri have afforded some insight into the history of physical education in Græco-Roman Egypt. The method of ephebic training originated at Athens spread rapidly through the neighboring countries, and this was especially true in Asia Minor. Everywhere that the ephebic organizations were founded, there was organized physical education. While the existence of a gymnasium in any given locality does not guarantee that it was there used as a school of physical education for the young, yet this was surely true in a large percentage of cases; and since gymnasia are known to have existed in nearly 140 localities,[1] it is

[1] See the useful list of 128 compiled by Oehler *RE* VII. 2005-8. Ten more are to be added: Arsinoë (*BGU* III. 760); Catana (Plut. *Marc.* xxx.); Hermopolis (*PRyl.* II. 101); Istria (*Rev. Philol.* LIII. [1927] 167 n. 2); Lete, Macedonia (*SEG* i. 276); Oxyrhyncus (*POxy.* XVII. 2127, 2147); Philadelphia, Egypt (*PSI* IV. 391); Sebennytus (*Sammelb.* 1106); Sidyma (*TAM* ii. 1. 201); Theadelphia (*Sammelb.* 6157-8).

safe to say that, wherever the Greeks went, they carried their love of gymnastics with them, and made physical exercises part and parcel of the common education.

To assemble the data on this wide spread of physical education was a laborious undertaking; many things must have escaped the author's notice. How best to present the material was also a troublesome problem; after considerable deliberation, it was determined to follow in the main the geographical rather than the topical method. That either method would lead to difficulties and inconsistencies was inevitable; whether the writer has avoided or encountered more by the course chosen, is hard to say. Chronological indications will be given where they are of importance. Our itinerary will take us first to Thebes and Bœotia. Then we will take a glimpse of other localities in Greece, principally in the Peloponnese, and pass thence to the lands farther north, then to the islands of the Ægean. Asia Minor will be the scene of long excursions, then will follow a brief trip across the Black Sea to the Greek colonies of South Russia. From there we will pass to Magna Græcia and Sicily, thence to Syria, and end our journey at the foot of the pyramids, in a land that was already ancient before any one ever heard of Athens or Sparta. From the Sphinx of Thebes to the Great Sphinx of Egypt—this in short will be our course.

Gymnastics, it was commonly believed, were overemphasized in Thebes,[1] to the neglect of the intellect. As a result, the Bœotians became proverbial for their stupidity; the ancients attributed this to the crass atmosphere, but I doubt if modern students of the relation of climate to civilization would accept this theory. Nepos saw the truth of the matter:[2] "All the Bœotians strive harder for physical soundness than for intellectual acumen," and again:[3] "That people has more brawn than brains." In other words, it was their one-sided education that was at fault, and the result was mental dullness such as we found in Sparta. Nor was stupidity the sole effect of carrying on gymnastics to excess; the Bœotians were so well-trained, in military as well as in gymnastic exercises proper, that their enemies criticized them as overeager for fighting, prone to wranglings and strife.[4] A third evil effect of their gymnastics was pæderasty, practiced to such an extent that it evoked a sharp rebuke from Plato.[5]

Plutarch, a Bœotian by birth, was proud of the

[1] Their passion for gymnastics was recognized by Ephorus (*FGrHist.* lxx. F97), who said that the Athenians were interested in sea-power, the Thessalians in horses, and the Bœotians περὶ τὴν γυμνασίας ἐπιμέλειαν. See too the interesting anecdote of Athenæus (xii. 47) about Alcibiades, who believed in the motto: "When in Bœotia, do as the Bœotians do," hence trained in gymnastic exercises to such an extent as to outdo the Bœotians themselves.
[2] *Alcib.* xi. 3.
[3] *Epam.* v. 2.
[4] Plat. *Legg.* i. 636B. Perhaps Alcidamas *Odysseus* i. (*Orat. Att.* II. 197 Didot) had Bœotia in mind when he spoke of the frequency of quarrels and harsh words in the palæstra.
[5] *l. c.*

outcome of the battle of Leuctra, in which Epaminondas and his Thebans thoroughly vanquished Sparta. His theory was that the Thebans won the battle because they were "well-trained in the palæstra."[1] History shows, however, that the battle was not a wrestling match, and had it been, the Spartans would hardly have been outdone by the Thebans. Rather the victory was due to the excellent generalship of Epaminondas, whose aversion for gymnastics and utter abomination for athletics were such that he told the Thebans: "If you would rule over Greece, frequent the camp and not the palæstra."[2] In spite of his blunt advice, the Bœotians spent as much time as ever at their exercises,[3] and in their enthusiasm erected three gymnasia at Thebes, one named in honor of Apollo Lykeios, the others called the Iolaus gymnasium and the Heracleum.[4] The magistrate who controlled the gymnasia and those who exercised there, was the gymnasiarch.[5]

In the third century before Christ, the cities of Bœotia proper, and some of those in the Bœotian League outside the borders of the land, had a system of ephebic training which closely resembled that of Athens. It was severely military in character, as the

---

[1] *Quæst. Conv.* ii. 5. 2.
[2] Nepos *Epam.* v. 4. Pelopidas, the close friend of Epaminondas, was fond of hunting and of the palæstra exercises, at least when he was young: Plut. *Pelop.* iv.
[3] Xen. *Hell.* vi. 5. 23.
[4] Schol. Soph. *O. T.* 919. Paus. ix. 23. 1; ix. 11. 7.
[5] Diog. Laert. vi. 90. Plut. *Amat.* ix. (754D).

Athenian ephebia was originally, and probably had a duration of two years; at any rate, it ended at the age of twenty, whereupon the young men were at once enrolled among the hoplites, or in some other branch of the army. Beloch [1] estimated that from all the Bœotian towns there may have been a total of about 500 drilling annually. The towns for which the ephebia is attested are: Acræphia, Anthedon, Chæronea, Chorsiæ, Copæ, Hyettus, Lebadea, Orchomenus, Thebes, Thespiæ, and Thisbe.[2] Among the towns of the Bœotian League outside Bœotia's borders, Ægosthena and Megara [3] are known to have instituted an ephebia on the same principles. Of a nature more gymnastic than military was the ephebia of a later time at Platæa.[4] The leader of the ephebi, at least in Megara and Platæa, was not called *kosmetes*, but gymnasiarch. About the teachers next to nothing can be said: a teacher of tactics (τακτικός) was employed

---

[1] (1906) 48.

[2] Acræphia: *IG* vii. 2715–21. *BCH* XXIII. (1899) 193ff. nos. 1–8.

Anthedon: *IG* vii. 4172.

Chæronea: *IG* vii. 3292–4, 3297–8 (cf. 3295, 3299).

Chorsiæ: *IG* vii. 2389–90.

Copæ: *IG* vii. 2781–9.

Hyettus: *IG* vii. 2809–32.

Lebadea: *IG* vii. 3065–8, 3072 (cf. 3069–71).

Orchomenus: *IG* vii. 3174–5, 3178–80, 3188 (cf. 3176–7, 3181–7, 3189).

Thebes: *IG* vii. 2442 (cf. 2429–45).

Thespiæ: *IG* vii. 1447–50, 1756–7 (cf. 1751–5); *SEG* iii. 333 (cf. 339).

Thisbe: *SEG* iii. 351–3.

[3] Ægosthena: *IG* vii. 209–22.

Megara: *IG* vii. 27–9, 31.

[4] *IG* vii. 4239.

at Thebes,[1] and teachers of shooting and slinging at Acræphia;[2] for the rest we must use our imagination. We can hardly think that any of these places lacked a gymnasium, and we have direct testimony for the existence of one at Acræphia,[3] and two each at Thespiæ[4] and Megara.[5]

There are a few other traces of physical education in the Bœotian towns. At Tanagra there were two gymnasiarchs,[6] and the same was true of Thespiæ,[7] and probably of Platæa.[8] Since Thespiæ had two gymnasia, no doubt one gymnasiarch presided over each; perhaps the two gymnasiarchs of Platæa and Tanagra may indicate that the same was true there. We have the names of a gymnasium class of fifty-five adults at Thespiæ, among them being an artist, a tanner, and a man in the civil service (δημόσιος).[9] A gymnastic club of ephebi at Acræphia was in existence as late as the second century of our era.[10] Haliartus had a gymnasium, in which philosophers sometimes lectured to the ephebi.[11]

Passing to Locris, Bœotia's neighbor, we find that a

[1] *IG* vii. 2440, probably of the first century B.C.
[2] *Ibid.* 2714.
[3] *Ibid.* 2712, 4134.
[4] *Ibid.* 1777 (ἐν τῷ ἄνω γυμνασίῳ, an expression which assures us that there was a lower one also).
[5] Paus. i. 44. 2, the Old Gymnasium; *IG* vii. 31, the Olympieum.
[6] *IG* vii. 557.
[7] Plut. *Amat.* x. (755A); cf. Haase 389.
[8] IG vii. 1668.
[9] *Ibid.* 1777 (first century of our era).
[10] *Ibid.* 2725.
[11] *Ibid.* 2849.

club of "lovers of gymnastics" (φιλογυμνασταί) existed in the first century of our era at Opus.[1] What connection this club had with the ephebi, who also existed at Opus about the same time,[2] is not known; a gymnasiarch is named in connection with both organizations. One very popular gymnasiarch of the gymnastic club, Lucius Allius Taurus, is named in four inscriptions.[3] The ephebi numbered forty in the only list preserved, and required the services of an assistant gymnasiarch[4] as well as of the gymnasiarch.

Farther to the westward, in Phocis, there was an ephebia at Delphi, also led by a gymnasiarch.[5] It will be seen that the Greek cities, aside from Athens, usually called the leader of the ephebi, not *kosmetes*, but either gymnasiarch or ephebarch; at Nicopolis, for instance, still further westward, the appropriate term of ephebarch was used for the leader of the ephebi,[6] and it was often used in the northern parts of

---

[1] *IG* vii. 4165; *Jahresberichte* CLXXXIX. (1921) 6. Cf. Oldfather *RE* XIII. 1269.

[2] Ἀρχ. Δελτ. VI. (1920–1) 139.

[3] *Jahresberichte l. c.*; Ἀρχ. Δελτ. *l. c.* 140; *IG* ix. 1. 284–5.

[4] Called ἀντιγυμνασίαρχος, a term never used elsewhere; compare, however, the Athenian ἀντικοσμήτης.

[5] Michel (Suppl.) 1523 = *SIG*³ 697. Cf. *BCH* XXIII. (1899) 571; *SGDI* 2731.

[6] Epict. iii.1.34 τοιοῦτόν σε θῶμεν πολίτην Κορινθίων, κἂν οὕτως τύχῃ, ἀστυνόμον ἢ ἐφήβαρχον ἢ στρατηγὸν ἢ ἀγωνοθέτην;

This passage can not be taken to establish the existence of an ephebarch at Corinth, although it shows that Epictetus thought there well might have been one there; but, as it is a sample list of typical officials with whom Epictetus was no doubt familiar in Nicopolis, it proves that an ephebarch did exist in the latter place. Epictetus showed his familiarity with the ephebarch in another passage (iii. 7. 19), while no

Greece and in Asia Minor. To return to Delphi, we have record of the gymnasium there,[1] of a gymnastic club called the "Anointers,"[2] and of a club of *Neoi*, "young men," directed by a gymnasiarch.[3] The gymnasium has been laid bare by the French excavators, and the inscriptions prove that it existed as early as 331 B.C.,[4] and remained in use for six centuries. An *epimeletes* had charge of the building,[5] while the education was led by the gymnasiarch. Little is known of the palæstra, which at Delphi formed part of the gymnasium,[6] but among the temple records is an account of a palæstra attendant ($\pi\alpha\lambda\alpha\iota\sigma\tau\rho o\phi\dot{\upsilon}\lambda\alpha\xi$) being presented, along with other slaves, by King Nicomedes III. of Bithynia.[7] For the pecuniary support of their education, the Delphians were not harassed from about 160 B.C. on, for Attalus III. of Pergamum gave them an endowment of 18,000 drachmas (roughly about $3500) for teachers' salaries.[8] All in all, however, Homolle judged that the Delphians were not fond of gymnastics, being rather absorbed by the fascinating religious life of their city. Of the other

other Greek author ever used the word. That Nicopolis had an ephebia is somewhat supported by the statement of Strabo vii. 7. 6 (325 Cas.) that a gymnasium and stadium existed there. The author owes this suggestion to Dr. Oldfather.

[1] Paus. x. 8. 8; *BCH* XXIII. (1899) 572.
[2] *BCH l. c.* 570 (about 170 B.C.) οἱ ἀλειφόμενοι.
[3] *BCH* XLIX. (1925) 81 no. 8.
[4] Homolle (1899) 561 and 563.
[5] *Ibid.* 575.
[6] *Ibid.* 564.
[7] This was in 92/1 B.C., *SGDI* 2738 l. 22.
[8] *SIG* ³ 672.

Phocian towns, we simply know that Anticyra and Elatea had gymnasia, the latter with a gymnasium club.[1]

At Corinth, on the Isthmus, physical exercises were practiced with some zeal.[2] Pausanias (ii. 4. 5) speaks of the Old Gymnasium there, which leads us to infer that there was a new one as well. In near-by Sicyon, if we may believe the account of Herodotus,[3] a *dromos* (running track) and palæstra were erected in the early sixth century before Christ. The tyrant Cleisthenes desired to wed his beautiful daughter, Agariste, to the best man in all Greece. One of the methods he took to determine who was the best man, is a fine illustration of the Greek fondness for gymnastics: he made trial of the ability of her suitors in the various athletic sports. As places where the sports might be conducted, he built the *dromos* and palæstra. It seems that Hippocleides must have been proficient in gymnastics, for he became the favorite; but he foolishly "danced away his marriage" and, on being rejected, he made the famous but flippant remark "Hippocleides doesn't care." In the time of Demosthenes, there was a *paidotribes* at Sicyon, but apparently, to our surprise, only one.[4] The third century saw an ephebia flourishing there, headed as usual by a gymnasiarch;[5] this ephebia was destined to endure

---

[1] Anticyra: Paus. x. 36. 9, cf. *IG* ix. 1. 7; Elatea: *IG* ix. 1. 128.
[2] Dio Chr. xv. 92 Budé.
[3] vi. 126.
[4] Ps.-Demosth. xvii. (*Fœd. Alex.*) 16; see Dumont I. 180 n. 3.
[5] Plut. *Arat.* liii.

for more than four centuries.¹ The gymnasiarch directed the gymnastic education of the boys, as well as of the ephebi, and was therefore a real superintendent of schools.² The city had two gymnasia,³ one being for general use, the other reserved for the ephebi.

Achæa was not markedly devoted to physical training, and Pellene is the only town in that district known to have had a gymnasium and an ephebia. As in the earliest days of the ephebia at Athens, it was made obligatory for every one to take the ephebic training; and the penalty invoked on the "slackers" was the forfeiture of citizenship.⁴ Elis had three gymnasia, but they were principally for the use of athletes training for the Olympic games;⁵ Olympia had a gymnasium for the same purpose.⁶ Of Messene we only know that it had a gymnasium,⁷ and the same may be said of several Laconian towns: Acriæ, Asopus, Gythium, and Las.⁸ Cythera, the island just off

¹ Paus. ii. 10. 7 καὶ παιδεύουσιν ἐνταῦθα ἔτι τοὺς ἐφήβους.
² Plut. *l. c.*
³ Paus. ii. 10. 1 and ii. 10. 7.
⁴ *Ibid.* vii. 27. 5. The Pellenian ephebia existed in the time of Pausanias (2nd century of our era), and, as the gymnasium reserved for them was called "old" in that period, the ephebi may have been organized centuries earlier.
⁵ Paus. vi. 23. 1–5, cf. v. 15. 8 and Strab. viii. 3. 2. (337 Cas.). A gymnasiarch existed at Elis: Paus. v. 4. 4.
⁶ *Ibid.* vi. 21. 2.
⁷ *Ibid.* iv. 32. 1.
⁸ *Ibid.* iii. 22. 5; iii. 22. 9; iii. 24. 7. Gythium: *IG* v. 1. 1208. For an ephebia at Therapne in Laconia there is no evidence. Oehler *RE* V. 2742 inferred the existence of one from Paus. iii. 20. 2, but a comparison of content and language with Paus. iii. 14. 9 shows that the ephebi who sacrificed to Enyalius in the Phœbæum were those from Sparta, not from Therapne. Poland (90), in his list of places where ephebi existed,

the coast of Laconia, had a gymnasium, with a gymnasiarch as director.[1]

At Colonides, in Messenia, an ephebic inscription of the late second century before Christ has been found;[2] a gymnasiarch was the head of the college, and was assisted by a deputy gymnasiarch and a secretary. Other Messenian localities, Thuria and Corone, had ephebic colleges with a like personnel.[3] For the most part, the inscriptions of these colleges date from the second or third century of our era; but at Thuria the ephebic organization was founded, with the example and inspiration of Sparta, in the second century before Christ. The Spartan influence is seen in the name given to one class of the ephebi: *tritirens* (τριτίρενες). It seems safe to conjecture that *tritirens* were *eirens* who were serving for the third year, and were about the age of the older Spartan *eirens*. Whether they served still longer than three years, and how close the parallel to Sparta was, our present data leave doubtful. This, by the way, slight as it is, is the only trace of Spartan educational influence in Greece proper. Beside the gymnasiarch at Corone stood the archephebus (a Peloponnesian equivalent for ephebarch).[4] Asine and Methone had gymnasiarchs,[5]

---

recorded Therapne with a question mark; the writer would go a step further, and not record it at all.

[1] *IG* v. 1. 938.
[2] *Ibid.* 1402.
[3] Thuria: *IG* v. 1. 1384, 1386; Corone: *ibid.* 1398.
[4] Oehler *RE* V. 2736.
[5] Asine: *IG* v. 1. 1410; Methone: *ibid.* 1417.

and there well may have been ephebic colleges in those towns, too. All in all, Messenia's activity in physical education was considerable.

The two famous old cities, Argos and Mycenæ, had ephebic colleges, in the former place headed by an archephebus.[1] At Argos, under the Empire, slaves were sometimes permitted to enjoy the privileges of the gymnasia,[2] contrary to the practice of Athens, Crete, and Sparta. The Cylarabis Gymnasium, which the Argives built, was unusually famous, and is noticed in many authors.[3] Trœzen, a city under Athenian influence, had an ephebic organization which dated back to a period almost as early as that of her great neighbor;[4] I believe it has the distinction of being the first ephebia founded directly on the Athenian model, and it certainly gives us our earliest testimony regarding a gymnasiarch who was a magistrate at the head of the physical education.[5] The under-gymnasiarch existed here, too. The Trœzenians called their gymnasium the Hippolyteum[6] in honor of the Hippolytus whom Euripides immortalized. Two inscriptions[7] mention the "Anointers," an organization which may have included with the ephebi all others who exercised in the Hippolyteum. The young men (νέοι) who came to the gymnasium were still ac-

---

[1] Argos: *IG* iv. 589; Mycenæ: *ibid.* 497 (197/5 B.C.).

[2] *IG* iv. 597. 606.

[3] Paus. ii. 22. 8–9; Liv. xxxiv. 26; Lucian *Apol.* 11.; Plut. *Cleom.* xvii. and xxvi.

[4] *IG* iv. 749, 753 (with addenda p. 381).   [5] Busolt I. 496 n. 1.

[6] *IG* iv. 754.   [7] *Ibid.* 790, 792.

counted under the gymnasiarch's authority. Epidaurus has left no record of ephebi, but at all events the city had gymnasia and gymnasiarchs.[1]

Of the ephebia at Tegea, in Arcadia, we know more details than for any other Peloponnesian locality save Sparta. Created in the second century before Christ, or even earlier, it lasted into the third century of our era. Sixteen inscriptions [2] furnish us with our data. The number of ephebi was not slight, running as high as seventy-one in 155/6 of our era, a total comparing favorably with that of the Athenian ephebia in the same period. On account of having such a number of lads to handle, the gymnasiarch was assisted by an under-gymnasiarch and one or two archephebi as well. The organization was gymnastic rather than military, as witness the repeated mention of the "oil-furnisher," [3] and one mention of the *paidotribes*, while no military instructors of any sort are named. A gymnasium at Tegea, however, is not attested, and the ephebic training was carried on in a palæstra.[4] Hunting, for which the Arcadian mountains furnished an ideal opportunity, was one of the principal activities of the Tegean lads, and one of their officials was called the "leader of the hunt" (κυναγός). The hunting probably was practiced in a gentlemanly and fashionable way, somewhat after the Eng-

[1] *IG* iv. 1432, 1467.
[2] Grouped together by Hiller von Gärtringen, *IG* v. 2. 43–58.
[3] ἐλαιοπάροχος; but ἐλαιοθέτης in no. 50, l. 77.
[4] So we may judge from the παλαιστροφύλαξ of the ephebic inscriptions.

lish tradition, and as Xenophon would have it, for there are many signs that betoken the aristocratic character of the Tegean ephebi. Among the officials and attendants who are named in the records, are a bath attendant (σινδονοφόρος), and a boy to run the bath furnace (καμινίων); hence bathing surely played a large part in the daily life of the lads. The care that they devoted to their personal appearance is brought out in a way that is almost ludicrous, by the fact that they even had an official barber. What a proud man must Zosimus, son of Mysticus, have been in the year of our Lord 155, when he was made "barber of the ephebi," and his name and function engraved on a stone, where future generations might read it—and smile! What function the "palm-bearer" [1] had is not clear; possibly we should connect him with the curious exercise of "setting up the palm," which is alluded to by Epictetus (iii. 12. 2). Finally, there was a college secretary and a college doctor. Of the other Arcadian towns, Mantinea, Heræa, Megalopolis, and Phigalia are known to have had gymnasia.[2]

If Pausanias had ventured into Macedonia, Thrace, and the other lands north of Greece proper, he would have found gymnasia and physical education in many of the larger towns, wherever Greeks had congregated in sufficient numbers to bear the expense. The Thessalian Heraclea and Hypata, the Illyrian Apollonia,

---

[1] Φοινεικοφόρος or σπαδεικοφόρος.
[2] Paus. viii. 9. 8 and *IG* v. 2. 268; Paus. viii. 26. 1; viii. 31. 9; viii. 39. 6.

the Thracian Amphipolis, the Mœsian Callatis and Istria, the Macedonian Lete and Dium had gymnasia;[1] several of these towns and others had clubs of *neoi* ("youths") headed by gymnasiarchs.[2] A palæstra must have existed at Abdera, in Thrace, since Hippocrates[3] spoke of a palæstra keeper (παλαιστροφύλαξ) there. The Thracian town Selymbria produced the famous *paidotribes* Herodicus.[4] Ephebic organizations were formed in a dozen places—the island Corcyra, Thessalonica, Deuriopus, Edessa, Celetrum, Callipolis, Perinthus, Byzantium, Philippopolis, Odessus, Tomi, an undefined place in upper Mœsia, and Sestos.[5] In

---

[1] Heraclea: Liv. xxxvi. 22; Hypata: *IG* ix. 2. 31, 56; Apollonia: Strab. ix. 3. 16 (424 Cas.); Amphipolis: *Jh. Österr.* I. (1898) 180ff.; Callatis: *SEG* i. 327; Istria: *Rev. Philol.* LIII. (1927), 167 n. 2; Lete: *SEG* i. 276; Dium: Polyb. iv. 62. 3 (this was destroyed by King Philip).

[2] Amphipolis (see previous note); Callatis: *AEM* VI. (1882) 4 no. 4; Serdica: Kalinka *Ant. Denkm. in. Bulg.* no. 138; Odessus: *AM* IX. (1884) 228f. no. 13; X. (1885) 314f. no. 2; Siris: *CIG* 2007; Callipolis: Dumont-Homolle 435 no. 100x; Sestos: *Br. Mus. Inscr.* 1000; Byzantium: Dethier-Mordtmann 77 no. 3. At Larissa (*IG* ix. 2. 620–1) and Phalanna (*ibid.* 1238) the term νεανίσκοι was used for νέοι.

[3] *Epidem.* vi. 8. 30 (V. 354 Littré; XXIII. 630 Kühn).

[4] Plat. *Resp.* iii. 406A.

[5] Corcyra: *IG* ix. 1. 372.
Thessalonica: Duchesne-Bayet 13 no. 2; 44 no. 60.
Deuriopus: Laum *Stift.* II. no. 36.
Edessa: Duchesne-Bayet 102 no. 135; *CIG* 1997c.
Celetrum: *CIG* 1957g.
Callipolis: Dumont-Homolle 435 no. 100x.
Perinthus: Dumont-Homolle 397 no. 74z.
Byzantium: Dethier-Mordtmann 75 no. 2; 79 no. 17.
Philippopolis: Dumont-Homolle 336 no. 43.
Odessus: *Rev. Arch.* II. 35 (1878 I) 112ff. nos. 5 and 6.
Tomi: *AEM* VI. (1882) 24 no. 47.
Mœsia Superior: *CIL* iii. 8175.
Sestos: *Br. Mus. Inscr.* 1000.

Perinthus and Byzantium the ephebi were called by the unusual name of *systatai* ("those who stand together"). An ephebarch ordinarily directed the ephebi in these northern lands, but Thessalonica, Celetrum, and Sestos had both ephebarch and gymnasiarch at the same time.[1] At Tomi the ephebi were divided into two classes, the upper being called the "seniors."[2]

The long inscription from Sestos, dating from about 120 B.C., earlier than most of the others, affords an interesting glimpse into the school activities of the town on the Hellespont. The decree honors the gymnasiarch, Menas, who had served twice and merited the praise of his city. We read (l. 31ff.): "Being chosen gymnasiarch, he took thought for the orderly behavior of the ephebi and the *neoi*, and generally showed himself an excellent and careful disciplinarian in the gymnasium. He conducted tactical exercises for both ephebi and *neoi*, arranged at his own expense contests in javelin throwing and archery, and in his zeal supplied oil for anointing, encouraging the young men to exercise diligently." In his second gymnasiarchy he outdid himself, never failing in times of stress, giving money generously for sacrifices, oil, and prizes. The exercises mentioned as practiced on Sestos, in addition to javelin throwing and archery, were fighting in armor (hoplomachy) and a long race in armor. Menas gave prizes of arms to those of the boys who

[1] Thessalonica even had two gymnasiarchs working in conjunction with the ephebarch.
[2] The Greek is ἔφηβοι τῶν προηγουμένων.

excelled in discipline (εὐταξία), diligence (φιλοπονία), and good physical condition (εὐεξία); the first two of these virtues are frequently found on modern elementary school report cards, but the last-named never. The whole inscription shows a reasonable and laudable emphasis upon physical education at Sestos.

We turn now to the Ægean islands, and then to Cyprus. Ægina offers little to interest us. The island's ancient hostility for Athens prevented it from imitating its neighbor by establishing an ephebic college. It did have two gymnasia, with clubs called the Anointers and the Gymnasium Club.[1] Other clubs of Anointers existed at Delos, at the town of Minoa in Amorgos, on Patmos, Thera, Samos, and Salamis,[2] while the town of Citium in Cyprus had a Gymnasium club,[3] and Patmos had an organization of "Torch-racers."[4] The *neoi* were banded together on many of the islands, Eubœa, Lesbos, Chios, Delos,

[1] Two gymnasia: *REG* XV. (1902) 138 no. 3. Anointers Club: *ibid.* and *IG* iv. 4. Gymnasium Club: *IG* iv. 43, 46, 47b. Gymnasiarch: *IG* iv. 4. Poland (104) doubted if οἱ ἐκ τοῦ γυμνασίου meant a club at all, and thought the term embraced all who were active in the gymnasium; possibly they were not a closed corporation, yet they performed some corporative acts, e. g., making dedications.

[2] Delos: *BCH* VII. (1883) 371 no. 20; XV. (1891) 265 nos. 6-7; XXXVI. (1912) 217 no. 48, 395ff. no. 9, l. 32, 426 no. 21, 431ff. nos. 25-8, 663, no. 33.

Minoa: *IG* xii. 7. 235 (τὸ κοινὸν τῶν ἀλειφομένων, directed by a gymnasiarch).

Patmos: *SIG*³ 1096.

Thera: *IG* xii. 3. 331.

Samos: *BCH* V. (1881) 480f. no. 3.

Salamis: *IG* ii. 1². 1227.

[3] *Rev. Arch.* III. 6 (1885 II.) 345.

[4] *SIG*³ 1096.

Thera, Cos, Rhodes, Tenos, and Samos.[1] Astypalæa had a gymnasium by the third century or earlier, and later a *paidonomos* who had charge of the education of the boys.[2] Thasos had both palæstræ and gymnasia in the fifth century,[3] and in the fourth century and later there were gymnasiarchs officiating there.[4] A gymnasiarch at Anaphe[5] implies a gymnasium there; the same may be said of Siphnos, Lemnos, Samothrace, and Peparethus.[6]

Eubœa had an ephebia in three of its towns, Carystus, Eretria, and Chalcis.[7] Of the one at Carystus we know only that it was late, and was headed by an ephebarch. The ephebarch, by the way, was rare on the islands, found only here, at Mytilene on Lesbos,[8] on Icaria,[9] and in a couple of Cyprian towns.[10] At

---

[1] Eubœa (Eretria): *IG* xii. 9. 235.
Lesbos (Mytilene): *IG* xii. 2. 134; (Methymne) 'Αρχ. Δελτ. VI. (1920–1) 99f.
Chios: *SIG*³ 959.
Delos: *BCH* XIII. (1889) 413ff.; XXXVI. (1912) 429 no. 24.
Thera: *IG* xii. 3. 331, 496.
Cos: *Inscr. Cos.* 108, 109, 110, 111, 114.
Rhodes: *IG.* xii. 1. 96.
Tenos: *IG* xii. 5. 818.
Samos: *AM* XXVIII. (1903) 357ff. no. 2; *SEG* i. 366.
[2] *IG* xii. 3. 193, 202.
[3] Hippoc. *Epidem.* i. 1.
[4] *IG* xii. 8. 377, 458, 459.
[5] *IG* xii. 3. 253.
[6] *IG* xii. 5. 484; *IG* xii. 8. 25, 27; *ibid.* 238; *ibid.* 642.
[7] For Carystus we have only one piece of evidence: *IG* xii. 9. 20. For Eretria see *IG* xii. 9. 191A, 234, 235, 240, 243 and 'Αρχ. Δελτ. 1915, 169 no. 10. For Chalcis, *IG* xii. 9. 904, 916.
[8] *IG* xii. 2. 134.
[9] Collignon (1877) 81–2 no. 3.
[10] Lapethus *OGI* 583; Chytri *IGRom.* iii. 935.

Eretria, two long inscriptions and a few others tell us some details about the ephebi. The oldest of these records,[1] from the end of the fourth century before Christ, is a treaty, which makes it a requirement that every year the ephebi should swear before the *strategoi* to abide by its terms. The two long inscriptions [2] are from the first century before Christ, and both honor gymnasiarchs. I will give a partial translation of the longer one, following with slight modifications the version of Richardson and Heermance: [3] "Elpinicus, son of Nicomachus, elected gymnasiarch by the people, has in general honorably discharged the duties of his office, and, when a considerable number of boys and of ephebi and of others subject to his jurisdiction were brought together, he took thought for their training, abiding in the gymnasium throughout the year; and he furnished at his own expense an instructor in rhetoric and one in heavy armed fighting, who devoted themselves in the gymnasium to the boys and the ephebi and all others who wished to receive profit from such training; and he took thought for the oil, also, that it be of the finest quality, himself defraying the expense incurred for this; he also instituted many *dolichoi* ("long races"), and at each *dolichos* performed a sacrifice to Hermes." The inscription proceeds to enumerate his generous benefactions, performed while

---

[1] *IG* xii. 9. 191A. *Ibid.* 240 gives us a list of about 37 ephebi for one year in the fourth century.
[2] *Ibid.* 234, 235.
[3] *AJArch.* XI. (1896) 175–6.

he was in office. Its companion record honors Mantidorus in similar terms; the latter, however, instead of furnishing an instructor in rhetoric and a *hoplomachos* secured a Homeric scholar from Athens.[1] It is interesting to note that the gymnasium of Eretria was excavated in the early nineties by the American archæologists. As for Chalcis, two or more gymnasia existed there from the middle of the third century,[2] but our earliest knowledge of the ephebia is from the second century.[3] The whole educational system there was entrusted to a gymnasiarch, who was thus in reality a superintendent of schools.

Ceos has furnished us three inscriptions on gymnasiarchs,[4] all from the third century before Christ. The longest (no. 647) refers to the introduction of the gymnasiarchy, a magistracy for which the age requirement was established as thirty; we may compare with this the Athenian law that the *sophronistai* be over forty years of age. We read on: "And the gymnasiarch shall hold a torch-race of the youths at the festival, look after the affairs of the gymnasium in general, and take his charges out three times a month to practice javelin throwing, archery, and the use of the catapult; whoever of the youths fails to appear when he is able to do so, shall be fined not more than one drachma."

---

[1] Ὁμηρικὸς φιλόλογος Διονύσιος Φιλώτου Ἀθηναῖος. The curious may read a translation of the entire inscription in *AJArch.* XI. (1896) 189.

[2] Ps.-Dicæarch. *GGM* I. 105. See also Plut. *Flam.* xvi.

[3] *IG* xii. 9. 904.

[4] *Ibid.* 5. 620, 621, 647.

The state not only furnished the catapult and other weapons but gave prizes for the best shooting. Surely the Cean law-givers had read Plato's *Laws*, for Plato had recommended, among his other schemes for state education, the reservation of open places for the practice of archery and throwing the javelin.[1] Another reason for believing that Ceos was in sympathy with Plato's *Laws*, is that the girls there exercised and even wrestled with the boys in the gymnasia.[2] Surely the philosopher would have been not a little delighted to see compulsory state education of a military character, in full swing a century after his death, on an island so close to the city where he had taught in the Academy.

On Naxos the ephebic alumni were organized to carry on the gymnastic training which they had enjoyed during their ephebia.[3] They were much more systematic about it than were the *neoi* generally. All who had just graduated from the ephebic college were banded together under the title of "last year's ephebi,"[4] and those who were one year out had a separate group called the "ephebi of year before last."[5] The one record we have shows about eighteen

---

[1] 804C.
[2] Ath. xiii. 20. The MSS. read ἐν Χίῳ, but Wilamowitz emended to Κέῳ, comparing Plut. *Mul. Virt.* xii. This emendation has been confirmed by Oldfather *RE* XIII. 1349, who observed that Ceos had close relations with the Locrians, and at Locri girls exercised in the gymnasia.
[3] *IG* xii. 5. 39.
[4] ἔφηβοι περυσινοί; cf. Poll. ii. 9.
[5] ἔφηβοι προπερυσινοί.

in the former class, and thirteen in the latter, an indication that the young men kept dropping out; indeed there is no indication of any class at all in the third year. The Naxian youths had, besides the gymnasiarch and under-gymnasiarch, a teacher of some sort (καθηγητής), and a gymnasium servant.

Paros had its ephebi,[1] and contests were held in running and wrestling, and especially the torch-race.[2] While the gymnasiarch and under-gymnasiarch headed the gymnastics of the island,[3] a *lampadarch* was appointed especially to take charge of the torch-race.[4] Metics were allowed the privileges of the gymnasium.[5] One feature that we meet here for the first time is a woman gymnasiarch.[6] Her name was Aurelia Leita, and she held her office at the end of the third century of our era. At Athens, where women were so completely excluded from public life, this would have been impossible, but Asia Minor and some of the islands in Roman times were more liberal in their attitude concerning women.[7] Naturally, a woman gymnasiarch

---

[1] *IG* xii. 5. 144, 145, 173, 232.
[2] *Ibid.* 137, 138.
[3] *Ibid.* 232, 1026.
[4] *Ibid.* 173, 174, 176.
[5] *Ibid.* 290.
[6] *Ibid.* 292.
[7] Oehler *RE* VII. 1983 lists sixteen localities, all in Asia Minor save Paros and Cyrene, which had, at one time or another, woman gymnasiarchs. It is now possible to add to his list Miletus (*Milet* i. 7 no. 265), Pergamum (*IGRom.* iv. 1687), the Pamphylian town Attalea (*SEG* ii. 696), and Mytilene on Lesbos (*IG* xii. 2. 232). See also the work of Braunstein: *Die politische Wirksamkeit der griechischen Frau*, Leipzig, 1911.

did not have as her province the direction of the exercises, but the furnishing of the oil and other necessaries; in the Christian era, the latter was the usual function of gymnasiarchs everywhere.[1]

In Amorgos, the town of Arcesine admitted boys to be ephebi at the age of sixteen.[2] Combining with this bit of information an inscription of Ægiale on the same island, which speaks of a lad being "just out of the *chlamys*" at eighteen,[3] we may deduce that the duration of ephebic service on Amorgos was two years, from sixteen to eighteen. Rarely are we given such precise data, and where we lack it, we presume that the usual ephebic period was only one year, from eighteen to nineteen, as was the practice at Athens in the third century and thereafter. The ephebi of Ægiale, of whom we have several lists,[4] numbered only six or ten a year; yet they had both a gymnasiarch and under-gymnasiarch set over them. One long inscription [5] tells of the foundation of a festival by one Critolaus, in memory of his dead son Aleximachus. Provision was made that in the sacred procession the ephebi should march, led by the gymnasiarch, and followed by all the younger boys: the ephebi, obviously, were too few to make an impressive line of march. Contests, including a torch-race, were ordered to form a part of the festival, and both young

[1] Ramsay II. 444.
[2] *IG* xii. 7. 115. Censorinus *de Die Nat.* xiv. 8 named sixteen as the ephebic age in Greece.
[3] *Ibid.* 447. [4] *Ibid.* 421–7. [5] *Ibid.* 515.

and old were to enter the contests. The gymnasiarch, whose charge was here only over the ephebi, was empowered to force the boys under the ephebic age to take part in the procession and the torch-race. Probably Aleximachus had been killed while engaged in a pancratium contest, for the command was given that the pancratium should not be included among the other contests, but announcement should be made, as if it were held, that the victor was Aleximachus, son of Critolaus. As for the town of Minoa, on the same island, no record is left of ephebi, and the Anointers Club established there, directed by a gymnasiarch and under-gymnasiarch, has already been spoken of.[1]

For Icaria we are poorly informed. An inscription [2] lists seventeen ephebi, headed by a gymnasiarch and an ephebarch. An epitaph [3] practically establishes the existence of a palæstra there in the first or second century after Christ; Philocrates, the gravestone says, died at the age of twelve, and thereby was prevented from "casting the *chlamys* about his body and gazing on Hermes, president of the gymnasium." In prosaic language, then, Philocrates was too young at the age of twelve to enter the gymnasium, much less the ephebic college (symbolized by the *chlamys*, as often), and we may therefore adduce the analogy of Athens once more, where boys entered the palæstra at seven, and the gymnasium at about fourteen.[4] We shall not,

[1] *IG* xii. 7. 232–5. See above, page 195.
[2] Printed in Collignon (1877) 81f. no. 3.
[3] Kaibel *Epigr. Gr.* 295.   [4] Ziebarth (1914) 83 n. 1.

I think, be wrong in judging this the almost universal practice.

Certainty regarding the existence of ephebi in Melos is dependent on a conjectural restoration of one inscription;[1] the only confirmation of this is the reference to an under-gymnasiarch in a second inscription.[2] Tenos had, besides the *neoi*, ephebi and gymnasiarchs.[3] Chios had three classes of ephebi, younger, middle, and older;[4] hence the ephebia there probably had a duration of three years. Three gymnasiarchs were chosen each year, one each for the boys, the ephebi, and the *neoi*. In addition to a gymnasium for the adults,[5] there was one named in honor of Homer,[6] for Chios was one of the chief claimants in the dispute over the place of Homer's nativity. Lesbos had its ephebi, with gymnasiarch, under-gymnasiarch, and ephebarch.[7]

Thera, besides having the usual ephebia with exactly the same leaders as on Lesbos,[8] offers one or two other points of interest. In 229 B.C., in the middle of a period when Thera was under the sway of the Ptolemies, the island's garrison was quartered in the gymnasium. Apparently the gymnasium was old, and

[1] *IG* xii. 3. 1074.
[2] *Ibid.* 1091.
[3] *Ibid.* 5. 818, 880–6, 911.
[4] *SIG*³ 959.
[5] τὸ πρεσβυτικόν: *IGRom.* iv. 1703.
[6] *CIG* 2221. On the Chian gymnasia see also *CIG* 2240; 'Αθηνᾶ XX. (1908) 164 no. 3B.
[7] *IG*. xii. 2. 134, 232, 241, 244, 258.
[8] *Ibid.* 3. 330, 338–40, 496, 517, 524.

the soldiers were moved to take up a subscription among themselves for its repair. The subscription list of ninety names is still preserved.[1] A class preparatory for the ephebia existed, comparable to the *mellephebi* (preparatory ephebi) of Piræus, but they were called by the unusual name of *parephebi*,[2] a term employed elsewhere only at Samos.[3] They used the gymnasium instead of the palæstra. For a palæstra at the town of Œa on Thera we have abundant proof; the boys who attended it frequently united to honor a benefactor or teacher.[4] The members of the gymnasium in Œa made similar dedications.[5] Besides the directors of the ephebic college, Thera had a *paidonomos* to direct the education of the boys.[6] Still a further noteworthy circumstance is that the under-gymnasiarch was in two cases the son of the gymnasiarch.[7] A responsive chord is struck in the hearts of school-boys everywhere on learning that the ephebi of Thera were wont to scratch their names on the walls of the gymnasium and carve them in the solid rock of a near-by cliff;[8] dozens of these boyish records have outlasted the centuries, and may still be seen.

[1] *IG* xii. 3. 327.
[2] *Ibid.* 339, 340. Cf. Oehler *RE* V. 2744.
[3] Wilamowitz *Nordion. Steine* 62 no. 21.
[4] *IG.* xii. 3. 526, 527, 529, 531. The dedications were made by οἱ μετέχοντες τῆς ἐν Οἴᾳ παλαίστρας.
[5] *Ibid.* 528, 534. Oehler *RE* VII. 2010 refuted the notion of Poland (103) that the members of the palæstra were identical with the members of the gymnasium.
[6] *IG* xii. 3 Suppl. 1299.
[7] *Ibid.* 1306, 1314.
[8] Ziebarth (1914) 100–1.

Quite similar to the school system of Thera was that of Cos: the same gymnasiarch, under-gymnasiarch, and *paidonomos* or "manager of boys."[1] The ephebarch is missing in our records, but on the other hand there was a priest of the ephebi,[2] a functionary unknown in Thera; we are reminded at once of the ephebic priest at Athens, called the *hypozakoros*. One case crops up of the gymnasiarchy being inherited by the son from the father;[3] such families of gymnasiarchs existed at Aphrodisias, Attalea, and Termessus.[4] School-boy scrawls from Cos have come to light in considerable numbers, recording the athletic victories of various ephebi.[5]

Samos not only had the ephebi, but had two preparatory groups, the *parephebi* and *pallekes* (πάλληκες)[6]. No way is known to determine which of these two groups consisted of older boys; neither do we know of their instructors. The ephebi and *neoi* were led by a gymnasiarch,[7] who was certainly director of the gymnasium, and was chosen by a show of hands in the assembly. Quite like the Athenian *kosmetes*, he looked out for the orderliness (εὐκοσμία) of the ephebi (and

---

[1] *Inscr. Cos* 34, 46, 107–11, 114, 119, 371–92. For the *paidonomos* Ziebarth (1914) 144 referred to two unpublished inscriptions.

[2] *Ibid.* 106.

[3] *Ibid.* 107.

[4] Liermann 65ff.; where the references are given.

[5] *Inscr. Cos* 65 Νίκη Κάσσου ἐφήβου. Herzog has found many of them: Ziebarth (1914) 105.

[6] *Parephebi:* Wilamowitz *Nordion. Steine* 62 no. 21; πάλληκες: *SIG*³ 1061.

[7] *SEG* i. 266.

neoi). The gymnasium was called the Eros Gymnasium.[1] Several victor lists found in Samos give a full picture of the various kinds of gymnastics and sports there employed. The *pallekes* trained in the use of the catapult, *lithobolos* (an artillery engine for hurling stones; not identical with the catapult), javelin, bow and arrow; they also trained in hoplomachy, in fighting with a large shield (θυρεαμαχία), in the stadium race, double race, and long race, and in diligence, discipline, and physical fitness. The last three were frequently the subjects of contests among the Greeks, as has been seen already. Contests other than these, for different ages, were wrestling, boxing, and the pancratium.[2] At Athens, as we were at great pains to show, the palæstra was always private, and was a school for boys; on Samos the reverse was true. A decree is preserved,[3] which was made in honor of a gymnasiarch by the Anointers Club of the men's (strictly "old men's") palæstra. That this was a state palæstra is made quite certain by the fact that its members decreed honors for the gymnasiarch, a state official.

A public educational system, centered around the palæstra and gymnasium,[4] prevailed on the island of

[1] Ath. xiii. 12.

[2] *AM* XXVIII. (1903) 353f. *JHS* VII. (1886) 148ff.

[3] *BCH* V. (1881) 480f. no. 3. Γερόντειαι παλαίστραι were also mentioned by Antiphanes *Fr.* 332 (I. 135 Kock). Cf. Schömann-Lipsius I. 551; Oehler *RE* VII. 2010.

[4] Dio Chr. xiv. 162 Budé. The gymnasium was referred to also by Polyb. v. 88. 5; Strab. xiv. 2. 5 (652 Cas.); *IG* xii. 1. 3.

Rhodes. In the second century before Christ, the Rhodians accepted from King Eumenes the royal gift of 280,000 medimni of grain; the proceeds from the sale of this were put out at interest, and the whole income used to pay the teachers, who were hired by the state. This was not an isolated case, and education in the Hellenistic period was public in numerous places, for the younger boys as well as for the ephebi. At Rhodes, the state superintendent of elementary education was not called by the usual name of *paidonomos*, but rather the "overseer of the boys."[1] The public gymnasium had existed in Rhodes from the early fifth century; but the people were hardly able to support it after a severe earthquake, which wrought havoc on their island. In modern times, international generosity in such a time of disaster is common, nor was it unknown in antiquity. The generous individuals this time were Hiero, the tyrant of Syracuse, and his brother Gelo, who sent to the Rhodians seventy-five silver talents to insure that plenty of oil might be supplied in the gymnasium.[2] That the gift was made for such a purpose, instead of for aiding the inhabitants of the island in recovering from the material effects of the earthquake, is an admirable illustration of the Greek passion for gymnastics. The Greeks were always ready to stint themselves in matters of personal luxury for the sake of erecting and maintaining struc-

---

[1] ἐπιστάτης τῶν παίδων. *IG* xii. 1. 43, 1. 22, and *AM* LI. (1926) 3.
[2] Polyb. v. 88. 5.

tures that glorified their city, a temple like the Parthenon, or a gymnasium like that of Rhodes. The common weal was put first, and individual comfort last. Rhodes also had organized ephebi,[1] but our scanty inscriptional evidence does not show whether they were led by the gymnasiarch. Foreigners were often admitted to the gymnasiarchy, and a single inscription[2] records two from Antioch and one each from Amphipolis and Soli. When Cæsar and Cicero studied at Rhodes, it had become an educational center comparable to the University of Athens. The relation of the ephebic college to the growth of university education at Rhodes can be traced still less than at Athens.

From half a dozen towns of the large island of Cyprus, we have documents which allow us to conclude that physical education enjoyed considerable favor there. The Gymnasium Club at Citium has been spoken of already (above, page 195); probably it was directed by the gymnasiarch, who is named in other inscriptions[3] of the same town. Paphos, the town so famed for the worship of Aphrodite, had a gymnasiarch,[4] hence, without doubt, a gymnasium. Chytri and Lapethus had ephebi, directed by ephebarchs.[5]

---

[1] *AM* XXI. (1896) 42 no. 9; *Jh. Österr.* VII. (1904) 92f.; *IG.* xii. 1. 95.

[2] *IG* xii. 1. 127.

[3] *CIG* 2626; *IGRom.* iii. 980, 982.

[4] *CIG* 2620, 2637; *OGI* i. 164–5; *IGRom.* iii. 950.

[5] *IGRom.* iii. 935; *OGI* ii. 583. An ephebic organization at Salamis was dubiously admitted by Poland (91), but Ziebarth ([1914] 95 n. 1) would supplement θιασῶται instead of ἔφηβοι in the inscription, Le Bas iii. 2756.

Lapethus had as superintendent of elementary education the gymnasiarch, and the same was true of Cerynia, where the boys of the palæstra united in honoring him.[1] Salamis had three gymnasia in the second century before Christ, but the groups who exercised there are unknown.[2]

For the small but important island of Delos, a vast number of inscriptions enable us to reconstruct the system of physical education in more detail than for any other island. Delos was a miniature Athens,[3] and one would therefore expect *a priori*, a close resemblance to the capital city in a phase of life so important to the Greeks as education. For the education of boys we should expect to find palæstræ, and to find that they were private. This was actually the case, and it corroborates the rule established in Chapter IV, that Athenian palæstræ were only for boys, and were owned and operated by private individuals.

There were, however, we hasten to add, two palæstræ on Delos which were owned by the temple, and the temple accounts from as early as 301 B.C. give us interesting little details of purchases for the palæstræ and outlay for their repair. Usually no distinction was made as to which palæstra was the one in question, but we are sure there were two, called the "lower

---

[1] *CIG* 2627. Cerynia also had a gymnasium, directed by a gymnasiarch; *REG* XVII. (1904) 212.

[2] Le Bas iii. 2756; gymnasiarch at Salamis: *CIG* 2630; *IGRom.* iii. 993–4.

[3] Ferguson 409.

palæstra" and the "old palæstra."[1] There was a well in the palæstra or near by, where the boys got their drinking-water. In 301 the temple officials bought a machine for raising water out of the well.[2] In the years immediately following, various repairs were made.[3] In 274 one Theophantus contracted to roof over several parts of the palæstra, which was unusually elaborate, as befitted a structure owned by the temple of Apollo; the rooms to be roofed over were the bath, the room for the *paidagogoi* or slave attendants, the anointing-room, the hall or *exedra*, the south porch, and two other porches which had formerly been roofless.[4] Other men in the same year contracted for the masonry, plastering, and tiling. In 250 some of the expenses were for ropes, anointing-oil, a victory fillet, sponges, and forty-five roof-tiles.[5] The rope was for the windlass of the well.[6] In 246 the well had to be cleaned out,[7] and about 224 this was done again.[8] Frequently the accounts record the purchase of a new spade for the palæstra; no doubt the spade was used to dig up the earth in the jumping and wrestling pits.[9] Again a

[1] *IG* xi. 2. 154A, l. 5 and 7 ἡ παλαίστρα ἡ κάτω; [*IG* xi. 3] 354, l. 76 ἡ ἀρχαία παλαίστρα. The author will refer to Durrbach *Inscriptions de Délos, Comptes des Hiéropes*, nos. 290–371 (Paris, 1926) as [*IG* xi. 3].

[2] A γαυλός: *IG* xi. 2. 146A, l. 29. See the new Liddell and Scott *s. v.*

[3] *Ibid.* 147A, l. 4; 154A, l. 5, 7, 8, 29; 156A, l. 58, 61ff., 65; 156B, l. 21f.

[4] *Ibid.* 199A, l. 104f.

[5] *Ibid.* 287A, l. 46, 74, 81, 113, 131, 133.

[6] [*IG* xi. 3] 354, l. 60 σχοινίον εἰς τὸν γαυλὸν τὸν ἐν τεῖ παλαίστραι; cf. l. 71, 78.

[7] *Ibid.* 290, l. 95.

[8] *Ibid.* 338A, l. 37.

[9] *Ibid.* 290, l. 76.

bar, or a lock and key, were purchased to secure the building at night.[1] The acquisition of a hoop (solemnly recorded on the books of a temple) gives proof from an unexpected source of the continuance of childhood games in the early palæstra training (see above, page 62). All these details, so trifling in themselves, have been thought worthy of record here, because they give a more concrete notion of the palæstra in its external features than we get anywhere in literature.

The janitor and general "handy man" about the palæstra was called, as in many other places, a *palaistrophylax*. The earliest record of one for Delos is in the accounts of 246 B.C.,[2] where the story runs that a "boy" was bought from Cimolus; seemingly he did not give satisfaction, for by public decree he was sold, and another was bought in the slave-market. In 231 a certain Papus was in service, and he did his work so well that he was retained for seven years or more.[3] The position carried an annual salary, or rather pittance, of 120 drachmas.[4]

Several private palæstræ on the island are known, and the *paidotribai* who owned them were sometimes foreigners, as we have conjectured was the case in Athens. One was owned by Niceratus & Son of Alexandria,[5] and a very popular one by Apollonius, son of Demetrius, from Laodicea.[6] Other foreign *pai-*

---
[1] *IG* xi. 2. 199A, l. 111; [*IG* xi. 3] 316, l. 72.
[2] [*IG* xi. 3] 290, l. 113ff.   [3] *Ibid.* 316, l. 117; 338A, l. 67.
[4] Homolle (1890) 488.   [5] *BCH* XV. (1891) 264 no. 5.
[6] *BCH* XIII. (1889) 420f. See Ziebarth (1914) 36.

dotribai, of unknown provenience, were Theodorus and Numenius.[1] The latter was too poor to buy or build a palæstra, and so he hired a house from the temple for 76 drachmas, making it serve as a palæstra. He taught there at least twelve years.[2] Not all the *paidotribai* who owned palæstræ were foreigners; Nicias and Staseas came from Athens.[3] The boys who attended the palæstræ were drawn from many countries, for Delos was a thoroughly cosmopolitan center. A single class of Nicias' comprised two boys from Athens, one from Laodicea, and another from the island of Myconus, north-east of Delos. Of a class of forty-two in the palæstra of Staseas, twenty-two came from Athens, others from Rome, Chios, Elea, Pelusium, Pitane in Æolis, Alexandria, Salamis, Thera, Ephesus, Chalcis, Patara, and the town of Carpasia in Cyprus. It is interesting to find that these boys loved to copy the organization of their city, wherefore they called themselves priests, *agonothetes* (directors of games), *lampadarchs* (directors of torch-races), and gymnasiarchs. In their palæstra life, moreover, they formed friendships and cliques which continued in the ephebia, to which we now turn.

While the ephebia was closely patterned after the Athenian model, it was on a smaller scale, and not all

---

[1] Theodorus is named in the fragmentary inscription *BCH* X. (1886) 38; Numenius, *BCH* XXXV. (1911) 75 no. 47.

[2] Ziebarth (1914) 36.

[3] Nicias: *BCH* XV. (1891) 263 no. 4; XXXII. (1908) 415f. nos. 3 and 4; XXXVI. (1912) 426 no. 20; Staseas: *Ibid.* XV. (1891) 255f. no. 2.

the details were the same.¹ A gymnasiarch served instead of a *kosmetes* at the head of the college, with the corresponding substitution of an under-gymnasiarch for an *antikosmetes*. The under-gymnasiarch was sometimes son of the gymnasiarch,² as at Thera; and after 166 we hear of him no more. The gymnasiarch was sent out from Athens, and was vested with great authority and importance.³ Like the Athenian *kosmetes*, he was concerned with all phases of the ephebic activity and the life that centered about the gymnasium.⁴ Not only was he a magistrate,⁵ but he conjoined with his duties some liturgical expenses;⁶ and indeed this was true in dozens of other places. On relinquishing office at the end of the year, he was obliged to submit to an accounting.⁷

The ephebic *paidotribes*,⁸ while not so grand a personage as the gymnasiarch, meant a great deal to the ephebi, and frequently remained in office several

---

¹ It had existed before the Athenian occupation in 166 B.C., but all that is known of it in this earlier time is that it was led by a gymnasiarch and under-gymnasiarch, and held a torch-race: *IG* xi. 4. 1151. *BCH* XV. (1891) 252.

² *BCH* XXXVI. (1912) 391 no. 5.

³ *IG* ii. 2. 985; Fougères (1891) 268–9. A complete and valuable list of these gymnasiarchs from 166/5 to 112/1 has been found: *BCH* XXXVI. (1912) 395ff. no. 9.

⁴ Fougères *l. c.* Oehler *RE* VII. 1990.

⁵ Elected annually: *BCH* XIII. (1889) 420 οἱ ἀεὶ χειροτονούμενοι γυμνασίαρχοι.

⁶ *BCH* XIII. (1889) 413ff.

⁷ *Ibid.*

⁸ Fougères (1891) 274 did not distinguish the ephebic *paidotribes* from the *paidotribes* who headed the boys' palæstra. Roussel, *BCH* XXXII. (1908) 373, naturally objected to this.

years in succession,[1] while a new gymnasiarch was sent out from Athens every year. The *paidotribes* taught all the exercises himself, and was so busy that he occasionally required a colleague;[2] it may be that pupil-teachers aided him, too. Nothing prevented a foreigner from getting a position[3] as ephebic *paidotribes;* two came from Alexandria. Other gymnastic teachers probably did not exist; yet there may have been a *hoplomachos* occasionally, for one inscription says that Apollonius of Laodicea, about 138 B.C., "supervised the ephebi for several years in their armed drill."[4]

The ephebi, like the pupils of the palæstra, came from all over the Mediterranean world. While the largest percentage was Athenian, others were from Rome, Tarentum, Sidon, Tyre, Damascus, Ascalon, Seleucia, Laodicea, Megalopolis, Alabanda, Phaselis, Sinope, Byzantium, Cnossus, Chios, Tenedos, Naxos, Thera, Chalcis, Thebes, and Nicopolis. Certainly Delos can take its stand among the most prominent educational centers of the ancient world. From the dedications made by the Delian ephebi, the national spirit is discernible. Some cliques were all Athenian,[5] some all Syrian[6] (for Syria sent many ephebi to Delos, as well as to Athens). Some were

[1] Fougères (1891) 273.
[2] *BCH* XV. (1891) 252 no. 1.
[3] *Ibid.* 261 no. 3; XXXII. (1908) 414f. no. 2.
[4] *Ibid.* XIII. (1889) 420.
[5] *Ibid.* XV. (1891) 252 no. 1.
[6] *Ibid.* XVI. (1892) 159 no. 17.

made up of foreigners from everywhere,[1] some had foreigners and Athenians commingled.[2] A noteworthy case, as showing how closely related the ephebia of Delos was to that of Athens, is that of Simalus, son of Simalus, from Tarentum. In 102/1 he was enrolled among the ephebi at Delos,[3] but in 101/0 he enrolled for his second year's training at Athens.[4] Probably the ephebic training at Athens was considered more valuable, although personal reasons of one kind or another might have been the determining influence, as often nowadays in passing from one school to another. The Delian ephebic organization lasted only a century and a half, too, while that of Athens lasted six centuries or more. As Fougères observed,[5] the history of the Delian ephebia was linked with the island's prosperity, and after the looting by the pirates in 48 B.C., the island was too impoverished to support it any longer.

As a corollary to Delos might be added Salamis, another Athenian cleruchy to which a gymnasiarch was sent. Our single inscription on the subject [6] honors the gymnasiarch Theodotus, from the Piræus, because he performed the fitting sacrifices, entertained the Anointers Club at the sacrificial feast, expended money on oil in addition to the funds entrusted to

---

[1] *BCH* XXXII. (1908) 414 no. 2.
[2] *Ibid.* 415 no. 3; for other instances see Ferguson 409 n. 4.
[3] *Ibid.* XV. (1891) 261 no. 3.
[4] *IG* ii. 1². 1028 col. 2, l. 145.
[5] (1891) 288.
[6] *IG* ii. 1². 1227.

him for that purpose, led the practice marches every month on the appointed days, built up the south wall of the gymnasium porch, conducted himself justly and zealously, and rendered a satisfactory account of his actions at the close of his term of service.

Leaving the multitudinous islands, we turn to Asia Minor. Here physical education was extraordinarily widespread, carried on privately and publicly, by boys, and in some places by girls, by ephebi and *neoi*, and even sometimes by the older men of the *gerusia* (senate). From dozens of towns we have but one or two paltry records, all much alike, proving the existence there of *neoi*, or ephebi, or a gymnasium and gymnasiarch. For the sake of clear presentation, let us first discuss as fully as possible the organized physical education of three cities, from which we have relatively abundant records, and then treat the rest topically and summarily.

The great and powerful city of Pergamum may serve as our first illustration. The educational system there was wholly public. Separate gymnasia were erected for the boys, ephebi, and *neoi*, the gymnasium of the boys [1] taking the place of the Athenian palæstra. Elementary education was shared by boys and girls alike, and the numbers in attendance were such that one superintendent, or *paidonomos*, was insufficient, and from two to four were required.[2] When parades

[1] τὸ γυμνάσιον παίδων: *Inscr. Perg.* 467.
[2] Two: *AM* XXVII. (1902) 126 no. 145; XXXIII. (1908) 388f. no. 6; four: *AM* XXIX. (1904) 171.

were held, the *paidonomoi* marched at the head of their charges.[1] Slaves were excluded, the education being, as in many other places, for the "free boys."[2] The teachers of the girls had as their task the moulding of their pupils to suppleness and grace. While the Spartans made the girls of their country perform even heavy exercises, with the purpose of producing a buxom, hardy, athletic type, the Pergamenes had rather the aim of modern boarding schools and colleges for girls, namely to produce a type that was light and slender, by means of the more polite exercises. Hence dancing and light gymnastics were prescribed for the maidens of Pergamum,[3] and their teachers were called "instructors in propriety."[4] The divisions which they formed were called *speirai* or "bands."[5] Their examinations were made a formal affair, directed by the teachers, and in the presence of the priests and high officials of the city.[6]

A second gymnasium was exclusively for the ephebi.[7] At the age of fifteen, considerably earlier than in Athens, the boys were enrolled on the ephebic lists.[8] The only list still preserved, the one for 147/6 B.C., records 178 ephebi, a total rarely reached even in Athens, at any time after compulsory service was

[1] *AM* XXXII. (1907) 243 no. 4, l. 45.
[2] *OGI* ii. 764, l. 3 and 19.
[3] See the comments of Fränkel on *Inscr. Perg.* 463.
[4] οἱ ἐπὶ τῆς εὐκοσμίας, *Inscr. Perg.* 463; *AM* XXXVII. (1912) 277 no. 1.
[5] *AM* XXXVII. (1912) 286 no. 13.
[6] *Ibid.* 277 no. 1.
[7] *Inscr. Perg.* 458. [8] *AM* XXIX. (1904) 171ff.

abandoned. Not alone the boys of Pergamum were enrolled, but if the sons of the *parœci* or people who lived anywhere in the Pergamene realm, cared to come, they were welcome.[1] We may consider Pergamum, therefore, as a local educational center, while Athens and Delos were international. So numerous were the ephebi that more than the ordinary number of officials were set over them; besides the gymnasiarch and under-gymnasiarch,[2] there were ephebarchs[3] and *ephebophylakes* ("ephebic guards").[4] How all these divided the labor and responsibility is not known. The gymnasiarch was the highest educational official, ranking above the *paidonomoi*, and no other was so often and so highly honored as he.[5] "So-and-so was a zealous gymnasiarch of both the gymnasia; he looked after the discipline and education of the *neoi* and ephebi, as the law demanded and his ambitions prompted."[6] "Strato took thought that the ephebi should be serious in their studies, . . . and in addition to the two teachers, he brought in other two

---

[1] *AM* XXXV. (1910) 422 no. 11. Any foreigner had the privilege of exercising in the gymnasium of the *neoi*: *AM* XXXII. (1907) 274ff. no. 10, l. 19.

[2] *Inscr. Perg.* 256, 323, 458, 465. *AM* XXXII. (1907) 243f. no. 4; XXXIII. (1908) 338f. no. 6.

[3] *Inscr. Perg.* 273B, 465.

[4] *Ibid.* 486B; *AM* XXVII. (1902) 105 no. 108. Found also at Priene: *Inscr. Prien.* 313.

[5] His praises are sounded in fairly brief and simple terms in the following inscriptions: *Inscr. Perg.* 440, 457, 459; *CIG* 3551 (supplemented by Fränkel *Inscr. Perg.* Vol. 2, p. 513); *AM* XXXIII. (1908) 382 and 407 no. 37.

[6] *Inscr. Perg.* 458.

at his own expense, that the ephebi might not be deprived of any of the necessary subjects, . . . and all the year long he distributed oil liberally at his own expense." [1] "So-and-so, being appointed gymnasiarch, . . . took care of the discipline and orderliness of the ephebi and *neoi*, giving prizes for scholarship, and exercising much forethought for training the lads in all the studies; he supplied an abundance of all sorts of arms, and brought in a teacher at his own expense." [2] "Agias when gymnasiarch put aside all his other affairs, and, thinking his watchful presence in the gymnasium most desirable, never neglected anything in his oversight of the discipline of the ephebi and *neoi;* with an austere loathing for evil, he made provision for the observance of good order and good behavior around the gymnasium." [3] "The gymnasiarch Athenæus was crowned with golden crowns at the Hermæa, by the ephebi, the *neoi*, and the teachers." [4] These are only samples, but they help us to form a conception of the activities, and the importance in the public eye, of the highest educational officer in ancient Pergamum. The usual rule was that a gymnasiarch served only one year, but those who served twice were not infrequent; [5] one inscription calls C. Aulus Julius Quadratus a life-long gym-

[1] *AM* XXXII. (1907) 279ff. no. 11.
[2] *Ibid.* XXXIII. (1908) 376f.
[3] *Ibid.* 380.
[4] *Ibid.* XXXV. (1910) 401ff. no. 1b.
[5] *Ibid.* XXXIII. (1908) 407 no. 37. An under-gymnasiarch, also, might serve twice: *Inscr. Perg.* 468.

nasiarch,[1] but this was in late Roman times, when the gymnasiarchy consisted in nothing but supplying oil. It was in this same period that a woman was allowed to hold the gymnasiarchy.[2]

The ephebi were divided into three groups as soon as they were enrolled, the basis of the grouping being their past record and an examination on entrance to the ephebic college. The groups were the Orderly (εὔτακτοι), the Industrious (φιλόπονοι), and the Fit (εὐέκται).[3] Already at Sestos and Samos we have found emphasis laid on these same qualities, and prizes offered for excellence in them. As for the exercises of the ephebi, little is known. A torch-race is referred to in one inscription,[4] and contests in armor repeatedly. The teachers were not individualized, but were simply called *paideutai;* we may, however, feel reasonably sure that a *hoplomachos* or teacher of heavy-armed fighting is referred to in the inscription quoted above where it is stated that the gymnasiarch supplied all sorts of arms and a teacher. Parades, processions, and sacrifices formed part of the ephebic life in Pergamum as at Athens.[5]

How long the lads of Pergamum remained in the ephebia, the records do not say. Entering the *neoi,*

[1] *Inscr. Perg.* 440.
[2] *IGRom.* iv. 1687.
[3] εὔτακτοι and εὐέκται, *AM* XXXIII. (1908) 388f. no. 6; φιλόπονοι, *Inscr. Perg.* 562 (as supplemented by Jacobsthal *AM l. c.*).
[4] *AM* XXIX. (1904) 152 no. 1, l. 43.
[5] See *AM* XXXII. (1907) 243ff. no. 4, l. 43ff. for a parade of ephebi, led by gymnasiarch and under-gymnasiarch.

which was the next step, was not an official act under state supervision, as was the enrolment among the ephebi. The *neoi* were not strictly a part of the state educational system, but the state did supply a gymnasium for them,[1] and that the finest and largest of all. This gymnasium the *neoi* used as a sort of club-house, as well as a place in which to carry on exercises. The political strength of the organization of *neoi* was well recognized, and in this respect they played far more of a rôle than the ephebi.[2] So important were they that the emperor Antoninus Pius once wrote them a letter;[3] if we will let our imagination play a little, we may realize the thrill that came with that imperial letter. As has been seen already, the gymnasiarch led the *neoi* as well as the ephebi, and he exerted himself magnanimously in their behalf. In 127 B.C. the gymnasiarch Diodorus found the gymnasium of the *neoi* so out of repair that it could not be used; he set to work energetically and soon restored the structure to its former splendor.[4]

These three gymnasia formed a great and unified school system, of which the excavations at Pergamum have enabled us to get a material concept. While in Athens the gymnasia were scattered, and the ephebi spent many hours in travelling from one to another, Pergamum had a centralized grouping. Off the prin-

[1] *Inscr. Perg.* 278 and many other inscriptions.
[2] They called themselves "the august synod of the young men" ἡ σεβαστὴ σύνοδος τῶν νέων: *Inscr. Perg.* 440. Their "synod" had a secretary: *ibid.* 571.
[3] *Inscr. Perg.* 275.
[4] *OGI* ii. 764. See Ziebarth (1914) 71-2.

cipal street of the city, one entered the school grounds through an ornamental gateway. There towered the three gymnasia, built on terraces, one above the other. Fittingly, the elementary school was on the lowest terrace, above it was the gymnasium of the ephebi, and still higher rose the gymnasium of the *neoi*, a structure so large that it contained an assembly hall capable of seating a thousand persons.[1] Nor were the citizens of Pergamum content with three gymnasia; in the reign of Attalus III. Philometor (138–3 B.C.), a fourth existed,[2] a century and a half later a fifth.[3] Athens was the only city in the ancient world that had more gymnasia, and it had only two more.[4] What disposition Pergamum made of the two additional gymnasia is not known, but they help prove the enthusiasm of this great city for physical education.

Another city which deserves to engage our attention is Miletus. Even before Hellenistic times, the Milesians were famed above the other Ionians for their gymnastics, as Plato remarked;[5] but most of our

[1] Dörpfeld in *AM* XXXIII. (1908) 335. Cf. Ziebarth (1914) 80–1.

[2] *AM* XXIX. (1904) 152 no. 1, l. 58 τέσσαρα γυμνάσια.

[3] *Ibid.* XXXII. (1907) 321f. no. 50. There was a sixth ἐν τῷ κοινῷ τῆς ’Ασίας (see *Inscr. Perg.* Vol. 2, p. 194, in commentary on no. 260), but it was not necessarily in Pergamum. See Oehler *RE* VII. 2007.

[4] Oehler *RE* VII. 2012 reckoned nine gymnasia at Athens, but the separate existence of a "gymnasium of ephebi" is hardly tenable (above, page 155, note 3), and the γυμνάσιον Διὶ Κεραιῶι καὶ Ἄνθαι of *BSA* III. (1896–7) 106 probably existed in Bœotia, whence the inscription concerning it strayed to Athens: such is the sagacious judgment of Adolf Wilhelm *Jh. Österr.* VIII. (1905) 278; cf. Ziebarth (1914) 52 and 72.

[5] *Legg.* i. 636B.

information is from the inscriptions of a later time. Physical education was commenced in the palæstra,[1] under the supervision of *paidotribai*.[2] The palæstra was not a private school but part of the public school system, and the *paidotribai* were salaried by the state. Our most interesting and extensive document concerning the Milesian elementary schools dates from 200/199 B.C.[3] A citizen named Eudemus gave the state ten silver talents, or some $12,000 in our currency (with of course a much greater purchasing power), "for the education of the free boys."[4] A civic decree was made, providing for the expenditure of the income from this endowment. The salaries of the teachers were probably raised, and there was bound to be more competition for their positions: hence the ruling was made that any who wished to be *paidotribai* or teachers of grammar and literature, should make a written declaration of their candidacy to the *paidonomoi*-elect. The latter posted their names in a public place and a few days later a public assembly gathered in the theater for the choice of the teachers. In the orchestra of the theater was set up a tripod and censer; around it stood to offer the gods an odor of sweet incense, the priest of Hermes Enagonios, whose shrine was in the boys' palæstra, the priest of the Muses, representing the

[1] ἡ παιδικὴ παλαίστρα *Milet* I. 7, no. 203. A fine epigram on a pupil of the Miletus palæstra, who died at the age of eight, was published by Haussoullier *Rev. Philol.* XXXIII. (1909) 6.

[2] *Milet* I. 7, no. 305.

[3] *SIG*³ 577.

[4] εἰς παιδείαν τῶν ἐλευθέρων παίδων.

grammar-school cult, the priestly herald, the *paidonomoi*, who had been elected at a previous assembly by a show of hands and now were about to assume their magistracy, and finally Eudemus (or, after his death, the oldest representative of his line). As incense burned in honor of Hermes, the Muses, and Apollo, the herald offered prayer: "Whoever chooses as *paidotribai* and grammar-school teachers the ones who will, as he believes, best lead the boys, whoever is not swayed by unjust and partisan motives in fixing on his choice, on that man may blessing come; if one does not so act, may the opposite of a blessing befall him." Next, the *paidonomoi* handed to the secretary of the senate a list of those who were making application for the teaching positions; as the secretary called their names, one by one they stepped forward and were sworn by the priests and herald according to this formula: "I swear by Hermes that I have not prevailed upon any one of he Milesians to vote for me, nor have I commanded any one to electioneer for me." The prospective *paidotribai* swore by Hermes in this oath, the others by Apollo and the Muses. Then came the show of hands, electing four *paidotribai* and four teachers of grammar and literature.

The monthly salary of the *paidotribai* was established at thirty drachmas, that of the other teachers at forty drachmas; the *paidotribai*, it appears were not valued quite so highly as the teachers of the mental disciplines. The examinations and general activity of the schools were regulated by a school law (παιδονομικὸς νόμος). If the *paidotribai* had excellent pupils, whom they wished to take out of town to games in another locality, they could be granted a few days leave of absence by the *paidonomoi*, provided that they offered a satisfactory substitute. The *paidonomoi* were compelled by law to sacrifice a steer annually to Apollo at the nearby Didyma; in the procession which went to make the offering, chosen boys marched, led by the *paidonomoi*, the eight teachers, and the benefactor Eudemus, or, after his death, his oldest descendant. The fifth of every month was ordained as a holiday, Eudemus Day, in addition to other holidays that came irregularly.

The one thing that stands out most in the decree, the text of which I have followed closely in the above, is the surpassing importance attributed to the elementary education. The choice of the teachers was made with great solemnity, and was based strictly on merit, not on political, partisan, or personal grounds. Certainly every effort was made to impress on the teachers their responsibility, and the Milesian *paidotribai* and palæstræ must have been models of their kind. It is refreshing to find a case of a city devoting such extreme care to the education of its children.

The ephebi of Miletus had been organized since 260 B.C. or earlier, and our first record of them [1] refers to the ephebic oath which they took at the end of

[1] *Milet* I. 3, no. 139, l. 47ff.

their service: "I will abide by the decrees of the people, and observe the alliance of friendship with King Ptolemy and his descendants." Such oaths were surely universal among the ephebi of Greece and the Greek world, even where our documents have not preserved the evidence.[1] We have already noticed the ephebic oath in Crete and at Athens, and we have knowledge of it also in Ephesus,[2] Eretria on Eubœa,[3] and Cibyra.[4] Gymnasiarchs headed the ephebi, and offered sacrifice with them at the beginning of the year, an act in which they were supported by their immediate predecessors and the class that had just graduated.[5] The ephebi shared the gymnasium of the *neoi*, although the latter had separate gymnasiarchs.[6] The term *neaniskarch* ("leader of the youths") was employed among the *neoi* as an honorary distinction[7]; perhaps the *neaniskarch* was like the president of a modern college class. Miletus had two other gymnasia, besides the one which served for ephebi and *neoi*; one was for the *gerusia*, and one for

---

[1] Busolt I. 224.
[2] Ziebarth (1910) 108.
[3] *IG* xii. 9. 191A, l. 44ff.
[4] Liermann *Analecta* pp. 60–1, part C. This oath was so different from any other exacted of ephebi that we quote it: ὀμνύτωσαν δὲ καθ' ἕκαστον ἐνιαυτὸν οἱ ἔφηβοι ἐν τῷ γυμνασίῳ τὸν πάτριον ὅρκον συνφυλάξειν τὴν γυμνασιαρχίαν καὶ πάντας τοὺς πόρους αὐτῆς. "Let the ephebi take the traditional oath every year to help in protecting the gymnasiarchy and all its revenues." See Ziebarth (1914) 164.
[5] *Milet* I. 7, no. 203.
[6] *Ibid.* no. 265, with the commentary by Rehm.
[7] *Ibid.* no. 212, with the commentary by Rehm. Far different was the *neaniskarch* of S. Russia and a few other places.

the citizenry in general. The three were called the Big Gymnasium, Capito Gymnasium, and Faustina Gymnasium.[1] A remarkable case was that of a woman who served as gymnasiarch of the *neoi*, gymnasiarch of the *gerusia*, gymnasiarch of the citizens, and *paidonomos*.[2] That the members of the *gerusia* exercised strenuously we need not believe, but no doubt they exercised a little, and, for the rest, used their gymnasium as a club.

A good parallel to the educational system of Miletus is that of the much smaller Ionian town, Teos. In the second century before Christ, a wealthy man named Polythrus saw that the money for teachers' salaries was often lacking, and made an endowment of 34,000 drachma "in order that all the free boys might be educated."[3] As in Miletus the teachers were to be elected by the people, and not by a school board or superintendent. Three men to teach grammar and literature to both boys and girls, were to receive as annual salary 600, 550, and 500 drachmas, the amount varying with their rank. Two *paidotribai* were to receive 500 drachmas apiece, and the one music teacher was to get 700 drachmas. Of less importance were the *hoplomachos*, *akontistes*, and *toxotes*, wherefore they were not chosen by the people, but were hired by the gymnasiarch and *paidonomos*, subject, however, to confirmation by the people. The latter three taught the older boys and the

[1] *CIG* 2881.   [2] *Milet* I. 7, no. 265.   [3] *SIG*³ 578.

ephebi; the *hoplomachos* received a salary of 300 drachmas, the *akontistes* and *toxotes* 250 apiece. Apparently the *hoplomachos*, at least, never taught more than a portion of the year, for the decree provided that he must earn his 300 drachmas by teaching at least two months. The *paidonomos* was charged by law to see that the boys and girls were capably trained, and the gymnasiarch was given the same charge over the ephebi. The law also required that public examinations or exhibitions should be conducted by the teachers, in order that the parents and friends of the pupils might know what proficiency the latter were attaining. Like the more important teachers, the *paidonomos* and gymnasiarch were chosen by the people, and it was made a rule that no *paidonomos* should be under forty years of age, the same rule that applied to the *sophronistai* at Athens.

Noteworthy in these arrangements is the instruction of girls in the school subjects, but apparently not in physical education. As at Miletus, the *paidotribai* were not so highly paid as the teachers of music and the mental disciplines, but the instructors in the military arts fared still worse. Humanistic education in this late period was everywhere driving the physical, and especially the military, training out of the curriculum.

The ephebia had more of a military character at Teos than in most parts of Asia Minor, for three separate military teachers are found nowhere else. Besides the teachers we have named and the gymnasiarch, they had an ephebarch.[1] The *neoi* existed there, as is attested by some fifteen inscriptions,[2] but no details about them are known.

That the primary education was public in many other cities of Asia Minor is certain. Wherever a *paidonomos* existed, the state at least had direct oversight of the palæstræ and primary schools, and probably owned them. In addition to the places already mentioned, *paidonomoi* are attested for Colophon Nova, Ephesus, Magnesia on the Mæander, Priene, Tralles, Mylasa, Stratonicea, Iasus, Eriza, Themisonium, Pessinus, Termessus, Smyrna, Elæa, and Cyzicus.[3] Of these cities, Ephesus, Priene, Magnesia, and Smyrna, like Pergamum and Miletus, had schools so flourishing that two or more *paidonomoi* were needed constantly, while Stratonicea assigned to the *paidonomos* special

[1] *CIG* 3085.
[2] E. g., *SEG* ii. 610-2.
[3] Colophon Nova: *Jh. Österr.* VIII. (1905) 162f.
Ephesus: *Br. Mus. Inscr.* 481. l. 170, 174.
Magnesia on the Mæander: *Inscr. Magn.* 98.
Priene: *Inscr. Prien.* 104, 108, 111.
Tralles: Papakonstantinu Τράλλεις nos. 40, 148.
Mylasa: Contoleon Μικρασιαναὶ ἐπιγραφαί no. 57.
Stratonicea: *CIG* 2715.
Iasus: *BCH* XI. (1887) 215f. nos. 6-7.
Eriza: *BCH* XIII. (1889) 335f.
Themisonium: Michel 544.
Pessinus: *AM* XXV. (1900) 441 no. 69.
Termessus: Lanckoronski II. 199 no. 34; II. 201 no. 44.
Smyrna: *CIG* 3185.
Elæa: *Inscr. Perg.* 246, l. 36.
Cyzicus: *SIG*[3] 798.

Of the islands, Cos, Thera, and Astypalæa had *paidonomoi;* so of course had Sparta and Crete at a much earlier time.

slave assistants (παιδοφύλακες). The freedman who held the office of *paidonomos* at Iasus [1] must have been specially qualified, for customarily men of high rank were chosen as school leaders. Smyrna imitated Pergamum in having an "instructor of propriety" for the girls; [2] hence we may add it to the brief list of towns which allowed girls to share in the public education. Magnesia on the Mæander must be added, too, for there the *gynaikonomoi* ("superintendents of the women"), headed the education of the girls.[3] Even where there was no *paidonomos*, the authority of the gymnasiarch could be extended over the boys, rendering us equally certain that the palæstra education was public: this was true at Attalea in Pamphylia.[4] We hear of *paidotribai* in Smyrna, Iasus, Lampsacus, and Ilium,[5] and of palæstræ in Magnesia, Mylasa, Theangela, Cnidus, and Halicarnassus.[6] The one at Mylasa was founded by some king, perhaps Philip V,[7] and the one at Theangela by the people in honor of some king. The Halicarnassus palæstra was public, and when the gymnasium of the *neoi* fell into disrepair, the *neoi* were temporarily allowed the use of the palæstra.

[1] *BCH* XI. (1887) 215 no. 6.
[2] *CIG* 3185.
[3] *Inscr. Magn.* 98 l. 20.
[4] *IGRom.* iii. 777, 783; *SEG* ii. 696. See Busolt I. 496.
[5] Smyrna: *CIG* 3384; Iasus: Ziebarth (1914) 117; Lampsacus: *CIG* 3644; Ilium: *CIG* 3620.
[6] Magnesia: *Inscr. Magn.* 102; Mylasa: *CIG* 2692, 2693d; Theangela: *AM* XII. (1887) 334; Cnidus: *Br. Mus. Inscr.* 797; Halicarnassus: *Jh. Österr.* XI. (1908) 56f. no. 2.
[7] Ziebarth (1914) 37 n. 2.

In the Hellenistic period even slaves were occasionally permitted to share in the privileges of the gymnasium. This has already been noticed at Argos; and at Gythium in Laconia slaves were allowed to exercise in the gymnasia, receiving their share of the oil, six days in a year, "neither archon nor senator nor gymnasiarch preventing." [1] At Priene the generous Dioscurides "shared the gymnasium with those whose ill fortune gave no right to it," [2] and Zosimus in his gymnasiarchy was equally magnanimous to the slaves of Priene.[3] At Dorylæum in Phrygia, Asclepiades was gymnasiarch of free men and slaves, while his wife Antiochis was gymnasiarch of the women.[4]

Of the highest significance for physical education in this period, in Asia Minor as at Athens, were the ephebi. The spread of ephebic organizations, always forming part of the state education, was greater in Asia Minor than in Greece. Oehler in 1905 [5] listed forty-five cities and towns in Asia Minor alone which had ephebi; Poland's list had forty-two.[6] We may now add Miletus and the Lycian town, Lydæ.[7] Concerning the entrance age, information is generally lacking. If the standard was eighteen, as at Athens, it was not strictly observed; in Cius, Bithynia, there

---

[1] *IG* v. 1. 1208.
[2] *Inscr. Prien.* 123=*CIG* 2906.
[3] *Ibid.* 112, l. 99f.
[4] *OGI* ii. 479.
[5] *RE* V. 2742-3.
[6] Besides pages 90-2, see his *Nachträge*, pp. 537-8.
[7] *TAM* ii. 1. 132.

are seven cases of brothers among fifty-six ephebi, and one case of three brothers.¹ At Iasus similar laxity prevailed.² A poor authority, the romancer called Xenophon of Ephesus (i. 2. 2), gave sixteen as the age for entering the ephebia at Ephesus. The customary length of time spent in the ephebia was presumably one year, as was the case at Cyzicus, Priene, and Iasus; a boy who repeated the course at the former place was placed at the head of the register as a mark of honor.³ At Halicarnassus and the Pontic Heraclea there were classes of younger ephebi, a fact which indicates a two-year ephebic service;⁴ the same was true at Apollonis in Lydia, where there were three classes, one each for the first semester, the second semester, and the second year.⁵ The utter disproportion between the numbers of the first and second year, however, shows that the second year was voluntary. Of a special school to prepare the future ephebi (*mellephebi*), we hear only at Mylasa.⁶

¹ *AM* XXIV. (1899) 416ff. no. 14, with the commentary by Körte.
² Reinach (1893) 163.
³ *CIG* 3665. The unusual lad was termed β' ἔφηβος (ephebus for the second time). At Priene (*Inscr. Prien.* 147) four out of about twenty-one in one list were β' ἔφηβοι. For Iasus see Reinach (1893) 162.
⁴ Halicarnassus: *SBWien Ak.* CXXXII. (1895) 29 no. 2; Heraclea Pontica: *BCH* XXII. (1898) 493f. no. 2.
⁵ *BCH* XI. (1887) 86f. no. 6; *Denkschr. Wien. Ak.* LIII. (1910) 47ff. no. 97; *REG* III. (1890) 69 no. 22. The Greek names for these divisions were ἡμετεῖς, ἐφέτειοι and διετεῖς.
⁶ *BCH* XII. (1888) 33 no. 13. Girard (1891) 58, n. 3, declared that the word *mellephebus* was here used in a non-technical sense. Possibly this is true, yet there was an ephebia at Mylasa: *SBWien Ak.* CXXXII. (1895) 12 no. 1, and the author sees no clear reason for not agreeing with Poland (97) in thinking the term here used technically.

Much less frequently than in Greece and the islands were the ephebi of Asia Minor headed by gymnasiarchs. Besides the three cities already discussed, Pergamum, Miletus, and Teos, the author knows only four others where it is certain that the ephebi were under gymnasiarchal direction; Cibyra, Colophon Nova, Elæa, and Priene.[1] Wherever the gymnasiarch did lead the ephebi, he corresponded exactly with the Athenian *kosmetes;* this is well evidenced by an inscription of Priene,[2] which says that he "maintained orderliness (εὐκοσμία), making the teachers coöperate with him in this." The same inscription shows his authority over the teachers: "Zosimus (the gymnasiarch) held contests in the literary studies and in the gymnastic activities, obliging the teachers to give the exhibitions in these as was required by law." Again like the Athenian *kosmetes,* the gymnasiarch was always a leading citizen, one who held public office and was highly esteemed by all.[3] The assistant gymnasiarch (ὑπογυμνασίαρχος) was not common in Asia Minor, but did exist in Cius, Bithynia, where, however, the gymnasiarchy was of a liturgical nature and a *kosmetes* led the ephebi.[4] In another Bithynian town, Nicæa, and in Ilium, the leader of the

---

[1] Cibyra: Liermann *Analecta* pp. 60–1; Colophon Nova: *Jh. Österr.* VIII. (1905) 162f.; *BCH* XXXVII. (1913) 241 no. 48; Elæa: *Inscr. Perg.* 246 (l. 35); Priene: *Inscr. Prien.* 99, 104, 108, 111 (l. 193), 113 (l. 114f.).

[2] *Inscr. Prien.* 113 (l. 26f.).

[3] Collignon (1877) 40.

[4] *AM* XXIV. (1899) 416ff. no. 14. The ὑπογυμνασίαρχος was also to be found in Apollonis: *Denkschr. Wien. Ak.* LIII. (1910) 47ff. nos. 96–7; and in Halicarnassus: Le Bas iii. 502.

ephebi was a *kosmetes*.[1] Dumont remarked in 1876 (I. 174) that "the *kosmetes* figures only in the inscriptions of Attica;" so rich have been the epigraphical finds since he penned those words that we now find the *kosmetes* figuring in three inscriptions of Asia Minor, not to mention dozens of inscriptions and papyri of Egypt.[2]

The more usual head of the ephebi in Asia Minor was the ephebarch. Granting that the ephebarch was in a few places only an honorary official, there is yet plenty of testimony to prove the general rule that he was a real magistrate, the equivalent of the Athenian *kosmetes*. At Apollonis, in Lydia, there were peculiar and unusual circumstances. In one ephebic list, the ephebarch is inscribed among the eponymi, but, strange to say, among the second-year ephebi his name recurs, plainly marked as "the ephebarch already mentioned."[3] Since a gymnasiarch also is among the eponymi, we come to the conclusion that he must have been the ephebic leader. Unfortunately, another inscription[4] of the same town, listing both gymnasiarch and ephebarch among the eponymi, goes on to shatter our logic, by making "the gymnasiarch already mentioned" the first one among the ephebi. We must conclude that either of these titles at Apollonis could be,

---

[1] Nicæa: *Bull. Inst.* 1848, 74; Ilium: *CIG* 3631.

[2] See Oehler *RE* XI. 1492: "*Überall war der Kosmetes Leiter der Epheben.*"

[3] *BCH* XI. (1887) 86 no. 6. The Greek is ὁ προγεγραμμένος ἔφηβος. A parallel to this is found in Odessus, Thrace: *Rev. Arch.* II. 35 (1878 I) 115f. no. 6.

[4] *Denkschr. Wien. Ak.* LIII. (1910) 47ff. no. 96.

on occasion, merely honorary; perhaps the fathers of the ephebi did the work, and let their sons have the glory. In the case of the gymnasiarch of the second inscription this was certainly true, for record is made that Demetrius, the father of Demonicus, "anointed" (i. e., performed the gymnasiarchal duties) in his son's behalf. At Iasus it can not be denied that the title of ephebarch was sometimes merely honorary, for two epheberchs of the year 85 of our era were so young that they did not become ephebi until seven years later.[1] At Philadelphia, too, a mere boy was named ephebarch, and his father performed in his stead the duties of the office.[2] Yet the ephebarch Melanion at Iasus was evidently a real magistrate and commander of the ephebi, for an inscription says that he took charge of the gymnasium and watched over the good behavior of the ephebi and the *neoi*.[3] The *cursus honorum* of a citizen of Colossæ reads as follows: "secretary, treasurer, ephebarch, guardian of the laws;" plainly enough these were not functions exercised by mere ephebi.[4] So at Ephesus a man was

[1] *REG* VI. (1893) 193f. nos. 40–1. Reinach (162) observed that these, as well as several other epheberchs at Iasus, were sons of the gymnasiarchs.

[2] *IGRom.* iv. 1633.

[3] *Br. Mus. Inscr.* 925b, l. 26f. This inscription was considered by Hicks to belong to Branchidæ, but has since been claimed for Iasus by Laum, according to Ziebarth (1914) 85 n. 2.

[4] *IGRom.* iv. 870 γραμματεύσας, ταμιεύσας, ἐφηβαρχήσας, νομοφυλακτήσας. The same was true at Philadelphia: *CIG* 3421, and at Apamea: *IGRom.* iv. 788. See Grasberger III. 472; Dumont I. 174; Collignon (1877) 51–4; Hirschfeld in *Br. Mus. Inscr.* IV. p. 97.

a senator before he became ephebarch,[1] and the financial responsibilities of the latter office were such as would be entrusted only to a magistrate.[2] Epictetus named the ephebarch in a group of magistrates,[3] and spoke of him as an educational official.[4] Finally, an inscription of Philadelphia says in so many words that the ephebarchy was a magistracy.[5] It might seem unnecessary to argue the point, but the opposite view, that the ephebarch was only the leading ephebus, *primus inter pares*, has been too often expressed.[6]

Where the ephebarch and gymnasiarch existed side by side, as at Cyzicus, the former led the ephebi, and the latter had a higher position, in supreme charge of the gymnasia and of all the young men, both ephebi and *neoi*.[7] Subordination to the gymnasiarch was the rule at Acmonia, too, for the ephebarch there erected a statue in his honor.[8] At Cyzicus the ephebarch had a subordinate, called the under-ephebarch; but the latter was his brother, and this was surely a special case, for we never find an under-ephebarch again at

[1] *Br. Mus. Inscr.* 579.
[2] *Ibid.* 481, l. 149ff.
[3] iii. 1. 34.
[4] *Ibid.* 7. 19 τίς αὐτοὺς παιδεύσει; τίς ἐφήβαρχος; τίς γυμνασίαρχος;
[5] ἀρχή, *IGRom.* iv. 1633.
[6] Duchesne-Bayet 100, Fränkel (following Foucart) on *IG* iv. 589, Poland 90.
[7] *SIG*³ 798. Dittenberger *ad loc.* abandoned his former view, expressed in 1863 (p. 40), that the gymnasiarch and ephebarch were identical, in favor of that of Grasberger III. 472. See also Oehler *RE* V. 2736.
[8] *CIG* 3858.

Cyzicus or elsewhere. Like the gymnasiarch, the ephebarch could be reëlected.[1]

It has been pointed out on earlier pages that certain places like Athens, Delos, and Pergamum had ephebic organizations so excellent that lads from other cities or countries were attracted. Three more cities of Asia Minor should be added to complete this list of educational centers. Priene, like Pergamum, limited its hospitality to the *parœci*, or people of the neighboring towns and country-side.[2] At Lampsacus a definite attempt to attract foreigners was made about 300 B.C. by exempting from taxes both students and teachers who came from other cities.[3] Cyzicus had an ephebia so famous that one of the proud citizens devoted three volumes to the discussion of it,[4] and several princes were sent there to be educated.[5]

All over Asia Minor it was a regular occurrence for ephebi still to keep together after graduation, for the purpose of carrying on their physical exercises. College life, in those days as in our own, had a special aptitude for forming associations and friendships which lasted through life.[6] The bands of ephebic graduates nearly always called themselves *neoi*. While they had no teachers, the city magistrates, the gymnasiarch,

[1] *Inscr. Prien.* 147 ἐφηβαρχοῦντος δὲ τὸ β′ Εὐφράνορος.

[2] *Ibid.* 113 (l. 43), 123 (l. 8).

[3] *BCH* XVII. (1893) 555 no. 57, according to the reading of Wilhelm *Neue Beitr. zur gr. Inschriftenkunde* I. 46.

[4] Suidas *s. v.* Τεῦκρός.

[5] Hasluck 258.

[6] The comedies of Terence give ample proof of this for Athens.

or, less often, the ephebarch took charge of them; so close was their relation to the state that they became cogs in the municipal organization of the Roman Empire. Poland in 1909 [1] listed forty-four places in Asia Minor which had colleges of *neoi*, and one may now add Laodicea, Eriza, and Prusa.[2]

Even when one became too old to belong to the *neoi* any longer, he could join the *gerusia*, a body of middle-aged and elderly men, who frequently had their meeting place in the gymnasia, and either had a gymnasiarch of their own,[3] or shared one with some of the younger groups. While they carried on exercises in a mild way,[4] they hardly belong in a history of physical education. Their importance in the municipal life of Asia Minor was, of course, far greater than that of the ephebi or *neoi*.

Before leaving Asia Minor, let us add that physical education suffered under the Roman Empire. Imperial Rome did not share the Greek ideals with regard to the gymnasium, and discouraged rather than fostered the system of education which had flourished in the gymnasium and palæstra. For the conveniences of life and for everything that contributed to ease and luxury, Rome was willing to spend her time and energies, but not for education.[5] The general trend of the

---

[1] 95; see also *Nachträge* 538.

[2] Laodicea: Ramsay I. 64; Eriza: *BCH* XIII. (1889) 334ff.; Prusa: *SEG* ii. 663.

[3] Sidyma: *TAM* ii. 1. 175; Pergamum: *AM* XXVII. (1902) 99 no. 98; Magnesia on the Mæander: *Inscr. Magn.* 164.

[4] Ramsay II. 440; Mommsen I. 383.

[5] Ramsay *l. c.:* "The educational system is the finest side of the

ephebic organizations was, as had been true at Athens, away from the military and gymnastic side, towards pomp, display, and mere tinsel.

Crossing now the Black Sea, we find that the Greek colonies in that far-distant land had built for themselves gymnasia, and started organizations of ephebi. Olbia, Tanais, Gorgippia, Panticapæum, Phanagoria, and Chersonesus are the places which furnish us records of gymnastic activity. Olbia had a gymnasium and gymnasiarch [1] as early as the third century before Christ. Panticapæum had both gymnasiarch and *neaniskarch* [2] ("leader of the youths"); the latter was very common as a gymnastic official of the youth in South Russia. We find gymnasiarch and *neaniskarch* side by side in Tanais,[3] while Gorgippia and Chersonesus had the gymnasiarch.[4] One chance allusion to a gymnasium at Phanagoria is all we know of gymnastics there.[5] Most interesting is the *paidotribes* named Pharnaces, who strayed away from his birthplace in Sinope across the Black Sea, came to Panticapæum, and liked the place so well that he remained there, teaching the young men in the gymnasium. He died before his prime, and a poetical

---

Greek city constitution; and we do not find any proof that it received as much attention in the Roman period. . . . As home-rule in the cities decayed, the educational system decayed also."

[1] *IPE* i. 22; iv. 459.
[2] *Ibid.* ii. 58; iv. 210, 211.
[3] *Ibid.* ii. 439–42, 445–8, 451, 454–5.
[4] Gorgippia: *IPE* ii. 403; Chersonesus: *IPE* iv. 153; *CIG* 2097.
[5] *IPE* ii. 360.

epitaph has preserved his memory. Interesting, too, is the possibility that there was an ephebic college at Gorgippia; Bœckh published a list of names found there,[1] which he suspected to be an ephebic list, and a gymnasiarch is mentioned in connection with a similar list.[2] This is only a possibility, however, which Latyschev [3] was inclined to doubt.

Leaving the inhospitable land made famous by Iphigenia, we go far westward, to Magna Græcia and Sicily. Our attention here is earliest attracted to the use made of gymnastics by Pythagoras. In his doctrine, the harmony of the soul was virtue, that of the body health. It seems, therefore, that he made gymnastics required in the training of his followers, in order to promote their health and physical harmony.[4] This is brought out in the Golden Verses (32-3): [5] "Nor must you disregard the health of the body; but use moderation in food and drink and gymnastics, too." Pythagoras also realized that gymnastics form a useful outlet for surplus physical energies, and that the appetites of the body can well be regulated and held in check by plentiful exercise.[6] According to his biographer Iamblichus, he extended the requirement of physical education to the girls, perhaps with the

---

[1] *CIG* 2130 = *IPE* ii. 402.
[2] *IPE* ii. 403.
[3] On *IPE* ii. 402.
[4] Williams 148. Schol. Theoc. xiv. 5 (in Diels *Vorsokr.*³ 373) οἱ μὲν Πυθαγορικοὶ πᾶσαν φροντίδα ποιοῦνται τοῦ σώματος. Elbern 242: "*Gymnastik . . . im pythagoreischen Unterricht eine bedeutende Stelle einnahm.*"
[5] *FPG* I. 195.   [6] Iambl. *Vit. Pythag.* xxxi. 205.

Spartan model in mind,[1] and least of all exempted his own daughter, of whom it is said that when a maiden she led the maidens in the dances, and when a woman led the women in processions to the altar.[2] He arranged the curriculum of his school to have three parts: gymnastics, music, and mathematics. Of these the humblest was gymnastics, which simply strengthened the pupils and made them healthy, while music purified, and mathematics perfected them.[3]

Croton, where the Pythagorean school especially flourished, enjoyed a high repute for her athletes, among whom Milo was of course most famous.[4] The sensible physical training, which was generally not pushed too far in this era, resulted in making Croton proverbial for the health of its inhabitants.[5] In the sixth century, more victors in the games came from Croton than from any other one place.[6] A palæstra existed at Croton, but for the use of athletes rather than for the instruction of boys, as the anecdote told by Athenæus[7] shows: "And once, at Croton, some Sybarites were standing by one of the athletes who was digging up dust for the palæstra, and said they

---

[1] Iambl. *op. cit.* xxxi. 209 δεῖν οὖν τούς τε παῖδας καὶ τὰς παρθένους ἐν πόνοις τε καὶ γυμνασίοις καὶ καρτερίαις ταῖς προσηκούσαις τρέφειν, τροφὴν προσφέροντας τὴν ἁρμόττουσαν φιλοπόνῳ καὶ σώφρονι καὶ καρτερικῷ βίῳ.

[2] *Ibid.* xxx. 170; Porphyr. *Vit. Pythag.* iv. quoting Timæus; cf. K. O. Müller II. 298.

[3] Davidson (1894) 100.

[4] Strab. vi. 1. 12 (263 Cas.) Μίλων, ἐπιφανέστατος μὲν τῶν ἀθλητῶν.

[5] *Ibid.* (262 Cas.).

[6] I. Müller 138.

[7] xii. 15 (from Timæus) tr. Yonge.

marvelled that men who had such a city had no slaves to dig the palæstra for them." The lazy and luxurious Sybarites, at least according to unfriendly tradition, did not overexert themselves in performing physical exercises. Athenæus related [1] that they took little Maltese dogs to the gymnasia with them, the implication being, perhaps, that they played with the dogs in preference to exercising and working up a perspiration.

At Locri gymnastics were carried on zealously, and some notable athletes came from there. The girls seem to have been allowed to practice gymnastics at Locri, in the same exercise grounds with the boys, and clad almost as scantily as those of Sparta.[2] Such special privileges were rarely accorded to women in the Greek colonies of the West.[3] Tarentum was another city that was zealous for gymnastics, and here again the Spartan influence was at work, causing the boys to be divided into troops, headed by troop-leaders.[4] Justin asserts [5] that the Lucanians were wont to bring up their children by Spartan methods, but his description shows that he was thinking of the general mode of life rather than of schools. Altogether, then, the Spartan influence on educational methods

---

[1] xii. 16.

[2] See the Locrian vase-painting, *Notizie* 1917, 110, with the commentary of Orsi.

[3] Oldfather *RE* XIII. 1349.

[4] Hesych. *s. v.* βειλαρμόστας: βειλάρχας. Ταραντῖνοι. The term βειλάρχας is equivalent to ἴλαρχος, or troop-leader. See K. O. Müller II. 297.

[5] xxiii. 1. 7.

was stronger in Magna Græcia than anywhere else, showing itself at Croton, Locri, Tarentum, and in Lucania. The only two places elsewhere that betray traces of imitating the Spartan system of education are Thuria in the Peloponnese [1] and Cyrene in Africa; the discussion of Cyrene must be postponed for the moment.

Rhegium had a gymnasiarch,[2] or two working conjointly,[3] and those who used the gymnasium[4] were banded together in an Anointers Club. Petelia, a town under Greek influence, also had two gymnasiarchs at once.[5] Thuria was noted for physical education in the fifth century, but later degenerated in this respect.[6] Cumæ was never enthusiastic for physical education,[7] and the tyrant Aristodemus finally did away with the gymnasia and military exercises altogether.[8] Naples not only had gymnasia and a gymnasiarch, but an ephebic organization as well.[9] The island of Capri, near Naples, had its ephebic organization, too, and the Emperor Augustus, when residing there, "was wont to watch the exercising ephebi, of whom there were

[1] The τριτίρενες, already discussed above, page 189.
[2] *IG* xiv. 616.
[3] *SEG* i. 218.
[4] Its existence is expressly attested by Theophrast. *H. P.* iv. 5. 6 and Plin. *N. H.* xii. 1. 7.
[5] *IG* xiv. 637.
[6] Plat. *Legg.* i. 636B.
[7] Fr. Cramer I. 305.
[8] Dion. Hal. vii. 9. 3.
[9] Gymnasiarch: *IG* xiv. 745; gymnasia and ephebia: Strab. v. 4. 7 (246 Cas.). Meineke's text of Strabo reads ἐφηβεῖα, but Jüthner *RE* V. 2737 is surely right in suggesting ἐφηβεία, "ephebia."

still fair numbers in Capri according to the old usage."[1]

In Sicily several towns and cities had gymnasia and made provision for physical training. At Syracuse stood the Timoleon gymnasium mentioned by both Nepos and Plutarch,[2] and in the third century King Hiero was enthusiastic for gymnasia.[3] Hiero founded a gymnasium at Netum, and the youths who exercised there, under the two gymnasiarchs so commonly found in the West, were called the "Hieronian youths."[4] At Catana, Marcellus founded a gymnasium.[5] Other towns with gymnasiarchs at the head of gymnasia were Acræ, Lilybæum, Tauromenium, and Tyndaris.[6] Clubs of Anointers were unusually frequent in Sicily,[7] which was markedly deficient in clubs of other kinds; since emphasis was laid by these clubs on bathing and anointing rather than on exercising, Olivieri (170) was justified in calling them a degenerate offspring of the ephebi. Phintias and Soluntum both had ephebic organizations led by gymnasiarchs.[8] The decree in behalf of the gymnasiarch at Phintias is sufficiently important for the latter's duties in the third century

[1] Suet. *Aug.* 98.

[2] Nepos. *Timol.* v. 4; Plut. *Timol.* xxxix. Liv. xxix. 19 also referred to the gymnasium at Syracuse, and Cicero (*II Verr.* ii. 14. 36) called it a palæstra.

[3] Ath. v. 40.

[4] *IG* xiv. 240.

[5] Plut. *Marc.* xxx.

[6] Acræ: *IG* xiv. 213; Lilybæum: *IG* xiv. 276; Tauromenium: *IG* xiv. 422; Tyndaris: Cic. *II Verr.* iv. 42. 92.

[7] Cephalœdium: *IG* xiv. 349; Haluntium: *IG* xiv. 369-71; Tauromenium: *IG* xiv. 432.

[8] Phintias: *IG* xiv. 256; Soluntum: *IG* xiv. 311.

before Christ to be worth quoting: "Since Heracleidas, son of Zopyrus, being chosen gymnasiarch for the present year, has looked out for the ephebi and *neoi* and the others who strip in the gymnasium, and has performed well everything else that relates to the gymnasium, acting in a manner worthy of his own and his ancestors' virtue, therefore it is fitting to crown with an olive crown the gymnasiarch Heracleidas, son of Zopyrus, because of his care and diligence about the gymnasium."

The farthest western point which Greek physical education reached was Massilia, the modern Marseilles. Massilia was the leading representative of Greek culture in Gaul, and did not fail to have an ephebic college. We would be curious to know all the details, but a pair of inscriptions [1] simply inform us that gymnasiarchs led the college, and that there was competition in orderliness (εὐταξία).

Now that we have followed the spread of the ephebic system to its very end in the West, let us turn and see how far eastward it went. At Antioch the existence of ephebi under the superintendence of a gymnasiarch is vouched for by a thrice-recorded anecdote about the younger Cato.[2] Approaching Antioch with a coterie of friends, Cato saw a multitude drawn up on either side of the road just outside the gates, and among them the ephebi, headed by their gymnasiarch

[1] *IG* xiv. 2444, 2445.
[2] Plut. *Cat. Min.* xiii, *Pomp.* xl; Jul. *Misop.* 358Aff.

and other officials. Thinking this was a reception arranged for him, Cato bade his friends dismount, and they approached on foot. As they drew near, the gymnasiarch, who was master of ceremonies, ran up to Cato and said: "Stranger, where is Demetrius?" Finding to his disgust, that all the pomp and display was for a mere freedman of Pompey's, Cato affronted the gymnasiarch with a curse on his city, and made off. His friends had a good laugh over it, and in later years the humor of the situation appeared to Cato himself. Now, to doubt that the word "ephebi" is here used in its technical sense is impossible. Any who have read the foregoing pages know that one of the reasons why Greek cities liked to have an ephebic organization, was that they might have the ephebi convenient for just such pomp and display as was prepared on this occasion for Demetrius. So in the third century before Christ, when King Ptolemy Euergetes came to Antioch, there met him, together with the satraps, priests, dignitaries, and soldiers, "all the young men from the gymnasium."[1] Besides, these ephebi were clad in the *chlamys*,[2] the official uniform which originated at Athens, and had been universally adopted. They were commanded by the gymnasiarch, who, here as everywhere else, had a

[1] Col. 3, l. 19ff. of the Gurob papyrus: *BCH* XXXIX. (1906) 332ff.

[2] In Plut. *Cat. Min.* xiii. all the manuscripts and most editors read χλαμύσι; the ingenious, nay too ingenious, Cobet emended to χλανίσι, and was followed by Sintenis. The reason for so emending, when the ephebi always wore the χλαμύς, is not clear to one less brilliant than Cobet.

staff (ῥαβδός) as a symbol of his authority. All the details, in short, fit in to show that this was a regularly organized ephebia; yet, strange to say, it was not listed by Girard, Oehler, nor Poland.[1] The most recent list of localities which had the ephebi is that of Poland; as it suffers a little from incompleteness, the author will add an appendix listing more than a score of localities, supplementing his list.

Farther up the Orontes river, at Apamea, there was a corps of teachers which reminds us of those who taught the Athenian ephebi: the riding-teacher (*polodamnes*), *hoplomachos*, and "all the teachers of the military art."[2] In Phœnicia at Byblus there was an ephebic college, and a tombstone inscription has been found there, which reads: "This is the tomb of Serapion, teacher of ephebi."[3] Testimony of an ephebic teacher at Berytus has also come to light;[4] he was an instructor in rhetoric rather than in physical exercises, but none the less his existence establishes also that of an ephebic college, and ephebi everywhere performed gymnastics with more or less diligence. Gymnasia were built by Herod at Tripolis, Damascus, and Ptolemais.[5] Generally speaking, we may doubt if the cities of Syria were enthusiastic exponents of

[1] Girard Dar.-Sagl. II. 634; Oehler *RE* V. 2741-3; Poland 90-2 and *Nachträge* 537-8.

[2] Strab. xvi. 2. 10 (752 Cas.).

[3] *Philol.* XIX. (1863) 137.

[4] *Rev. Arch.* II. 33 (1877 I) 61 no. 9.

[5] Jos. *B. J.* i. 21. 11 (422). The gymnasium at Damascus was mentioned again by Josephus *op. cit.* ii. 20. 2 (560).

physical education, for Posidonius[1] declared that they used their gymnasia as baths, after the Roman style, and anointed themselves with expensive oil and myrrh.[2]

Not the least interesting is the case of Jerusalem. Onias and the sons of Tobias, about 175 B.C., tired of the Jewish mode of life, and decided to turn Greek. Their very first thought was to build a gymnasium in Jerusalem, for how could they be Greeks without that indispensable factor in Greek life?[3] Apparently they did not do it, but the high-priest Jason, about the same time, obtained from King Antiochus Epiphanes the privilege of introducing Greek customs into Jerusalem. He wished to build a gymnasium and start an ephebic college. That the Jews were opposed to this goes without saying, but he carried his project through, nevertheless. "Gladly he established a gymnasium at the foot of the acropolis itself, and by his authority made the noblest of the ephebi[4] wear the *petasos*. . . . No longer were the priests zealous for the services of the altar, but scorning the temple and the sacrifices, they hurried to take part in the unlawful displays of the palæstra, after the announcement of the discus-throw, holding of no

[1] *FGrHist.* lxxxvii. F10.
[2] Cf. Polyb. xxx. 26. 1.
[3] Jos. *A. J.* xii. 5. 1 (241).
[4] *II Macc.* iv. 9ff. In verse 12 Swete reads ἐφ' ἡμῶν for ἐφήβων, but the mention of the *petasos*, which was as characteristic of the ephebic uniform as was the *chlamys*, makes the author incline to ἐφήβων as the true reading.

account what their forebears had honored, but esteeming above all else the things in which the Greeks gloried."[1] Of the history of this gymnasium and ephebic college we are not informed, but of course they must have disappeared during the powerful reaction under the fanatical Maccabees.

After discovering that there were ephebi in the stronghold of the Jews, we are hardly capable of further astonishment at finding them in the ancient city of Babylon. A record of 109/8 B.C.[2] names a gymnasiarch, and lists the ephebi who had won in various contests: archery, javelin throwing, hoplomachy with the round shield and the oblong shield, the long race, and the one-lap race. Then follows a fragmentary list of *neoi* who had won in their division of the same contests. Plainly, the ephebic organization at Babylon did not differ from the form so familiar elsewhere; it was headed by a gymnasiarch, and both physical and military exercises were employed. The remarkable thing about it is that it existed more than 1,200 miles from Athens, and marks the farthest eastern boundary of the recorded spread of Greek education, as Massilia the western. That the Greek colonies still farther eastward, in Persia, Bactria, and India, had gymnasia, is probable in the very nature of things, since physical training was so indispensable to the true Greek, no matter how far he might be

---

[1] The founding of a gymnasium in Jerusalem is briefly referred to in *I Macc.* i. 14 and *IV Macc.* iv. 20.

[2] *Klio* IX. (1909) 353 no. 1.

from the home land. The same might well be true of the colonies in Spain, but the records fail us.

One more place to be mentioned before entering Egypt is Cyrene. Eustathius, Aristophanes of Byzantium, and Hesychius assured us, even before we had the inscriptions, that there were ephebi in ancient times at this African city.[1] They were called by the singular name *triakatioi*,[2] a name indicating their division according to their *triakas* (a group of thirty families). They were led by *triakatiarchs*, as an inscription proves.[3] This inscription is of the third century before Christ, which shows that the ephebic college there was founded far earlier than in most countries. It was undoubtedly based on the Spartan, rather than the Athenian model, since Cyrene was a Doric colony. Hence we are not surprised to find that the girls there had contests in running, and watched the exercises of the young men.[4] In the first century of our era, four hundred years after the time of the early record (Michel 644) mentioned above, gymnasiarchs and the rest of the organization familiar elsewhere were existing in Cyrene.[5] The

---

[1] Eust. *Il.* p. 727. 18ff., *Od.* p. 1592. 56ff. Aristoph. Byz. (Miller *Mél. de la litt. gr.* 429); Hesych. *s. v.* τριακάτιοι.

[2] Hesychius gave the correct form of the word, but Eustathius perverted it to τριακάποι, and Aristophanes to τρικάποι.

[3] Michel 644.

[4] Grasberger III. 506.

[5] *CIG* 5129, 5132. The history of the ephebi at Cyrene is extended further into the Christian era, viz. to the year 224, by a recently discovered dedication, which the ephebi of that year made to Hermes and Heracles. See the *Journal des Savants* 1927, 319.

circumstance that one of the two gymnasiarchs of whom we have record was a woman, is a further trace of the Dorian influence.

In Egypt [1] the traces of palæstra education are few; yet Herondas [2] in enumerating the resources of Egypt, wrote "wealth, palæstra, power, etc.," and Polybius [3] mentioned palæstræ in Alexandria. We have record of *paidotribai* at Alexandria, and of how they, with the grammar teachers, were absolved from taxes.[4] A letter, the full sense of which the writer fails to grasp, written by an Alexandrian *paidotribes* in 257/6 B.C., speaks of opening a palæstra.[5] Another letter, from what city is unknown, speaks of a boy being sent to the palæstra.[6] At Hermopolis the boys of the palæstra were assigned a sort of Boy Scout duty, acting as a guard of honor for the *strategos*, gymnasiarch, *kosmetes*, and other officials.[7] Finally, at Naucratis an inscription has been found, by which Cleænetus and Mæandrius dedicated a palæstra to Apollo.[8]

Somewhat more data are furnished on the gymnasium and ephebic education. The gymnasia which

[1] See the works of Jouguet, San Nicolò, K. Fr. W. Schmidt, Smolka, and Wilcken, listed in the bibliography.
[2] i. 28.
[3] xv. 30. 6.
[4] *PHal.* line 260ff. (between 259 and 253 B.C.).
[5] *PSI* IV. 340.
[6] *Ibid.* 418; the diminutive παλαιστρίδιον, used in this papyrus, is ἅπαξ λεγόμενον.
[7] *PAmh.* II. 124 (2nd century of our era). They were called παλαιστροφύλακες, but manifestly were wholly different from the slaves who bore this title elsewhere.
[8] *Sammelb.* 355.

sprang up after Alexander's conquest were the center of Greek life in Egypt, and it seems certain that as a rule none but Greeks and the most aristocratic Egyptians were admitted to them.[1] Strabo declared that the finest of all the beautiful public edifices at Alexandria was the gymnasium.[2] An inscription found in the modern Cairo points to a gymnasium there early in the second century before Christ [3] with a gymnasiarch and a Gymnasium Club. At Sebennytus also, in the Ptolemaic era, there was a gymnasium, called the Heracleum, and a Gymnasium Club.[4] The gymnasiarch Leonidas in 150/49 dedicated a gateway and entrance to the gymnasium at Theadelphia.[5] In 136/5 there was a Gymnasium Club at Ombi, although this was a non-Greek city far up the Nile valley,[6] and in the third century of our era there was a gymnasium at Elephantine, still further up.[7] Arsinoë, a metropolis, probably had two gymnasia, as a papyrus refers to the Big Gymnasium.[8] Everywhere the gymnasia were endowed institutions, and not state-

---

[1] Jouguet 46; San Nicolò I. 31. The papyrus *BGU* IV. 1140 seems to assert that an Alexandrian Jew or his father had gymnasium education, but the text is uncertain. Jews were excluded from holding the office of gymnasiarch or *kosmetes: PLond.* 1912 l. 93 (Bell *Jews and Christians in Egypt* p. 25); but not so with Romans: van Groningen 33.

[2] Strab. xvii. 1. 10 (795 Cas.). Two gymnasia at Alexandria in the third or fourth century after Christ: *Sammelb.* 411.

[3] *Arch. Pap.* II. (1903) 548 no. 26.

[4] *Sammelb.* 1106.

[5] *Ibid.* 6157, 6158.

[6] *Arch. Pap.* V. (1913) 415f.

[7] *Philol.* LIII. (1894) 82.

[8] *BGU* III. 760.

owned, as they were at Athens and generally in the Greek world.

Ephebic organizations were formed in the Ptolemaic period, at least as early as the first half of the second century.[1] The directors of both gymnasia and ephebi in this period were annually elected gymnasiarchs,[2] who were men of the highest rank, as we have observed so often elsewhere. The particular director of the ephebi was the *kosmetes*,[3] who took rank under the gymnasiarch. The ephebi were divided into sections (αἱρέσεις).[4] The term *synephebi* was frequently employed to indicate their fellowship.[5] Those who had been ephebi together in a certain year retained an organization, and called themselves the "Class of such-and-such a year," exactly like our modern practice in America.[6] Each of these classes of alumni had a president and secretary.[7]

From Roman times we have more information on the Egyptian ephebi. Certainly the service was not compulsory, and the requirements for admission to the ephebia included free and legitimate birth and descent from a father who had been an ephebus.[8] The Roman

[1] *Arch. Pap.* II. (1903) 560 no. 44 (συνεφήβων).

[2] Wilcken 139. Annual magistracy: *Arch. Pap.* V. (1913) 162 no. 7.

[3] *Sammelb.* 1569 (88–80 B.C.): Apollonius became *kosmetes*, and later rose to the office of gymnasiarch. No record so far found mentions the *kosmetes* earlier than this.

[4] *OGI* 176, 178.

[5] *Arch. Pap.* II. (1903) 560 no. 44; *OGI* 188, 189.

[6] *OGI* 176, 178.

[7] *Ibid.* 178.

[8] *POxy.* III. 477, l. 9; *BGU* IV. 1084; *PFlor.* 79.

authorities assumed control of the education, and the prefect was charged with seeing that no one entered the ephebia unless he could meet the requirements.[1] At Alexandria certainly, and elsewhere probably, the ephebic training was a prerequisite to citizenship, as it originally was at Athens. The Emperor Claudius, at the beginning of his reign, wrote a letter to the Alexandrians, assuring that the citizenship would be taken away from no one who had been an ephebus, except in cases of servile birth, where the person concerned had no right to enter the ephebia.[2] The age for admission was fourteen,[3] but application for admission was frequently filed long in advance, when a boy was seven years old, or three, or only one.[4] The duration of service was either two or three years.[5] The name formerly used for the divisions ($αἱρέσεις$) was abandoned for *symmoriai*, and each *symmoria* was led by a *symmoriarch*.[6] A subdivision of the *symmoria* was the *plagion*.[7] The term *synephebi* was still

---

[1] *PFlor.* 57; Wilcken 142. In spite of this, some sons of slave mothers managed to dodge the prefect's vigilance: *PLond.* 1912 l. 53ff. (Bell *Jews and Christians in Egypt*, p. 53.)

[2] *PLond. l. c.*

[3] *PFlor.* 57 l. 78: Theon was 14 years, 17 days old when examined for entrance to the ephebi. Cf. Wilcken 141.

[4] *PTeb.* II. 316: Demetrius was registered at 3, Heliodorus at 7; *BGU* IV. 1084: Theon was registered at 1. A parallel case has come to the author's notice in America; a certain professor, on becoming a grandparent, almost immediately filed in behalf of the infant, an application for admission to the college where he had been teaching for many years.

[5] Wilcken 142.

[6] *PTeb.* II. 316. Cf. the Spartan herd-leaders or $βουαγοί$.

[7] $πλάγιον$ *BGU* IV. 1084; *Journ. Egypt. Arch.* XII. (1926) 246. Cf. San Nicolò 34.

REMAINDER OF GREECE AND THE GREEK WORLD 255

used.[1] In charge of the ephebi were the gymnasiarch and *kosmetes*, both of whom now belonged to the regular metropolitan functionaries.[2] Besides administrative duties, the gymnasiarch and *kosmetes* equally were obliged to make very heavy contributions, not to the gymnasium alone, but to the other expenses of the metropolis. At Hermopolis, during the reign of Trajan, the prefect was obliged to set a limit to the expenses entailed by the gymnasiarchy,[3] and in the year 250 a certain Hermophilus, who had served as *kosmetes* in the same city, wrote to Eudæmon, a former gymnasiarch, calmly informing him that he had been bankrupted by his office.[4] The burden was occasionally lightened by dividing the office among several people.[5] Only at Coptus, in the third century of our era, has the author found an under-gymnasiarch.[6]

The young men who visited, or had a right to visit, the gymnasium, and those who had taken the gymnastic education, together with their families (women

---

[1] *PAmh.* II. 124 l. 10.

[2] The gymnasiarchs were everywhere: see the list of van Groningen 3. The *kosmetes* is attested for Alexandria (*IGRom.* i. 1074; *Sammelb.* 5225), Hermopolis (*CPR* 20; *PRyl.* III. 77, 86, 116, 117, 181, 286; *PAmh.* II. 124; *Sammelb.* 5676), Arsinoë (*BGU* II. 362 p. xii. l. 6; Wilcken *Chr.* 193), Arsinoite nome (*PFlor.* 21), Oxyrhyncus (*POxy.* III. 477, 519; XIV. 1645, 1703; *PSI* VII. 803), Fayum (*CPR* 228; Wilcken *Chr.* 176), and two undefined localities (*IGRom.* i. 1097; *Sammelb.* 5676).

[3] *PAmh.* II. 70.

[4] *CPR* 20.

[5] Hence the ἐγ μέρους κοσμητής of *PFlor.* 21 (239 of our era); Preisigke *RE* XI. 1495.

[6] *Mnemos.* N. S. LV. (1927) 265. The word ὑπογυμνασίαρχος does not appear in the last fascicle of Preisigke's *Wörterbuch*, issued in 1927.

included), were grouped together as "the gymnasium people" (οἱ ἀπὸ γυμνασίου), and they formed a privileged class in the cities. Out of the number of this "intellectual aristocracy" were chosen the city magistrates.[1] To be an ephebus was therefore a coveted privilege, and if a boy was accidentally omitted from the annually prepared list of those eligible for the ephebia, his father was likely to raise a vigorous protest.[2] The son of Julius Cæsar by Cleopatra, Cæsarion, was enrolled in the Alexandrian ephebia, as was Mark Antony's son by Fulvia, Antyllus.[3] Of the gymnastics of the ephebi little is said, but the latest ephebic record[4] is a proclamation by a worthy named Dioscurides: "The contest of the ephebi will take place tomorrow, the 24th; and tradition, as well as the distinguished nature of the festival, indicates that it befits them to put their best foot forward in their gymnastic exhibition."

The proclamation to which allusion has just been made is the last trace of the existence of ephebi in Egypt, or indeed anywhere else in the world. The editors, Grenfell and Hunt, dated it A.D. 323, just about the time of the adoption of Christianity as the official religion of the Roman Empire. Significantly, the very last document concerns their gymnastic exer-

[1] Wilcken 144; Ziebarth (1914) 167.
[2] Well illustrated by *POxy.* IX. 1202.
[3] Dio Cass. li. 6. 1. Cæsarion's enrolment is mentioned also by Plut. *Ant.* lxxi.
[4] *POxy.* I. 42.

cises! This fact assures us that, wherever there were ephebi, there was physical education. Again, the close connection of the gymnasiarchs with physical education and the ephebi is manifested by their disappearance in the same century.[1] So at last Greek physical education comes to an end.

[1] The last record of a gymnasiarch is *POxy.* XIV. 632, dated A.D. 353. See van Groningen 2.

CHAPTER VIII

CONCLUSION

In this history of physical education among the ancient Greeks, the author has covered the Hellenic, Hellenistic, and Roman periods, using the available literary, epigraphical, and papyrological sources. The author believes that the chapters on Athenian and Spartan physical education constitute the fullest chronological and historical study of the subject. Moot points the writer has tried to settle, where it seemed possible, and hopes to have contributed something in this regard. The investigations have been in the records of three continents, extending over more than a thousand years. An educational movement which spread so widely in what the Romans called the *orbis terrarum*, and which endured even when Greek civilization was in decay, has merited a comprehensive study. As the length of the last two chapters testifies, the twentieth century trend in classical scholarship has been followed by assigning due importance to those centuries which followed the conquests of Alexander.[1]

[1] "Many years of close study of the history of the ancient world have convinced me that one of the most important epochs in the evolution of the world is the Hellenistic period."—Rostovtzeff *Journ. Egypt. Arch.* VI. (1920) 161. The works of Professors Wilamowitz and W. S. Ferguson, for example, bear witness to this change in emphasis.

It is to be hoped that the new knowledge imparted by the documents gathered around the shores of the Mediterranean will contribute to the understanding of the principles and practices of Greek physical education, and of how essential such education was to Greeks wherever they were. Alexander's victories promoted the extension of Greek gymnastics to distant lands, and especially in Asia Minor, and later in Egypt, they flourished to an extraordinary degree. If we may paraphrase a familiar saying: "When Greek met Greek, they founded a gymnasium."

It has not perhaps been as fully realized as the fact deserves that the Greek gymnasium, where instruction was eventually given for both body and mind, was the lineal ancestor of the German *gymnasium*, the French lycée, and the American academy. We saw how the Academy Lyceum, and the scores upon scores of other gymnasia which the Greeks built wherever they went, were originally for gymnastics only, but gradually the mental discipline gained an entrance; and at length, like Æsop's camel, they unkindly usurped the whole field, and turned physical education out into the cold.

The Greeks, the author is convinced, regarded physical education in a far different light from that in which we are wont to regard it. The great thinkers of our age busy themselves with the problems of sociology, philosophy, and science; how many of them have thought and written about the development of the body by rational gymnastic methods, as a means to foster a sound and sturdy race? Yet in ancient times, Plato, that philosopher supreme, both thought and wrote copiously on physical education. Aristotle, in his lectures on political science, included a discussion of the part that gymnastics should play in the constitution of a state. Pythagoras had set the example first, by making gymnastics compulsory in his school of philosophy. Protagoras, one of the greatest of the sophists, wrote a book *On Wrestling*. No better evidence than this could be furnished to show the importance ascribed by the Greeks to a program of physical education. As a community and as individuals, moreover, they were willing to make heavy sacrifices in the cause of physical education. Wealthy men volunteered, often repeatedly, to hold the expensive liturgical gymnasiarchy. Every self-respecting community erected a gymnasium at public expense, and scores of cities supported ephebic organizations. Even the eschatology of the Greeks was affected, so that they imagined the blessed dead hurling the discus and wrestling on the asphodel meadows of Elysium. The American Indians conceived paradise as a Happy Hunting-Ground, the Vikings as a Valhalla of warfare and carousals over the mead, the Greeks as an athletic field.

"An indispensable requisite for the continuance of Greek life and Greek freedom was the practice of gymnastics," said Friedrich Cramer.[1] If this statement

[1] I. 304.

should seem overbold, he bade us consider the history of the Greek colonies in Italy. Tarentum, Rhegium and Naples did not neglect physical education, and they flourished for a long time;[1] while Cumæ, although maintaining Greek traditions in most ways,[2] abandoned gymnastics and suffered a premature decline and fall. It would have gone less well with Philip, declared Libanius,[3] "had war been sweet to the Greeks and the practice of arms and the love of glory and physical exercise." In other words, the decline of gymnastics, which stirred the protest of Aristophanes, ran parallel with the decline of the glory that was Greece. So it was, not in Greece alone, but everywhere that the colonizing Greeks carried the civilization of their native land. As long as gymnasium and palæstra were crowded with healthy youths, the Greek city-state had nothing to fear; but when the blight fell on the exercises of the young, then it was time to be anxious for the future.

The causes which finally destroyed physical education in Greece were several. The Romans were particularly unsympathetic with this phase of Greek life, and did what they could in passive opposition. The Stoics preached scorn of the body, which was a mere detriment to the soul—$\sigma\hat{\omega}\mu\alpha$ $\sigma\hat{\eta}\mu\alpha$. The early Christians exhorted to a similar attitude. "Exercise thyself for holiness," we read in the *First Epistle to Timothy*, "for

---

[1] Strab. vi. 1. 2 (253 Cas.).
[2] *Ibid.* v. 4. 4 (243 Cas.).
[3] *Decl.* xvii. 50.

physical exercise is of little worth." Most insidious and deadly of all was athleticism, the striving for virtuosity in special exercises. Physical education and professional athletics are not friends, but irreconcilable foes.

In the finest days of Greece, as in the later centuries of Græco-Roman Egypt, a gymnastic education was the distinctive mark of culture. No man who lacked it could be called πεπαιδευμένος, "educated," or a καλὸς κἀγαθὸς ἀνήρ, "a man both beautiful and good." Lucian [1] speaks of the ideal Athenian lads as using good Greek and "breathing of the palæstra" and represents Solon as saying to Anacharsis, in explaining the Greek system of physical education: [2] "Especially and above all we bethink ourselves of this: that our citizens may be virtuous in soul, and strong in body."

[1] *Navig.* 2.   [2] *Anach.* 20.

APPENDIX

SUPPLEMENT TO POLAND'S LIST [1] OF LOCALITIES WHICH HAD ORGANIZED EPHEBI

1. Alexandria: *Sammelb.* 5069; *PTeb.* II. 316; *BGU* IV. 1084; *PSI* VII. 777; *Journ. Egypt. Arch.* XII. (1926) 246; Dio Cass. li. 6. 1.
2. Antioch: Plut. *Cat. Min.* xiii., *Pomp.* xl.; Julian *Misop.* 358Bff.
3. Arcesine (Amorgos): *IG* xii. 7. 115.
4. Arsinoë (Fayum): *BGU* II. 362, p. xii. l. 6 (*kosmetes*).
5. Ascarion: *BCH* XVIII. (1894) 541.
6. Babylon: *Klio* IX. (1909) 353 no. 1.
7. Capri: Suet. *Aug.* 98.
8. Carystus (Eubœa): *IG* xii. 9. 20.
9. Cedreæ: *BCH* XVIII. (1894) 27f. no. 6.
10. Chalcis (Eubœa): *IG* xii. 9. 904, 916, 952.
11. Delphi: Michel (Suppl.) 1523 = *SIG*³ 697.
12. Dreros: *SIG*³ 527.
13. Eriza: *BCH* XIII. (1889) 334ff., XIV. (1890) 103f. no. 7.
14. Haliartus: *IG* vii. 2849.
15. Hermopolis: *CPR* 20; *PAmh.* II. 124; *PFlor.* 57, 79; *PRyl.* I. 101.
16. Hierocæsarea: *BCH* XI. (1887) 105 no. 26.
17. Jerusalem: *II Macc.* iv. 9ff.
18. Lydæ: *TAM.* ii. 1. 132.
19. Miletus: *Milet* I. 3 (1914) no. 139; I. 7 (1924) no. 203; *Miletbericht* 7, p. 28.

[1] Pp. 90–2 and *Nachträge* 537–8.

20. Naples: Strab. v. 4. 7 (246 Cas.).
21. Nicopolis: Epict. iii. 1. 34.
22. Oxyrhyncus: *POxy.* I. 42; III. 477; VI. 705; IX. 1202; XIV. 1697, 1703, 1705.
23. Samos: *BCH* V. (1881) 480ff. nos. 3–4; *SEG* i. 266.
24. Theadelphia: *Sammelb.* 6159.
25. Thisbe: *SEG* iii. 351–3.

GLOSSARY

agelai herds, troops, companies. The boys and girls in the Spartan educational system were grouped into such divisions.

agelaoi Cretan ephebi, members of the agelai.

agoge leading, training, discipline. The ancient name for Sparta's educational system.

agonothetes an exhibitor or director of games.

akontistes a javelin-man, a coach in javelin throwing.

akontistikos same as foregoing.

aleiptes an anointer. Athletic coach or trainer.

ampaides those concerned with children. Educational officials at Sparta.

anoros immature. Technical name for a Cretan youth who had not yet come of age.

antigrammateus *see* **hypogrammateus.**

antikosmetes deputy kosmetes or vice-president of the ephebic college at Athens.

apageloi those not in the agelai (because too young). Cretan boys not yet seventeen years old.

aphetes instructor of the Athenian ephebi in the use of the catapult.

apodromos one too young to be admitted to the dromoi or gymnasia of Crete. Lads from seventeen to about twenty years of age.

archephebus leader of the ephebi. Equivalent to ephebarch.

archos leader. A Cretan official who directed a band of ephebi.

boua herd. A subdivision of a company (agela) of boys at Sparta.

chlamys cloak. Part of the ephebic uniform.

cleruch member of a cleruchy.

cleruchy a body of Greek citizens settled in a conquered country, where land was allotted to them.

deme one of the townships, or political subdivisions, of Attica.

diamastigosis thorough flogging. A Spartan rite, honoring Artemis Orthia, and training the lads to Stoical endurance of pain.

didaskaloi teachers. A name sometimes used collectively for the members of the faculty of the Athenian ephebic college in its early history.

didaskalos teacher. The term was employed in a special sense, during the Roman Empire, for a man who taught music to the Athenian ephebi.

dolichos a " long " race ($\frac{3}{4}$ to $2\frac{1}{4}$ miles).

dromeus a Cretan old enough to be admitted to the dromoi or gymnasia.

dromos running-track, athletic grounds, gymnasium.

eirens Spartan ephebi.

epengraphoi those enrolled in addition. A term used for the foreign students in the Athenian ephebia under the Roman Empire.

ephebarch a magistrate, head of the ephebi. Equivalent to archephebus.

ephebia military and gymnastic college for young men about 18–20 years of age (ephebi); the period of training in such a college.

ephebophylakes ephebic guards, officials at Pergamum and Priene.

ephebus a young man during the first years of puberty. Official term at Athens for youths 18–20 years of age; similar official limitation of the term elsewhere.

ephors the five Spartan magistrates who had supreme control of the state.

epimeletes a curator, overseer, as of gymnasia.

epistates same as foregoing.

eponymi the officials listed at the head of an inscription, fixing its date to a certain year.

exedra a hall, with seats, in a gymnasium.

gerusia a council of elders, senate.

gymnasiarch superintendent of the gymnasium, or of various groups who exercised there. Also, in the classical period at Athens, a director of the torch-race.

gymnasiarchy office, or term of office, of a gymnasiarch.

gymnastes director of exercises, athletic coach.

hegemon leader. An official who led the ephebi on parades.

hetairia band of comrades. In Crete an association of full-grown men who messed together.

hoplomachos a teacher of heavy-armed fighting.

hoplomachy fighting in heavy armor.

hypogrammateus assistant secretary, as of the Athenian ephebic college.

hypohoplomachos assistant to the hoplomachos.

hypopaidotribes assistant to the paidotribes.

hypotaktes a minor official of the Athenian ephebi. See page 168.

hypozakoros a subordinate priest, assigned to the ephebic college at Athens.

kapsarios a bath servant, employed by the ephebic college.

katapaltaphetes same as aphetes.

kestrosphendone a kind of artillery engine, used in practice by the ephebi.

kestrophylax the man who taught the use of the kestrosphendone.

kosmetes orderer, director, president of the ephebic college at Athens and elsewhere.

lampadarch director of the torch-race.

lentiarios an attendant who was put in charge of the clothing of the Athenian ephebi.

lithobolos an engine for hurling stones.

liturgy an expensive public service performed by wealthy citizens, lightening the burden of the state treasury.

lochagoi captains. Cadet officers of the Athenian ephebi.

mastigophoroi whip-bearers, disciplinary assistants of the paidonomos at Sparta.

medimni the medimnus was an Attic measure, approximately equivalent to 1½ bushels.

melleirens those about to be eirens, the thirteen-year-old boys at Sparta.

mellephebi those about to be ephebi (sometimes organized in a preparatory school).

metics resident aliens of Attica, who were granted some of the privileges of citizens.

mothakes illegitimate children of genuine Spartans (Spartiates) by helot women.

neaniskarch leader of the young men; in some places an honorary distinction, in others a real function.

neoi young men, beyond the ephebic age. Organized in groups, on the ephebic pattern, for the continuance of gymnastic exercises and other purposes.

pæderasty love of boys, a homosexual relation.

paidagogoi slave attendants of Athenian schoolboys.

paideutai educators, teachers. Sometimes used collectively for the corps of ephebic instructors at Athens.

paidonomos manager of boys, superintendent of schools.

paidotribes "boy-rubber," instructor of physical education.

palæstra wrestling-school, building used for physical education in general.

palaistrophylax palæstra keeper, usually a janitor. In Egypt, a sort of Boy Scout, used in the honorary guards of certain officials.

pallekes mellephebi, in Samos.

pancratium a rough exercise, which combined wrestling with boxing.

parephebi mellephebi, in Thera and Samos.

parœci neighbors; specifically applied to the inhabitants of the Pergamene realm who dwelt outside the capital city.

periœci a Spartan term for the free inhabitants of the towns in her dominions.

peripolarch a captain or leader of peripoloi.

peripoloi (peripolos in the singular) patrols. The ephebi were called peripoloi in their second year of service, when they patrolled the borders of Attica. In the fifth century, a mercenary corps of police at Athens.

petasos a broad-brimmed felt hat. Part of the ephebic uniform.

plagion a subdivision of the ephebic symmoria, in Egypt.

polodamnes horse-breaker, instructor in equitation.

prostates one who stands before, head man. An ephebic official, whose duties are unknown.

sideunai the younger eirens at Sparta, aged fifteen or sixteen.

skotioi a designation for Cretan boys under seventeen years of age. Synonym for apageloi.

sophronistai discipline masters, overseers of the ephebi at Athens.

speirai cohorts, bands, bevies. Divisions of girls in the educational system of Pergamum.

strategos general; an Athenian official with civil and political, as well as military, functions.

symmoria a division of ephebi, in Egypt.

symmoriarch leader of a symmoria.

synephebi fellow-ephebi, comrades in the ephebic organization.

syssitia common meals, public messes.

systatai those who stand together. Chums in the ephebia.

systremma (plural **systremmata**) a division of the Athenian ephebi, in the time of the Roman Empire.

systremmatarch student leader of a systremma.

thetes under Solon's constitution at Athens, the members of the fourth and lowest class, with scant property and few rights.

thyroros doorkeeper, concierge of the ephebic college at Athens.

toxotes archer, instructor of archery.

triakas a group of thirty families, in Cyrene.

triakatioi the ephebi of Cyrene, grouped according to their triakas.

triakatiarch leader of the ephebi, at Cyrene.

tritirens eirens serving for the third year, at Thuria.

trophimoi foster-children. Spartan designation for sons of foreigners who came to enter the agoge.

BIBLIOGRAPHY

* Indicates works which the author has not been able to examine.
† Indicates the more important works.

* Achtzehn, "*Sport bei den Griechen*," *Das humanistische Gymnasium*, 1924, p. 121.
* J. E. Adamson, *The theory of education in Plato's Republic*, London, 1903.

F. H. Ahrens, *De Athenarum statu politico et literario inde ab Achaici fœderis interitu usque ad Antoninorum tempora*, Göttingen, 1829.

* G. Allievo, *Delle idee pedagogiche presso i greci*, Cuneo, 1887.

Antonius van der Bach, *De institutione veterum Græcorum scholastica*, Bonn, 1841.

Ernest Barker, *Greek political theory, Plato and his predecessors*, London, 1918.

Henry Barnard, "*Aristotle and his educational views*," *American Journal of Education* XIV. (1864) 133–46.

————, "*Lycurgus and education among the Spartans*," *ibid.* 611–24.

Baron, *Geschichte der Leibesübungen. Eine kurz und populäre Darstellung der Gymnastik bei den Alten und ihrer Weiterentwicklung bis auf das Gegenwart*, Limbach, 1865.

Paul Barth, "*Die Geschichte der Erziehung in soziologischer Beleuchtung bei Griechen und Römer*," *Vierteljahrschrift für wissenschaftliche Philosophie und Soziologie* XXVII., 209ff.; XXVIII., 319ff. and 393ff.

————, *Die Geschichte der Erziehung in soziologischer und geistesgeschichtlicher Beleuchtung*, 3. Aufl., Leipzig, 1920.

* W. Baumgarten-Crusius, *Disciplina juvenilis Platonis cum nostra comparata*, Meissen, 1836.

* L. Baunard, *Quid apud Græcos de institutione puerorum senserit Plato*, Orléans, 1860.
* Jacob Becker, *Antike und moderne Erziehung*, Frankfurt, 1865.
† W. A. Becker, *Charikles, Bilder altgriechischer Sitte, zur genaueren Kenntniss des griechischen Privatlebens*, new ed. by H. Göll, Berlin, 1877-8, 3 vols.

H. Idris Bell, "*Records of entry among the ephebi*," Journ. Egypt. Arch. XII. (1926) 245-7.

* Julius Beloch, "*Bildung und Bildungsstätten im hellenistichen Altertum*," Zeitschrift für Staatswesen IV. (1901) 489-96.

—————, "*Griechische Aufgebote*," Klio V. (1905) 341-74; VI. (1906) 34-78.

Karl Benrath, *Das pädagogische System Platons in seinen Hauptzügen*, Diss., Jena, 1871.

G. Bernhardy, *Griechische Litteraturgeschichte*, 5 Aufl., Halle, 1892. (See Vol. I., pp. 62-104.)

K. F. C. Beutler, *De Athenarum fatis, statu politico et literario sub Romanis*, Göttingen, 1829.

Wilhelm Biehl, *Die Erziehungslehre des Aristoteles*, Innsbruck, 1877.

* M. Billia, *Acceni all' idea dell' educazione in Platone ed Aristotele*, Torino, 1900.

J. Bintz, *Die Gymnastik der Hellenen*, Gutersloh, 1878.

Br. Bischof, *Die körperliche Erziehung bei den Griechen im Lichte der griechischen Philosophie*, Gymn. Progr., Freudenthal, 1912.

* Blume, *De Platonis educandorum liberorum disciplina*, Halle, 1817.

Hugo Blümner, *Leben und Sitten der Griechen*, Leipzig, 1887, 3 vols.

August Bœckh, *Dissertatio prior, de ephebia Attica*, 1819; *Dissertatio altera, de epheborum tirociniis*, 1820. Most accessible in: *Kleine Schriften*, Vol. IV. (1874) 137–56.

————, *Die Staatshaushaltung der Athener*, 3 Aufl. von Max Fränkel, Berlin, 1886, 2 vols.

Hanns Bohatta, *Erziehung und Unterricht bei den Griechen und Römer*, Gutersloh, 1895.

Bomback, *Entwicklung der platonischen Erziehungslehre*, Rottweil, 1854.

Alexander Bondurant, *Ancient athletics, their use and abuse*, Banner Press, Emory University, Georgia, 1924.

* A. Bonvicini, *Sulla educazione dei greci*, Vicenza, 1864.

Bernard Bosanquet, *The education of the young in the Republic of Plato*, Cambridge, 1908.

† Alice Brenot, "*Recherches sur l'éphébie attique et en particulier sur la date de l'institution*," *Bibliothèque de l'École des Hautes Études*, fasc. 229, Paris, 1920.

Franz Breznik, *Erziehung und Unterricht bei den Griechen*, Rudolfswert, 1883.

† A. A. Bryant, "*Boyhood and youth in the days of Aristophanes*," *Harvard Studies in Classical Philology*, XVIII. (1907) 73–122.

* A. Buechle, *Die Pädagogik des Isokrates*, Progr., Baden-Baden, 1873.

Ferdinand Buesgen, *De gymnasii Vitruviani palæstra*, Diss., Bonn, 1863.

August Burk, "*Die Pädagogik des Isokrates als Grundlegung des humanistischen Bildungsideals*," *Studien zur Geschichte und Kultur des Alterthums*, Bd. XII, Heft 3–4, Würzburg, 1923.

John Burnet, *Aristotle on education*, Cambridge, 1903.

Cecil Delisle Burns, *Greek ideals, a study of social life*, London, 1917.

* W. Buseskul, *Die Schulverhältnisse bei den alten Griechen, auf Grund neuer Tatsachen*, St. Petersburg, 1911.

† Georg Busolt, "*Griechische Staatskunde,*" Müller's *Handbuch der klassischen Altertums-Wissenschaft,* IV., 1, 1, München, 1920–6, 2 vols., continuously paged. 2. Band bearbeitet von H. Swoboda.

A. G. Bussemaker, "*Gymnastes,*" Dar.-Sagl. II. 1698–9.

———, and G. Fougères, "*Gymnastica,*" Dar.-Sagl. II. 1699.

———, and E. Saglio, "*Aliptes,*" Dar.-Sagl. I. 185.

E. Caillemer, "*Agelai,*" Dar.-Sagl. I. 131–2.

* Aristide Calderini, "*Scuole e scolari di venti secoli fa,*" *Studi e Saggi di Antichità,* pp. 1–26, Milano, 1924.

V. Canet, *Les institutions de Sparte,* Lille, 1886.

———, *Les institutions d'Athènes,* Lille, 1887–8, 2 vols.

W. W. Capes, *University life in ancient Athens,* London, 1887.

* Caradec, "*Les palestres et les gymnases dans l'antiquité,*" *Culture Physique,* May 1, 1913.

L. Carrau, "*L'enseignement par l'état dans une république idéale: le système platonicien d'éducation,*" *Revue Politique et Littéraire* XXIX. (1882) 8–15.

* M. Carriere, "*Die Erziehung im Altertum,*" *Allgemeine Zeitung,* 1884, Beilagen nr. 145–51.

Victor Chapot, "*Quand fut instituée l'éphébie attique? à propos d'un travail récent,*" *Revue de Synthèse Historique,* XXXIV. (1922) 105–11. (Discusses the views of Alice Brenot, *Recherches,* etc.)

* E. Chauvet, "*Galien. Ce que les anciens ont pensé de la gymnastique,*" *Mémoires de l'Académie de Caen,* 1879, pp. 233–57.

Gaston Colin, "*Inscriptions de Delphes,*" *BCH* XXX. (1906) 161–328.

Léon Maxime Collignon, *Quid de collegiis epheborum apud Græcos, excepta Attica, ex titulis epigraphicis commentari liceat,* Paris, 1877.

* ———, "*Les collèges de 'Neoi' dans les cités grecques,*"

Annales de la faculté des lettres de Bordeaux II. (1880) 135–51.

A. Conze, "*Giuramento da efebo, rappresentato in pitture vascolari,*" *Annali* XL. (1868) 264–7 and Plates H and I.

* Edoardo Corsini, *Fasti Attici*, Florence, 1744–56, 4 vols.

* Adolph Cramer, *De educatione puerorum apud Athenienses*, Marburg, 1833.

Friedrich Cramer, *Geschichte der Erziehung und des Unterrichts im Alterthume*, Elberfeld, 1832–8, 2 vols.

Elwood P. Cubberley, *The history of education; educational practice and progress considered as a phase of the development and spread of Western civilization*, New York, 1920.

———, *Readings in the history of education; a collection of sources and readings to illustrate the development of educational practice, theory, and organization*, New York, 1920.

* Anton van Dale, *Dissertationes IX antiquitatibus, quin et marmoribus cum romanis tum græcis, illustrandis inservientes*, Amsterdam, 1702. (See Diss. VII. and VIII.)

Gustave Dantu, *L'éducation d'après Platon*, Paris, 1907.

A. Danysz, "*Pedagogika Arystotelesa,*" *Eos* X. (1904) 42–56.

Thomas Davidson, *Aristotle and ancient educational ideals*, New York, 1892.

———, *The education of the Greek people and its influence on civilization*, New York, 1894.

M. Defourny, "*Aristote et l'éducation,*" *Annales de l'Institut Supérieur de Philosophie* (Louvain) IV. (1920) 1–176.

G. Deile, "*Vergleichende Darstellung der platonischen und aristotelischen Pädagogik,*" *Pädagogische Studien*, N. F., XXIII. (1902), 229–38, 310–21.

H. Deinhardt, "*Über das Verhältniss des antiken und modernen Erziehungsprincips,*" *Jahrbücher für classische Philologie.* Supplementband IV. (1836) 390–401.

† W. Dittenberger, *De ephebis atticis*, Göttingen, 1863.

Adolf Dreinhofer, *Das Erziehungswesen bei Plato*, Marienwerder, 1880.

J. Drever, *Greek education, its practice and principles*, Cambridge, 1912.

A. Drygas, *Platons Erziehungstheorie nach seinen Schriften*, Schneidemühl, 1880.

† Albert Dumont, *Essai sur l'éphébie attique*, Paris, 1875-6, 2 vols.

E. Egger, Review of Dumont, *Journal des Savants*, 1877, 232-9 and 277-89.

J. B. Egger, *Begriff der Gymnastik bei den alten Philosophen und Medizinern. Ihr Verhältnis zur Iatrik, Diätetik, Hygieine, Paidotribik, und Athletik*, Freiburg in der Schweiz, 1902.

Benedikt Elbern, "*Die pythagoreischen Erziehungs- und Lebensvorschriften im Verhältnis zu ägyptischen Sitten und Ideen*," *Philosophisches Jahrbuch der Görresgesellschaft*, XXIX. (1916) 233-49.

† Nikolaus Exarchopulos, *Das athenische und das spartanische Erziehungssystem im 5. und 6. Jahrhundert vor Christen. Ein Vergleich*, Langensalza, 1909.

William Scott Ferguson, *Hellenistic Athens*, London, 1911.

Paul Foucart, "*Décrets en l'honneur des éphèbes de l'année 333*," *BCH* XIII. (1889) 253-71.

Gustave Fougères, "*Fouilles au gymnase de Délos*," *BCH* XV. (1891) 238-88.

―――, "*Gymnasium*," Dar.-Sagl. II. 1684-98.

―――, "*Paidotribes*," Dar.-Sagl. IV. 277-8.

Fournier, *Notices et observations sur l'éducation et l'instruction publiques chez les Grecs*, Progr., Berlin, 1833.

* B. Frank, *Die Lehren des griechischen Arztes Galen über die Leibesübungen. Nach der Quellen dargestellt*, Dresden, 1868. (Reprint from: *Neue Jahrbücher für Turnkunst.*)

† Kenneth Freeman, *Schools of Hellas, an essay on the practice*

and theory of ancient Greek education from 600–300 B.C., London, 1907.

E. N. Gardiner, *Greek athletic sports and festivals*, London, 1910.

Robert Geier, *Über Erziehung und Unterricht Alexanders des Grossen, Erster Theil*, Progr., Halle, 1848.

* Johannes Gennadius, *A sketch of the history of education in Greece*, Edinburgh, 1925.

Gustav Gilbert, *Handbuch der griechischen Staatsalterthümer*, Leipzig, 1881–5, 2 vols. Vol. 1, 2. Aufl. 1893.

† Paul F. Girard, *L'éducation athénienne*, Paris, 2nd ed. 1891.

† ———, "*Educatio*," Dar.-Sagl. II. 462–77.

† ———, "*Ephebi*," Dar.-Sagl. II. 621–36.

——— , "*Kosmètès*," Dar.-Sagl. III. 865.

——— , "*Paidonomos*," Dar.-Sagl. IV. 276–7.

——— , "*Sophronistès*," Dar.-Sagl. IV. 1399–1400.

F. Glaeser, "*De Pseudo-Plutarchi libro περὶ παίδων ἀγωγῆς*," *Diss. Philol. Vindobon.*, XII. 1. 1–107, Wien-Leipzig, 1918.

——— , "*Platos Pädagogik*," *Wiener Blätter*, II. (1924) 157–61.

G. Glotz, "*Gymnasiarchia*," Dar.-Sagl. II. 1675–84.

Marie Gothein, "*Der griechische Garten*," *AM* XXXIV. (1909) 100–44.

P. Graindor, "*Les cosmètes du musée d'Athènes*," *BCH* XXXIX. (1915) 241–401.

——— , "*Études sur l'éphébie attique sous l'Empire*," *Musée Belge* XXVI. (1922) 165–228.

——— , "*Liste d'éphèbes athéniens de 128/7*," *Rev. Belge* III. (1924) 13–17.

† L. Grasberger, *Erziehung und Unterricht im klassischen Altertum*, Würzburg, 1864–81, 3 vols.

F. P. Graves, *A history of education before the Middle Ages*, New York, 1909.

B. A. van Groningen, *Le gymnasiarque des métropoles de l'Égypte romaine*, Groningen, 1924.

J. Gröschl, *Antike und moderne Erziehung*, Progr., Linz, 1913.

Friedrich Haase, "*Palästra*" and "*Palästrik.*" Ersch und Gruber *Allgemeine Encyclopädie*, section 3, part 9, p. 360ff. (1837.)

* E. Haenisch, *Wie erscheint die athenische Erziehung bei Aristophanes?* Progr., Ratibor, 1829.

A. Harrent, *Les écoles d'Antioche*, Paris, 1898.

A. Hauvette-Besnault, *Les stratèges athéniens*, Paris, 1885.

D. H. Hegewisch, *Ob bei den Alten öffentliche Erziehung war?* Altona, 1811.

J. E. Heinrichs, *Der Kriegsdienst bei den Athenern*, Berlin, 1864.

K. F. Hermann, Review of a treatise by Roulez, *Göttinger Gelehrte Anzeigen*, 1844, no. 8.

——— and H. Blümner, *Griechische Privatalterthümer*, 3. Aufl., Freiburg i. B. and Tübingen, 1882.

W. Hobhouse, *The theory and practice of ancient education*, Oxford, 1885.

Théophile Homolle, "*Comptes et inventaires des temples déliens en l'année 279,*" *BCH* XIV. (1890) 389–511. (See p. 488.)

———, "*Le gymnase de Delphes,*" *BCH* XXIII. (1899) 560–83.

* T. Hudson-Williams, *An educational bill from ancient Greece*, Cambridge, 1917.

W. W. Hyde, *Olympic victor monuments and Greek athletic art*, Washington, 1921.

Friedrich Jacobs, "*Über die Erziehung der Hellenen zur Sittlichkeit,*" *Vermischte Schriften* III. 1–374, Leipzig, 1829.

O. H. Jäger, *Die Gymnastik der Hellenen*, Neue Bearb., Stuttgart, 1881.

F. A. Janke, *Aristoteles doctrinæ pædagogicæ pater*, Halle, 1866.

* G. Jaré, *Cenni sulla educazione spartana*, Mantova, 1878.

Jegel, "*Platos Stellung zu Erziehungsfragen*," *Archiv für Geschichte der Philosophie*, XXVI. (1913) 405–30.

Pierre Jouguet, "*Remarques sur l'éphébie dans l'Égypte gréco-romaine*," *Rev. Philol.*, XXXIV. (1910) 43–56.

J. Jüthner, "*Gymnastes*," *RE* VII. 2026–30.

† ———, "*Gymnastik*," *RE* VII. 2030–85.

——————, "*Hoplomachie*," *RE* VIII. 2298–9.

† ———, *Philostratos über Gymnastik*, Leipzig-Berlin, 1909.

† U. Kahrstedt, *Griechisches Staatsrecht*. I. *Sparta und seine Symmachie*, Göttingen, 1922.

H. Kalchreuter, "*Griechisches Schulwesen in hellenistischer Zeit*," *Korrespondenz-Blatt für die höheren Schulen Württembergs*, XXIV. (1917) 135–46.

H. Kanter, *Platos Anschauungen über Gymnastik*, Progr., Graudenz, 1886.

Alexander Kapp, *De legibus quas Plato in Republica de educatione tulit*, Erlangen, 1821.

————, *De Platonis re gymnastica*, Hamm, 1828.

————, *Platons Erziehungslehre als Pädagogik für die Einzelnen und als Staatspädagogik. Oder dessen praktische Philosophie. Aus den Quellen dargestellt*, Minden-Leipzig, 1833.

* ————, *Aristoteles Staatspädagogik als Erziehungslehre für den Staat und die Einzelnen*, Hamm, 1837.

A. D. Keramopoullos, Οἱ γυμναστικοὶ ἀγῶνες τῶν ἀρχαίων Ἑλλήνων, Athens, 1906.

A. Kirchhoff, *Rede zur Feier der 3 Aug. 1884*, Berlin, 1884.

H. Klauser, *Die Erziehung im Alterthum, besonders bei den Hellenen, und in der Neuzeit*, Progr., Czernowitz, 1899.

Ulrich Köhler, "*Attische Ephebenstele*," *AM* IV. (1879) 324–36.

† J. H. Krause, *Die Gymnastik und Agonistik der Hellenen*, Leipzig, 1841, 2 vols.

———, *Geschichte des Unterrichts, der Erziehung und Bildung bei den Griechen, Etruskern, und Römern*, Halle, 1851.

M. A. Krigel, *De Lycurgi legibus quas Lacedæmone de puerorum educatione tulit*, Leipzig, 1726.

*K. H. Lachmann, *Platons Vorstellungen von Recht und Erziehung*, Hirschberg, 1849.

D. Lampsas, *Die künstlerische Erziehung der athenischen Jugend im 5. und 4. Jahrhundert v. Chr.*, Langensalza, 1904.

F. H. Lane, *Elementary Greek education*, Syracuse, 1895.

W. Larfeld, *Handbuch der griechischen Epigraphik*, Leipzig, 1898–1907, 2 vols. (See vol. 2, pp. 324–59.)

S. S. Laurie, *Historical survey of pre-Christian education*, London, 1895.

Salomon Lefmann, *De Aristotelis in hominum educatione principiis*, Berlin, 1864.

Fred E. Leonard, *A guide to the history of physical education*, Philadelphia, 1923.

B. Leonardos, " 'Αμφιαρείου ἐπιγραφαί," 'Αρχ. 'Εφ. 1918, 73–100.

Th. v. Lerber, *Professoren, Studenten und Studentenleben vor 1500 Jahren*, Bern, 1867.

Ch. Letourneau, *Évolution de l'éducation dans les diverses races humaines*, Paris, 1898.

E. von Leutsch, "*Die Eidesformel der athenischen Epheben*," *Philologus* XII. (1857) 279.

Otto Liermann, "*Analecta epigraphica et agonistica*," *Diss. Philol. Halenses*, Vol. X, Halle, 1889.

Fr. Lindemann, *Dissertatio de utilitate artis gymnasticæ apud Græcos*, Progr., Zittau, 1841.

*G. Löbker, *Die Gymnastik der Hellenen. Ein Versuch*, Münster, 1835.

G. Löbker, *Charakter und Bestimmung der Gymnastik in Athen*, Münster, 1864.

J. O. Lofberg, "The date of the Athenian ephebeia," *Classical Philology*, XX. (1925) 330–5.

* Alois Luber, *Musik und Gymnastik als Erziehungsmittel bei Platon und Aristoteles*, Progr., Salzburg, 1872.

Georg Lüdke, *Über das Verhältnis von Staat und Erziehung in Platons* Πολιτεία, Berlin, 1908.

J. P. Mahaffy, *Old Greek education*, 2nd ed., New York, 1882.

Mann, *Die Grundlinien der aristotelischen Erziehungstheorie*, Brandenburg, 1873.

Clarence A. Manning, "Professionalism in Greek athletics," *Classical Weekly* XI. (1917) 74–8.

Alexandre Martin, "*Les doctrines pédagogiques des Grecs*," *Revue Pédagogique* III. (1879) 1–18, 217–46, 325–53, 457–69, 541–59 and IV. (1879) 1–22, 109–26.

B. May, *Die Mädchenerziehung in der Geschichte der Pädagogik von Plato bis zum 18. Jahrhundert*, Strassburg i. E.-Leipzig, 1908.

* A. Mazarakis, *Die platonische Pädagogik systematisch und kritisch dargestellt*, Diss., Zürich, 1900.

Erwin Mehl, *Antike Schwimmkunst*, München, 1927.

* Hieronymus Mercurialis, *De arte gymnastica libri sex*, Venice, 1573.

L. Meyer, *De virginum exercitationibus gymnicis apud veteres*, Clausthal, 1872.

* Michaelis, *Ideen über Erziehung nach der Politik des Aristoteles*, Leipzig, 1803.

Theodor Mommsen, *The provinces of the Roman Empire, from Cæsar to Diocletian*. Translated by Wm. P. Dickson, New York, 1887, 2 vols.

Paul Monroe, *Source book of the history of education for the Greek and Roman period*, New York, 1906.

S. Moraites, "Ἡ κατὰ Πλάτωνα τροφὴ καὶ παιδεία," Ἀθήναιον III. 415ff., 489ff., 601ff.

J. C. Morgan, "The transition period of Athenian education and modern education," Classical Journal XIII. (1918) 272–6.

* M. Moser, De puerili apud veteres Græcos et Romanos institutione, Sorau, 1856.

Iwan von Müller, "Griechische Privataltertümer," Müllers Handbuch der klassischen Altertums-Wissenschaft IV., 2, 2. 2 Aufl., München, 1893.

* Karl Müller, Körpererziehung des jungen Griechen, Göttingen, 1926.

K. O. Müller, Die Dorier, 2. Aufl., Breslau, 1844, 2 vols.

R. L. Nettleship, The theory of education in the Republic of Plato, Chicago, 1906.

Richard Neubauer, Commentationes epigraphicæ, Berlin, 1869.

August H. Niemeyer, Originalstellen griechischer und römischer Klassiker über die Theorie der Erziehung und des Unterrichts, 2. Aufl. besorgt von Rudolf Menge, Halle, 1898.

† Martin P. Nilsson, "Die Grundlagen des spartanischen Lebens," Klio XII. (1912) 308–40.

* J. Oehler, Epigraphische Beiträge zur Geschichte der Bildung im klassischen Altertum, Progr., Wien, 1909.

———, "Das humanistische Gymnasium im klassischen Altertum," Mitteilungen des Vereins der Freunde des humanistischen Gymnasiums, Heft 9, pp. 33–43, Wien, 1909.

———, "Ἐφήβαρχος," RE V. 2735–6.

† ———, "Ἐφηβία," RE V. 2737–46.

———, "Γυμνασίαρχος," RE VII. 1969–2004.

† ———, "Gymnasium," RE VII. 2004–26.

———, "Κοσμητής," RE XI. 1490–3 (completed for Egypt [1493–5] by Preisigke).

J. Oehler, "Σωφρονισταί," *RE* (2. Reihe) III. 1104–6.

A. Olivieri, "*Unti*," *Rivista Indo-Greca-Italica* VII. (1923) 169–73.

P. Østbye, *Die Schrift vom Staat der Athener und die attische Ephebie*, Christiania, 1893.

Lewis R. Packard, *Studies in Greek Thought*, Boston, 1886. (See pp. 65–76: "On Plato's system of education in the *Republic*.")

Christian Petersen, *Das Gymnasium der Griechen nach seiner baulichen Einrichtung*, Hamburg, 1858.

J. Polach, *Erziehungsideale bei Platon und Aristoteles*, Progr., Brunn, 1904.

† F. Poland, *Geschichte des griechischen Vereinswesens*, Leipzig, 1909.

Karl Prächter, *Die griechisch-römische Popularphilosophie und die Erziehung*, Progr., Bruchsal, 1886.

K. F. Preisigke, "Κοσμητής," *RE* XI. 1493–5 (the portion of the article dealing with Egypt).

J. G. Purmann, *De certaminibus gymnicis veterum*, Progr., Frankfurt a. M., 1793.

W. M. Ramsay, *The cities and bishoprics of Phrygia, being an essay of the early history of Phrygia from the earliest times to the Turkish conquest*, Oxford, 1895–7, 2 vols.

G. Rauschen, *Das griechisch-römische Schulwesen zur Zeit des ausgehenden Heidentums*, Bonn, 1901.

Théodore Reinach, "*Inscriptions d'Iasos*," *REG* VI. (1893) 153–203.

———, "*L'éducation athénienne et l'éducation française*," *Revue Politique et Parlementaire* LXXVIII. (1913) 189–214.

Emil Reisch, "*Aleiptes*," *RE* I. 1360–2.

F. Ribezzo, "'*Gymnasia*' e '*collegia*' greco-romani a Napoli. Iscrizione latina trovata a Baia," *Rivista Indo-Greca-Italica* VIII. (1924) 152–4.

* J. E. Rietz, *De puerorum educatione apud Græcos*, Lund, 1841.

* Josef Ritter, *Analyse und Kritik der von Platon in seiner Schrift vom Staate aufgestellten Erziehungslehre*, Deutz, 1881.

Fr. Ritzer, *Fichtes Idee einer Nationalerziehung und Platons pädagogische Ideal*, Langensalza, 1913.

J. P. Rossignol, *De l'éducation et de l'instruction des hommes et des femmes chez les anciens*, Paris, 1888.

C. Rüger, "*Das altgriechische Gymnasium*," *Das humanistische Gymnasium* XXXI. (1920) 81–91.

Robert R. Rusk, *The doctrines of the great educators*, London-New York, 1918.

Mariano San Nicolò, *Agyptisches Vereinswesen zur Zeit der Ptolemäer und Römer*, München, 1913–5, 2 vols.

Gaetano de Sanctis, "*Contributi alla storia ateniese dalla guerra lamiaca alla guerra cremonidea*," Beloch's *Studi di Storia Antica*, fascicolo 2, 1–63, Rome, 1893.

Simon Schiessling, *Wertschätzung der Gymnastik bei den Griechen und Würdigung der körperlichen Ausbildung der Jugend in neuerer Zeit*, Progr., Mies, 1891.

Hermann Schmidt, *Die Erziehungstheorie des Aristoteles*, Diss., Halle, 1878.

Karl Schmidt, *Geschichte der Pädagogik*, 3. und 4. Aufl. von R. Lange, Cöthen, 1873–8, 4 vols.

K. Fr. W. Schmidt, *Das griechische Gymnasium in Ägypten*, Halle a. S., 1926.

* Karl Schneider, *Die griechischen Gymnasien und Palästren nach ihrer geschichtlichen Entwicklung*, Diss., Freiburg in der Schweiz, 1908.

G. F. Schömann, *Griechische Alterthümer*. 4. Aufl. bearbeitet von J. H. Lipsius, Berlin, 1897–1902, 2 vols.

B. W. Schröder, *Platonische Staatserziehung*, Leipzig, 1907.

Bruno Schröder, *Der Sport im Altertum*, Berlin, 1927.

F. G. Schulze, *Die Erziehungstheorie des Aristoteles*, Naumburg, 1844.

P. G. Hermann Schween, *Die Epistaten des Agons und der Palæstra in Literatur und Kunst*, Diss., Kiel, 1911.

Franz Seitz, *Die Leibesübungen der alten Griechen und ihre Einwirkung auf Geist und Charakter der Nation*, Progr., Ansbach, 1872.

G. L. Selchau, "*De peripolis Atticis*," *Nordisk Tidskrift for Filologi* X. (1891) 209–16.

Max Seliger, *Das Interesse der Hellenen am Sport. Eine kulturgeschichtliche Studie*, Progr., Tilsit, 1905.

H. Bompas Smith, "*Plato and modern education*," *The Monist* XXXIII. (1923) 161–83.

Franciszek Smolka, *Szkolnictwo Greckie w Starozytnym Egipcie*, We Lwowie, 1921.

A. Spathakes, "Περὶ τῶν μέρων τῆς παρὰ τοῖς ἀρχαίοις Ἕλλησιν ἀγωγῆς ἰδίᾳ. Α. περὶ γυμναστικῆς," *Ἀθήναιον* I. (1873) 315–28.

F. Stadelmann, *Erziehung und Unterricht bei den Griechen und Römern*, Triest, 1891.

Lorenz von Stein, *Das Bildungswesen der alten Welt*, 2. Aufl., Stuttgart, 1883.

Paul Stengel, "*Griechische Kultusaltertümer*," Müllers *Handbuch der klassischen Altertums-Wissenschaft* V. 3, 3. Aufl., München, 1920.

Kurt Sternberg, *Moderne Gedanken über Staat und Erziehung bei Plato*, 2. Aufl., Berlin-Grunewald, 1924.

Fortunat Strowski, *De Isocratis pædagogia*, Albi, 1898.

* Johannes Sundwall, "*De institutis reipublicæ Atheniensium post Aristotelis ætatem commutatis*," Helsingfors, 1906, *Acta Societatis Scientiarum Fennicæ*, Vol. XXXIV.

Emil Szanto, "Ἀγέλαι," *RE* I. 769–70.

———, " Ἀγέλαστος," *RE* I. 771.

———, "Βίδεοι," *RE* III. 431.

Emil Szanto, "Βοαγός," *RE* III. 572.

———, "Διαβέτης," *RE* V. 302.

———, "Διαμαστίγωσις," *RE* V. 325.

J. W. Taylor, "The Athenian ephebic oath," *Classical Journal* XIII. (1918) 495–501.

* N. Terzaghi, *L'educazione in Grecia*, Palermo, 1912.

† T. Thalheim, "'Εφηβία," *RE* V. 2737–46 (in collaboration with Oehler).

J. L. Ussing, *Erziehung und Jugendunterricht bei den Griechen und Römer*, Neue Bearb., Berlin, 1885.

* F. Valletti, *La ginnastica in Grecia, studii storici*, Palermo, 1882.

La Rue Van Hook, *Greek life and thought*, New York, 1923.

* G. Vieth, *Versuch einer Encyclopädie der Leibesübungen*, Berlin, 1795.

K. Wachsmuth, "*Einige antiquarische Bemerkungen zu dem 'Codex des Privatrechts' von Gortyn*," *Nachrichten von der königlichen Gesellschaft der Wissenschaften zu Göttingen*, 1885, pp. 199–207.

J. W. H. Walden, *The universities of ancient Greece*, New York, 1909.

W. Wayte, "Ephebus." Smith's *Dictionary of Greek and Roman Antiquities* (3rd ed. 1890), I. 739–40.

* G. Wente, *Erziehung und Unterricht bei den Athenern*, Vechta, 1861.

K. M. Westaway, *The educational theory of Plutarch*, London, 1922.

* Ludwig A. Wiese, *In optima Platonis civitate qualis sit puerorum institutio quæritur*, Prenzlau, 1834.

U. von Wilamowitz-Möllendorff, *Aristoteles und Athen*, Berlin, 1893, 2 vols.

Ulrich Wilcken, "*Grundzüge der Papyruskunde*," Vol. 1, part 1 in Mitteis-Wilcken, *Grundzüge und Chrestomathie der Papyruskunde*, Leipzig-Berlin, 1912. (See pp. 138–45.)

Ulrich Wilcken, "*Ein Gymnasium in Omboi*," *Arch. Pap.* V. (1913) 410–16.

A. S. Wilkins, *National education in Greece in the fourth century before Christ*, London, 1873.

S. G. Williams, *History of ancient education*, Syracuse, 1903.

O. Willmann, *Aristoteles als Pädagog und Didaktiker*, Berlin, 1909.

* L. Wittmann, *Erziehung und Unterricht bei Platon*, Progr., Giessen, 1868.

F. A. Wright, *Greek athletics*, London, 1925.

A. Zamarias, *Die Grundzüge der aristotelischen Erziehungstheorie*, Diss., Leipzig, 1877.

* S. Zebelev, Ἀχαικά, St. Petersburg, 1903. (In Russian.)

Erich Ziebarth, *Das griechische Vereinswesen*, Leipzig, 1896.

———, "*Zum griechischen Schulwesen*," *Jh. Österr.* XIII. (1910), 108–16.

† ———, *Aus dem griechischen Schulwesen. Eudemos von Milet und Verwandtes*, 2. Aufl., Leipzig, 1914.

———, "*Schulen. A. In Griechenland*," *RE* (2. Reihe) II. 758–63.

Julius Ziehen, "Pädagogik," *Vom Altertum zur Gegenwart*, 2. Aufl., Leipzig, 1921, pp. 128–37.

Alfred Zimmern, *The Greek commonwealth*, 4th ed., Oxford, 1924.

ABBREVIATIONS EMPLOYED FOR PERIODICALS AND COLLECTED WORKS

AEM	Archäologisch-epigraphische Mitteilungen aus Österreich-Ungarn, 1877–97.
AJArch	American Journal of Archæology, 1885–.
AJP	American Journal of Philology, 1880–.
AM	Mitteilungen des deutschen archäologischen Instituts, Athenische Abteilung, 1876–.
Annali	Annali dell' Instituto di Corrispondenza Archeologica, 1829–85.
'Αρχ. Δελτ	'Αρχαιολογικὸν Δελτίον, 1915–.
'Αρχ.' Εφ	'Αρχαιολογικὴ 'Εφημερίς, 1910–.
Arch. Pap	Archiv für Papyrusforschung, 1900–.
BCH	Bulletin de Correspondance Hellénique, 1877–.
BGU	Ägyptische Urkunden aus den Königlichen Museen zu Berlin: Griechische Urkunden, Berlin, 1892–.
Br. Mus. Inscr.	Ancient Greek Inscriptions in the British Museum, Oxford, 1874–1916.
BSA	Annual of the British School at Athens, 1895–.
Bull. Inst.	Bullettino dell' Instituto di Corrispondenza Archeologica, 1829–71.
CGF	G. Kaibel, Comicorum Græcorum Fragmenta, Vol. 1, fasc. 1, Berlin, 1899.
CIG	Corpus Inscriptionum Græcarum, Berlin, 1828–77.

CIL	Corpus Inscriptionum Latinarum, Berlin, 1862–.
CPR	Corpus Papyrorum Raineri Archiducis Austriæ, Wien, 1895.
Dar.-Sagl.	Daremberg-Saglio, Dictionnaire des Antiquités grecques et romaines, Paris, 1877–1919.
Denkschr. Wien Ak.	Denkschriften der Akademie der Wissenschaften in Wien, philosophisch-historische Classe.
Dethier-Mordtmann	Epigraphik von Byzantion etc., in Denkschr. Wien Ak. XIII. (1864).
Diels Vorsokr.³	Hermann Diels, Die Fragmente der Vorsokratiker, 3. Aufl., Berlin, 1912.
Duchesne-Bayet	Mémoire sur une mission au Mont Athos, Paris, 1876.
Dumont-Homolle	Mélanges d'archéologie et d'épigraphie, Paris, 1892.
Ἐφ. Ἀρχ	Ἐφημερὶς Ἀρχαιολογική, 1883–1909.
FGrHist	Jacoby, Die Fragmente der griechischen Historiker, Berlin, 1923–.
FHG	Müller, Fragmenta Historicorum Græcorum, Paris, 1841–70.
FPG	Mullach, Fragmenta Philosophorum Græcorum, Paris, 1860–81.
GGM	Müller, Geographi Græci Minores, Paris, 1855–61.
HGM	Dindorf, Historici Græci Minores, Leipzig, 1870–1.
IG	Inscriptiones Græcæ, Berlin, 1873–.
IGRom	Inscriptiones Græcæ ad res Romanas pertinentes, Paris, 1906–.
Inscr. Cos	Paton and Hicks, The Inscriptions of Cos, Oxford, 1891.

Inscr. Magn.	Kern, *Die Inschriften von Magnesia am Mæander*, Berlin, 1900.
Inscr. Perg.	Fränkel, *Die Inschriften von Pergamon*, Berlin, 1900.
Inscr. Prien.	Hiller von Gärtringen, *Die Inschriften von Priene*, Berlin, 1906.
IPE	Latyschev, *Inscriptiones antiquæ oræ septentrionalis Ponti Euxini Græcæ et Latinæ*, St. Petersburg, 1885–1901.
Jahresberichte	Bursian, *Jahresberichte über die Fortschritte der klassischen Altertumswissenschaft*, 1873–.
Jh. Österr.	*Jahreshefte des österreichischen archäologischen Institutes*, 1898–1922.
JHS	*Journal of Hellenic Studies*, 1880–.
Journ. Egypt. Arch.	*Journal of Egyptian Archæology*, 1914–.
Kaibel *Epigr. Gr.*	G. Kaibel, *Epigrammata Græca ex lapidibus conlecta*, Berlin, 1878.
Lanckoronski	*Städte Pamphyliens und Pisidiens*, Wien, 1890.
Laum *Stift.*	B. Laum, *Stiftungen in der griechischen und römischen Antike*, Leipzig, 1914.
Le Bas	*Inscriptions grecques et latines recueillies en Grèce et en Asie Mineure*, Paris, 1847–77.
Liermann *Analecta*	O. Liermann, *Analecta Epigraphica et Agonistica*, Halle, 1889.
Michel	C. Michel, *Recueil d'inscriptions grecques*, Brussels, 1900 (with Supplément I, 1912).
Milet	Wiegand, *Milet. Ergebnisse der Aus-*

	grabungen und Untersuchungen seit dem Jahre 1899.
Miletbericht 7	*Siebenter vorläufiger Bericht über die in Milet und Didyma unternommenen Ausgrabungen*, in *Abhandlungen der Berliner Akademie*, 1911.
Mnemos.	*Mnemosyne*, 1852–.
Notizie	*Notizie degli Scavi di Antichità*, 1876–.
OGI	Dittenberger, *Orientis Græci Inscriptiones Selectæ*, Leipzig, 1903–5.
PAmh.	Grenfell and Hunt, *Amherst Papyri*, London, 1900–1.
PFlor.	*Papiri Fiorentini*, Milano, 1906–15.
PHal.	*Dikaiomata . . . , Papyrus des philologischen Seminars der Universität Halle*, Berlin, 1913.
Philol.	*Philologus*, 1846–.
PLond.	*Greek Papyri in the British Museum*, London, 1893–.
POxy.	Grenfell and Hunt, *Oxyrhyncus Papyri*, London, 1898–.
PRyl	*Catalogue of the Greek Papyri in the John Rylands Library at Manchester*, 1911–.
PSI	*Papiri greci e latini*, Firenze, 1912–.
PTeb.	*Tebtunis Papyri*, London and New York, 1902–7.
RE	Pauly-Wissowa-Kroll-Witte, *Real-Encyclopädie der classischen Altertumswissenschaft* (Neue Bearbeitung), Stuttgart, 1893–.
REG	*Revue des Études grecques*, 1888–.
Rev. Arch.	*Revue Archéologique*, 1844–.

Rev. Belge..........	*Revue Belge de Philologie et d'Histoire*, 1922–.
Rev. Philol...........	*Revue de Philologie*, Nouvelle Série, 1877–.
Riv. Filol...........	*Rivista di Filologia*, 1873–.
Sammelb...........	Preisigke, *Sammelbuch griechischer Urkunden aus Ägypten*, 1913–.
SB Wien Ak.........	*Sitzungsberichte der Akademie der Wissenschaften in Wien, philosophisch-historische Classe.*
SEG...............	*Supplementum Epigraphicum Græcum*, Leyden, 1923–.
SGDI.............	*Sammlung der griechischen Dialekt-Inschriften*, Göttingen, 1884–1915.
SIG[3]	Dittenberger, *Sylloge Inscriptionum Græcarum*, editio tertia, Leipzig, 1915–24.
TAM..............	*Tituli Asiæ Minoris*, 1901–.
Wilamowitz *Nordion. Steine*...	*Nordionische Steine*, in *Abhandlungen der Berliner Akademie*, 1909.
Wilcken *Chr.*.......	Vol. 1, part 2 in Mitteis-Wilcken, *Grundzüge und Chrestomathie der Papyruskunde*, Leipzig-Berlin, 1912.

INDEX

Abdera, 72 n. 2, 193
Achæa (Pellene), 188
Ægean islands, 195–216
Ægosthena, 183
Æschines, 54, 73–74, 118, 122, 124
Ætolia, 18
Age for entering school: Athens, 57, 74; Crete, 50; Sparta, 18, 31–32
Age terminology: Crete, 44–46; Sparta, 20–21, 37
Agela, 22, 29, 38, 44, 46–48, 50, 52–53
Agelaoi, 47–48, 50, 52
Agesilaus, 16, 23
Agis, 32–35
Agoge, defined and criticized, 12–13; inferior types, 18; falls into decay, 32; various vicissitudes, 32–40; complete downfall, 41; results, 41–43
Akontistes, 136, 140, 227–228
Alcibiades, 81, 87, 116, 181 n. 1
Aleiptes, 40, 66 n. 2, 67, 82, 91
Alexandria, 211–212, 214, 251–252, 255 n. 2, 256
Alumni, ephebic, 156, 160, 199, 237, 253
Ampaides, 39
Anacharsis, 4, 262
"Anointers," clubs of, 186, 190, 195, 202, 215, 243–244
Anoros, 45–46
Antikosmetes, 165, 170

Antioch, 160, 163, 208, 245–247
Apageloi, 46
Aphetes, 136, 140–141
Apodromos, 45, 47
Apollo, 7, 224–225, 251
Arcadia, 191–192
Archephebus, 189–191
Archery, 25, 52, 96, 101–102, 139–140, 184, 194, 198–199, 206, 249
Archos, 48, 50
Areopagus, 72–74, 141–142, 171
Argos, 190
Aristophanes, 54, 85–87, 261
Aristotle, 12–14, 42–44, 48 n. 2, 53, 55, 57, 59, 61 n. 3, 68–69, 75–76, 91, 105–108, 110–112, 118–119, 120 n. 5, 121, 127, 260
Asia Minor, 157, 159–160, 216–239
Athens: gymnasia, 5, 76–85, 221–222; physical education, 10–11, 14, 32, 42–43, 54–92; sphere of influence, 190, 209, 212–215; stages of education, 109; supervision of education, 72–76; varying interest in gymnastics, 85–89; views of philosophers on gymnastics, 93–108; *see also* Educational centers, Ephebi
Athletics, 5–6, 40–41, 65, 68–71, 77–78, 82, 89–91, 103, 106, 171, 241–242, 262

Babylon, 249
Ball, 15, 21, 30 n. 5, 62
Bathing, 30 n. 1, 80, 86, 92, 192, 244, 248
Berytus, 159, 247
Bœotia, 18, 42, 117, 118 n. 1, 122, 126, 181–184, 222 n. 4
Boua, 18, 20, 48
Boxing, 7 n. 1, 25, 49, 62, 206

Catapult, 135–136, 139–141, 159, 198–199, 206
Ceos, 29 n. 4, 198–199
Chiron, as gymnastic teacher, 8
Cleomenes, 15, 32, 34–35
Cleruch, 151
Cnossus, 53, 214
Compulsory education: Athens, 75; Ceos, 198; Crete, 49; Pellene, 188; Sparta, 12; in theory, 102
Corcyra, 193
Corinth, 187
Crete, 9–11, 14, 29, 44–54, 57, 140
Croton, 241–242
Cyprus, 195–196, 208–209, 212
Cyrene, 250–251
Cythera, 188–189
Cyzicus, 229, 232, 236–237

Dancing, 13 n. 2, 30 n. 5, 62, 101, 103, 217
Delos, 67, 72 n. 2, 195, 209–215
Delphi, 185–186
Demetrius of Phalerum, 142, 145
Demosthenes, 118, 123
Diamastigosis, 20, 23–24
Didaskalos, 167–168, 177; didaskaloi, 136
Diogenes the Cynic, 63, 65 n. 6

Diogeneum, 144, 155, 168, 173 n. 1, 175–177
Discus, 23, 30, 52, 62, 80, 248
Dorians, 8–11, 25–26, 44, 55, 251
Dreros, 52
Dress, 30, 31 n. 1, 42, 49, 150, 201–202, 242, 246, 248
Dromeus, 45, 47, 52
Dromos, 29, 45–48, 50 n. 3, 78, 80, 187

Educational centers: Athens, 17, 157, 159–163, 171–177; Cyzicus, 237; Delos, 212, 214–215; Lampsacus, 237; Pergamum, 218; Priene, 237; Sparta, 17–18
Egypt, 251–257, 262
Eirens, 20, 22, 23 n. 6, 27, 37, 48, 95, 189; *see also* Tritirens
Elis, 188
Endowments, educational, 126–127, 186, 223, 227, 252
Epaminondas, 91, 182
Epengraphoi, 173
Ephebarch, 185, 189, 194, 196, 202–203, 208, 218, 229, 234–238
Ephebi: Athens, 18, 37, 54, 70–71, 74, 108–179, 215; date of first organization, 112–124; number, 150–155, 157–162, 171–177; sources of information, 110–113; Crete, 44, 47, 52; other localities, 179, 182–185, 187–208, 212–222, 225–226, 228, 231–240, 243–257, 260; in philosophical theories, 95–97, 104–105

INDEX

Ephebic inscriptions, 110–112, 120 n. 5, 127, 134, 143, 154–155, 157; oldest, 130

Ephebic oath, 44, 52–53, 111–112, 123–124, 147–149, 197, 225–226

Ephebophylakes, 218

Ephesus, 212, 226, 229, 232, 235

Ephors, 27, 33–34

Epicrates, founder of Athenian ephebia, 126–127

Epicurus, 151–152

Epidaurus, 191

Epimeletes, 84, 164, 186

Epistates, 84

Eudemus, 223–225

Eugenics, 100, 106

Euripides, 91

Foreign students, *see* Educational centers

Galen, 69

Games, 62, 100–101, 107, 211

Gerusia, 226–227, 238

Girls, physical education of: Athens (not allowed), 57, 74; Ceos, 199; Crete (doubtful), 53; Cyrene, 250; Locri, 242; Magnesia on the Mæander, 230; Pergamum, 216–217; Smyrna, 230; Sparta, 28–32, 38, 41; in philosophical theory, 70, 98–99, 101, 103, 105, 240–241

Gods, connected with physical education, 7; *see also* Apollo, Hermes

Gortyn, 53; Law of, 45

Gradation of exercises by ages: Athens, 61–62; Sparta, 21; in philosophical theory, 107

Group instruction, 64

Grouping, Spartan system of, 18, 20, 22, 28–29

Gymnasiarch, 38–40, 75 n. 3, 84, 141, 145, 162–163, 169, 182–191, 193–198, 200–209, 212–216, 218–221, 226–231, 233–240, 243–247, 249–257, 260

Gymnasium, 5, 29–30, 38–39, 46, 54, 76–85, 101–102, 108 n. 1, 179, 182, 184, 186–209, 216–222, 226–227, 230–231, 235–236, 238–240, 242–249, 251–253, 255, 259–261

Gymnasium club, 185–187, 195, 208, 252

Gymnastes, 26, 54, 66 n. 2, 67–70, 82, 91

Health, 41, 55, 65, 68, 73, 78, 86–87, 89, 91–92, 100–101, 103, 106, 135, 167, 192, 240–241

Hegemon, 136 n. 5, 139 n. 3, 166, 168, 177

Helots, 13, 16

Heracles, 7–8, 25, 250 n. 5

Hermæa, 74–75, 79, 219

Hermes, 164, 197, 202, 250 n. 5; Enagonios, 7, 223–224

Herodicus, 91–92, 193

Hetairia, 48

Hierapytna, 53

Hippocrates, 68

Homeric period, 6–7, 55–56, 70

Hoplomachos, 26, 70–71, 136–137, 139–140, 164, 168, 177–178, 197, 214, 220, 227–228, 247

INDEX

Hoplomachy, 63, 70–71, 103, 116, 135, 156, 171, 194, 206, 249
Hunting, 8, 25, 50–51, 88, 96, 101, 191
Hypohoplomachos, 139
Hypokosmetes, 165
Hypopaidotribes, 72, 81, 138, 165, 168, 170, 177–178
Hyposophronistai, 168–169, 178
Hypozakoros, 167–168

Iasus, 76 n. 2, 78 n. 2, 229–230, 232, 235
Illyria, 192
Immorality, 42, 73–74
Ionians, 55, 222
Isocrates, 69, 113, 116–117
Itanus, 46

Javelin, 23, 25, 30, 52, 62, 71–72, 79–80, 96, 101–102, 139–140, 156, 194, 198–199, 206, 249
Jerusalem, 248–249
Jumping, 30 n. 5, 52, 62

Katapaltaphetes, *see* Aphetes
Kestrophylax, 164–165, 168, 170, 177–178
Kestrosphendone, 164, 171
Kosmetes, 115, 127–129, 131–135, 137, 139, 141–144, 146, 162–166, 169–171, 233–234, 251, 252 n. 1, 253, 255

Laconia (aside from Sparta), 188–189, 231
Lampadarch, 200, 212
Laodicea, 211–212, 214
Latus, 53
Leonidas, 16, 28

Leuctra, battle of, 32, 182
Lochagoi, 146
Locri, 29 n. 4, 199 n. 2, 242–243
Locris, 184–185
Lucian, 4, 54, 262
Lycurgus, 8, 10, 12, 24–25, 37

Macedonia, 192–193
Magna Græcia, 240–244
Magnesia on the Mæander, 229–230, 238 n. 3
Malla, 53
Massilia, 245
Mastigophoroi, 28
Megara, 183–184
Melleirens, 21, 37
Mellephebi, 163–164, 176–177, 204, 232
Menander, 151–153
Messenia, 188–190
Metics, 160, 200
Miletus, 78 n. 3, 163, 172–173, 222–229, 231
Military aspect of physical education, 8, 18, 23, 37, 42–45, 50–51, 53, 56, 70–71, 89–91, 94–97, 101–103, 109, 114–115, 118, 125, 127, 136, 142–144, 156, 170, 181–183, 199, 228
Mœsia, 193
Mothakes, 16–17
Mountain-climbing, 8
Mycenæ, 190

Neaniskarch, 226, 239
Neoi, 186, 190, 193–196, 199, 203, 205–206, 218–222, 226–227, 229–230, 235–238, 245, 249
Nicopolis, 185, 214

INDEX

Old men, exercises of, 83, 108, 206, 226–227, 238

Olympic games, 25–26, 90, 188

Orphans, education of, 76, 111, 125–126

Overseers, of education (Sparta), 39; of gymnasia (Athens), 84

Pæderasty, 73, 75 n. 2, 181

Paideutai, 136, 167, 220

Paidonomos, 27–28, 32, 34, 49, 107, 196, 204–205, 216–218, 223–225, 227–230

Paidotribes, 26, 54, 58, 62–70, 72–73, 75–81, 91, 136–139, 155, 165, 170, 187, 191, 193, 211–214, 223–225, 227–228, 230, 239, 251

Palæstra, 38–39, 54, 59–62, 65–68, 70, 72–82, 85–89, 101, 107, 137, 156, 181 n. 4, 186–187, 191, 196, 202, 204, 206, 209–212, 216, 223–225, 229–230, 241, 248, 251, 262; personified, 7

Palaistrophylax, 72, 186, 191 n. 4, 193, 211, 251 n. 7

Pallekes, 205–206

Pancratium, 25, 62, 171, 202, 206

Parephebi, 204–205

Paros, 159, 200

Pergamum, 78 n. 3, 216–222, 238 n. 3

Periœci, 18

Peripoloi, 115, 117, 119–122, 124

Philopœmen, 36, 71

Philostratus, 68–69, 171

Phocis, 185–187

Physical education: carried on in synchronism with mental training, 57–61; causes for decline, 261–262; defined, 5–6; Greek attitude towards, 3–5, 259–262

Pindar, 90

Plato, 4, 12, 31, 53–54, 56, 59, 68–72, 75, 83, 89, 91–93, 97–106, 113–116, 125, 181, 199, 260

Play, see Games

Plutarch, 12, 54, 123, 181–182

Polodamnes, 62, 71–72, 247

Pontus, 17

Priene, 229, 231–233, 237

Professionalism, 41, 68–69, 89–91, 262

Prostates, 166–167

Ptolemy Euergetes, 46, 246

Public education: Athens, 109, 113; Crete, 45; Sparta, 13, 19; elsewhere, 207, 216, 223, 227–231; in philosophical theory, 94–108

Pythagoras, 240–241, 260

Riding, 25, 62–63, 71–72, 87–88, 101, 135, 144, 162

Rome and Athens, 156–157, 160; and Sparta, 36–37; general, 212, 214, 238, 252 n. 1, 253–254, 261

Running, 8, 25, 30, 50 n. 3, 51, 62, 64, 84, 86–87, 90, 155, 171, 194, 197, 200, 206, 249–250

Russia, South, 239–240

Salamis, 195, 212, 215–216

Secretary (grammateus) of the ephebi, 139 n. 3, 141, 168, 170, 177, 192; assistant, 166, 168, 170, 177

Selymbria, 91, 193
Senate, Athenian, 128, 131, 133–134, 141, 155, 164
Sicily, 17, 244–245
Sicyon, 159, 187
Sideunai, 21
Skotioi, 46
Slaves, 49, 57, 72, 74, 128, 190, 211, 217, 230–231, 254
Slinging, 101, 184
Smyrna, 229–230
Socrates, 32, 81–82, 83 n. 4, 88–89, 91, 99, 116–118, 121–122, 126
Solon, 10, 58, 60–61, 73, 83 n. 2, 90, 262
Sophronistes, 26, 74, 115, 117, 128–133, 137, 146, 153, 168–170, 178, 198, 228
Sparta, 8–51, 53–55, 57, 85, 89–95, 97–98, 100–101, 115–116, 182, 189, 241–243, 250
Sphærus, 35
Strategoi, 141–144, 176 n. 4, 197, 251
Student officers of ephebi, *see* Lochagoi
Student-teachers, 72, 214
Superintendent of schools, 188, 190, 198, 207, 209; *see also* Paidonomos
Swimming, 62
Synephebi, 37–38, 124, 169 n. 4, 253–254
Syria, 157, 160, 214, 245–248
Syssitia, 35, 49–50, 104, 146
Systatai, 194
Systremma, 169

Tarantinarchs, 141
Tarentum, 214–215, 242–243, 261
Tegea, 191–192
Teos, 227–229
Terence, 153
Themistocles, 83
Theseus, 7, 142 n. 4; festival for 145, 156, 158
Thespiæ, 159, 183
Thessaly, 192–193
Thetes, 128, 151
Thrace, 192–195, 234 n. 3
Torch-race, 84, 87, 156, 171, 195, 198, 200–201, 213 n. 1, 220
Toxotes, 52, 136, 140, 227–228
Triakatioi, 250
Tritirens, 189
Trœzen, 190–191
Trophimoi, 17
Tyrtæus, 89–90

University: of Athens, 18, 178; of Rhodes, 208

Women, participate in gymnastics, 9, 231; hold gymnasiarchy, 200–201, 220, 227, 231, 251
Wrestling, 25, 30, 49, 62, 64, 70, 72 n. 2, 90, 101, 171, 199–200, 206

Xenophanes, 90
Xenophon, 12, 17, 54, 71, 80, 88, 93–97, 100, 105, 117–118, 121, 126